Conti...

Through ... Lens of Love

"Robin gives a voice to glioblastoma (GBM), a voice to caregivers of GBM and a voice that most people/doctors/nurses have never heard. Robin expresses trials, tribulations, fears and uncertainty that we have all felt. I understood with relief many of these experiences that I could never put into words, but she did. She told her story BUT also told Dick's—in such a way it became a lesson in surviving, a lesson in bravery, a lesson in the little things, a lesson of life and love, in sickness and in health."

—Stacie Guirguis, a warrior sister,
forever linked because of GBM

"This is truly an engrossing memoir, written with insight, fact and elegance. Robin's impassioned account of her valiant struggle through the fatal illness that took her husband, is potently written and awash with riveting candor. Robin's spellbinding voice is as compelling as any you are likely to encounter this season—or any season."

—Mel Yoken, Chancellor Professor Emeritus
of French Language and Literature,
author of _Breakthrough_ (Peter Lang, 2007)

"This is an unforgettable love story. Throughout their lives, Richard and Robin modeled devotion and care, not only for each other and their deeply connected family, but for a large friendship circle they developed through their dedicated, principled work in their professional and community involvements. That community returned it in countless, moving and memorable ways, showing once again that "love is something, if you give it away, you end up having more."

—Janet Freedman, Resident Scholar,
Womens Studies Research Center, Brandeis University,
author of *Reclaiming The Feminist Vision:*
Consciousness-Raising and Small Group Practice

"Why do we write books? In the hopes our story, experiences and lessons learned might help others. Kudos to Robin Gross for honoring her husband, family and community for their loving support through her dark night of the soul. You will be inspired and uplifted by the humanity demonstrated in this book—and will be motivated to reach out to those around you to re-establish what matters most in good times and bad—kindness, compassion and connection."

—Sam Horn, author of *SOMEDAY is Not a Day in the Week*

"Anyone who has been touched by glioblastoma will hear their own voices echoed somewhere in Robin's book. With gentle yet exquisite, and sometimes humorous style, she invites readers to explore her family, faith, & friendship. Robin takes us on a journey of making every minute count."

—Jo Simpson, MSN, Spouse of Glioblastoma Patient

THROUGH THE
LENS OF
LOVE

THROUGH THE
LENS OF
LOVE

FACING TERMINAL ILLNESS

A MEMOIR BY ROBIN GROSS

Printed in the United States of America

Disclaimer: The author has tried to recreate events, locales, and conversations from her own memory. In some instances, the author has changed the names of individuals, companies, and places in order to maintain their anonymity. Although the author has made every effort to ensure the information in this book is correct at press time, the author and publisher do not assume and hereby disclaim any liability to any party for loss, damage, or disruption caused by errors or omissions. Lastly, this book is a memoir and not intended as a substitute for the medical advice of physicians. The reader should consult a physician in matters relating to his/her health.

First Printing, 2020

ISBN: 978-1-952106-21-7 (paperback)
ISBN: 978-1-952106-22-4 (ebook)

Library of Congress Cataloguing Number: 2020904623

Published by Redwood Publishing, LLC (Ladera Ranch, California)
www.redwooddigitalpublishing.com

Author's Website: www.backyardadventurephotos.com

Book Design:
· Cover Design: Bonny Katzman
· Interior Design: Ghislain Viau
· Front and Back Cover Photo: Charles Needle
· Author Photo: Joanne Medeiros

For my beloved husband, Dick,
who made a difference in the lives of so many.

Table of Contents

Introduction

"These were the best two years of my life," Dick said to me.

In May 2012, my husband, Dick, was diagnosed with glioblastoma multiforme (GBM), an aggressive form of brain cancer. Despite the grim diagnosis, he described his last two years of life as the happiest he had ever experienced.

I wondered how that could be, but as I began to write this book and record the last two years we spent together, the reason for Dick's positivity became obvious. The immense love and support he received from family, friends, patients, and acquaintances carried him forward with hope and resilience. Beyond that, he felt fulfilled in his life's work. Dick spent thirty-four years as an internist in a small-town private practice, showing great care and concern for each and every one of his patients. When news of his diagnosis hit, his patients reached out with offers of help and beautiful, heartfelt letters. He felt gratified knowing his life work was appreciated and that he had made a difference in this world.

A year and a half after Dick's diagnosis, the cold, bitter winter seemed never-ending. It became challenging to leave the house as his health gradually declined. Despite the hardship of the disease, we tried to rejoice in every day. Our philosophy was to enjoy every moment and be grateful for each other and the people and love that surrounded us. We had recently moved to Plymouth, Massachusetts, so we saw less of our old friends. I felt like Dick's spirits needed a lift, so I wrote to my favorite columnist at the *Boston Globe* and requested she write an article. She eventually got back to me and responded that she would not be writing his story because there were *so very many similar ones* out there.

Each cancer patient is so different and such a precious soul. I felt that Dick's narrative was unique, in any case, because it was not his illness that defined the story. It was the people who helped him, his "helping hands family," and his strength and determination to make every day count. Perhaps *Globe* readers tire of hearing repetitive stories of violence, greed, and selfishness, but would they feel the same about stories of human endurance, kindness, and community? I was disappointed in the columnist's response but determined that someday I would write this story.

After my husband's death, I read of a twenty-nine-year-old woman who was diagnosed with GBM and chose to take her own life. While I respected her decision, I wanted people faced with glioblastoma to know that there are other choices—that the journey of glioblastoma can also be one of love, support, and fortitude. Dick and I created a caring community through a website called Lotsahelpinghands, where we were able to share our journey and ask for assistance. Because of that, we never felt alone or helpless.

A childhood Hebrew school classmate of mine from California signed up as a member of Lotsahelpinghands. I received a communication from her toward the end of our journey that made me realize our story could influence other people as well.

Barbara wrote:

Dear Robin,

I'm so sorry that I have not written to you sooner, but I have read each of your helping hands updates religiously. They are all so inspiring. I wish I lived closer and could be of some use to you—but your letters have made me much more aware of people in my community who are dealing with terminal illness . . . and have pushed me to reach out to them. Thank you for that.

This story goes beyond Dick, me, and our family. It is not just a book about life with glioblastoma. It is a story about the power of love and community—how the support of family, friends, and even strangers can come together to elevate one man's life.

CHAPTER 1

Empty Nesters
Tending the Nests

It was May 20, 2012, a day that will be imprinted on my mind forever. We'd been back home for three weeks from a photography trip to Monet's Garden in France, and we were still on a high. My husband, Dick, and I raised our four children in the small town of Lakeville, in southeastern Massachusetts. The last few years, Dick had a slower pace at his job as a physician in private practice, which enabled him to spend more time at home. Having just reached the stage of empty nesters, we were thoroughly enjoying more time to ourselves. We took photographs together, created canvas prints, went hiking in the woods, and enjoyed skinny dipping in the pool on a hot summer's night. We felt like newlyweds, falling in love all over again.

It was a glorious spring weekend with a cool, gentle breeze, and the sun was shining overhead. We were enjoying our own little Garden of Eden, which we had nurtured over the past thirty-three years to become a haven for butterflies and wildlife. Dick and I were eager to take photos of a family of chickadees who had taken up residence in one of our backyard birdhouses. Dick set up a tripod and we monitored the birds' activities. Although we couldn't see the chickadee nestlings inside the birdhouse, we photographed the parents busily feeding their babies. Every twenty minutes, like clockwork, the adult chickadees approached the birdhouse with a wriggly worm or caterpillar.

Earlier that week, I noticed that both a male and female cardinal were frequent visitors to our backyard. I tracked the male, who was tenaciously hunting for worms on the side yard near the woods that border our house. It didn't take long to spot the nest at the edge of the woods, where the cardinals were taking prey to feed their offspring. I excitedly showed Dick and he worked hard to set up a second tripod at just the right angle, even trimming some of the lower brush and vines, so we could get a better view.

The baby cardinals were captivating as they stretched out their heads and opened their beaks wide in anticipation of that next meal. The male and female cardinal took turns hunting and feeding, so we were able to capture the vibrant red of the male. Between the two active nests, we had our hands full.

Around one p.m., I walked over to the backyard, where Dick was photographing the chickadees.

I asked, "Would you like to switch and watch over the cardinal nest?"

"What about feeding the humans?" he responded, and we took a lunch break.

We had an absolutely delightful day, spending time with each other, enjoying the fruits of our beloved backyard, and doing what we both loved—photographing nature. It was one of those rare, perfect days that is forever etched in your memory.

In April we had gone on a photography trip to Europe to celebrate our fortieth anniversary. Right before we left on the trip, Dick had gotten an eviction notice from the owner of the medical building where he had rented his office for the past thirty-four years. The building had been sold and the tenants had to be out by July first. Since our return, we had been trying to figure out what to do about the impending loss of his office. Dick had just turned sixty-four, one year short of retirement age, yet it was a costly proposition to set up a private practice in another location at that stage of his career. Should he consider retiring early? That thought lingered in our minds, especially since Dick's brother, Sam, had died of glioblastoma just as he was approaching retirement age.

That evening we had plans to meet Dr. Bob McNamee ("Mac" among his peers) and his wife, Alex, for dinner at a restaurant in downtown Taunton. Mac was one of the physicians in Dick's coverage group. He had recently negotiated an agreement with Porter Health Care so that he could maintain his private office and oncology practice but work under the auspices of Porter. Dick had arranged the dinner meeting to talk with Mac about his contract with Porter Health Care in anticipation of setting up a similar agreement.

I reluctantly pointed out that it was 5:30 p.m. and we needed to leave soon to meet Mac and Alex. We got ready and Dick went to pull the car out of the garage. As is usually the case when I had five minutes to spare, I started pulling weeds by the side yard. All of a sudden, I realized a lot of time had gone by and I hadn't seen Dick drive out. I assumed he must have forgotten something and run back into the house.

Shortly after, Dick got out of the car and said, "My car won't start. We'll have to take yours."

"That's too bad. I'll drive," I offered. "We can bring your car in for servicing tomorrow."

I thought it was strange that Dick had been in the car so long, but I didn't question it at the time. On the ride to dinner, Dick was very quiet. He answered questions with short responses and didn't initiate conversation. It was not like him to be so reserved and passive.

I asked, "Are you okay?"

"I'm fine," he said.

I noticed he was wearing a jacket that was too heavy for such a warm evening.

"Aren't you uncomfortable? Do you want to take your jacket off?"

"No."

There was no explanation or joking around like usual.

During the ride I asked him more than once, "Are you sure you're feeling all right?"

Each time he responded with his winning smile, "I'm fine," but I was glad I was doing the driving as something just didn't feel right.

We got to the restaurant and were seated. Mac and Alex arrived right after us and the waiter came to take our drink orders.

The waiter asked Dick, "What would you like, sir?"

Dick responded, "Pickles."

There was a moment of silence.

The waiter asked again, "What would you like to drink?"

"Pickles," Dick repeated.

My heart skipped a beat.

I reiterated, "Dick, he's taking your order for what you want to drink."

Dick was smiling but I realized he was not joking. He had that same blank look he had in the car. I had a horrible feeling in the pit of my stomach.

I shouted to Mac, "Something's wrong. We need to get to the hospital right away!"

CHAPTER 2

Emergency Room

Mac immediately took Dick to Morton Hospital, a five-minute drive away. I followed in my car with Alex.

We got the royal treatment at Morton, where Dick and Mac were both on the medical staff. The emergency room personnel began performing tests right away. My growing fears were confirmed when Dick couldn't remember basic identifying information in the mental status exam.

"What is today's date?" the emergency room physician asked.

"May twentieth, 1970."

"What is your home telephone number?"

"508-947-7673."

"Dick, that's your office number," I interrupted.

"Can you tell me your home telephone number?" the doctor continued.

"508-947-7673."

"Thank you. What is your home address?"

"Bates Avenue."

That was the street Dick grew up on in Winthrop, Massachusetts. I was getting increasingly scared but I reassured myself, thinking, *It must be a stroke and nowadays strokes can be treated.*

"How old are you?" the ER physician continued.

"Sixty-three."

Dick had had a birthday one-month prior and had turned sixty-four years old.

Dick tried hard but he was confused about basic facts and sometimes just answered, "I don't know." Uncharacteristically, he didn't appear to be upset at all that he couldn't provide the information requested.

I started to cry, averting my face so Dick couldn't see my tears. Then I noticed that he showed no awareness at all that I was upset. He had a broad grin and a childlike demeanor. That was the moment I knew something was terribly wrong—when he didn't react to my tears. I felt an agonizing dread that this was not just a ministroke. Raw fear gripped my insides.

Alex asked me about calling someone to come over. My best friend, Ruth, seemed to arrive within minutes, and I grasped onto her strong hug for support. Ruth suggested I call the children. I had still been thinking we were dealing with a temporary problem that would right itself, but suddenly I recognized that that might not be the case. Ruth was right, I needed to call the kids. Samantha and Sarah responded, and I left messages for Sandra and Seth to call me back.

Samantha was at the park with her two young children when I reached her. She was quite shaken and had lots of questions. She said she would find someone to care for Aerin and Jacob and drive right to the hospital. Sarah's fiancé, Vivek, who was a second-year neurology resident at Duke, consulted with the Morton Emergency Room staff by phone. I could tell by Sarah's quivering voice that she knew this was serious, and she and Vivek also initiated plans to come to Boston.

The hospital staff did a CAT scan of Dick's head and discovered what looked like a tumor on the brain. Mac remembered that Dick's brother Sam had died of glioblastoma, the most aggressive type of brain cancer, a few years earlier. We were all wondering the same thing—could it possibly have struck twice in the same family? My fear turned into sheer terror. I had images of visiting Dick's brother in a Florida nursing home. Shortly after Sam's initial diagnosis, he had a massive seizure that caused brain damage. He was not a candidate for treatment and had to be placed in a nursing home because his care needs were so great. I could barely breathe thinking about the terrible progression of Sam's illness and the possibility that Dick could have the same disease.

The next step was arranging a transfer to one of the Boston hospitals and we chose Brigham & Women's Hospital, the top Boston hospital for the treatment of brain tumors.

As further updates were available, I communicated back and forth with the kids. I tried to keep the fear and panic out of my voice, but the facts spoke for themselves. My daughter Sandra was visiting her best friend in Boulder, Colorado, scouting out a living arrangement and job possibilities with the intention of moving there. When Sandra got word about her dad, she immediately made plans to return home. Seth was in the army, stationed in Seattle, Washington. When he called back, we decided to see how things progressed before he made a request for leave. I called Dick's sister, sister-in-law, and my own siblings. We all feared the worst but hung onto the unknowns. I left it to my sister to call my eighty-eight-year-old mother, as I knew I couldn't trust myself to hold steady when talking to her.

We were waiting in the ER for the ambulance when Dick gave out a deafening scream, like an animal wail. His arm shot up, and his body thrashed. I yelled for help and the emergency staff rushed into the exam room and ushered me out. Dick's agitation was in stark contrast to his previous mellow temperament.

I buried my head in my hands because I was afraid to look up. I was so scared that Dick might die. The staff quickly renegotiated plans to send Dick to Boston by helicopter. He was thrashing and fighting so hard they were afraid he would injure himself. His physician asked for permission to put him into an induced coma to protect him and I agreed.

It was agonizing to watch the ambulance personnel escort Dick to the helicopter and not be able to go with him. Although they explained the regulations, I hated being separated from him. I was blinded by tears as Ruth led me out to my car, which she insisted on driving to Boston. I prayed for Dick's safety all the way there and was relieved to be reunited with him when we arrived at the Brigham ER. He remained unconscious through the long wait for a bed on the neurology floor.

In the meantime, I found out the procedure to request that Seth come home from the army. I contacted the Red Cross, and after speaking to the Brigham medical personnel, the Red Cross intervened so that the army granted Seth an emergency medical leave. Ruth insisted on staying through the night, and I was grateful to have her calm presence. My daughter Samantha arrived from New York.

Medical personnel at the Morton ER had told me that the Brigham would do an MRI to confirm the diagnosis of a brain tumor. I was losing patience over the delay.

"My husband was supposed to get an MRI when we arrived. We've been here for over eight hours. What's going on? We need to get that MRI *now*."

The nurse finally got Dick scheduled and sent him down for the MRI. It was close to morning by then. None of us had eaten or slept, but we weren't thinking about food or sleep. I called our friend and Dick's colleague, Dr. Bharani Padmanabhan, a neurologist, and he said he would come right over. Our faithful friend Bharani remained with us throughout Dick's entire illness.

A few hours later, Dick began to stir and show signs of agitation, which is not uncommon when a patient comes out of an induced coma. I was just relieved and thankful that he woke up.

"I was so worried about you. I'm glad you are okay. I love you so much," I told him. I gave him a huge hug and kiss and said a silent prayer to God.

Dick was trying to get out of bed, insisting, "I have to go take care of my patients." We calmly explained where he was and what happened, but he wouldn't accept "no" for an answer. He insisted he had to go to work. He desperately tried to pull out his catheter.

At one point, he yelled, "I want to speak to the administrator of this hospital. I demand to see the administrator!"

It was a challenge to keep Dick calm. We had to hold his hands so he would not remove the catheter and the pulsometer. All those bootcamp workouts he'd been doing the past couple of years had made him pretty strong.

When Samantha, Bharani, and I were beginning to tire and became concerned that we could not keep Dick safe, we requested help from the staff in managing his agitation. The charge nurse responded that she could get Dick one-on-one staffing but then family would not be allowed to assist. She said only one family member could be in the room at a time and the rest would need to remain in the waiting room. We had already been spoken to a few times about having too many people in the room. The charge nurse was particularly rigid, which earned her the nickname "Nurse Ratched."

By the time my daughter Sarah and Vivek arrived from North Carolina, Nurse Ratched was antagonistic toward the family and refused to allow them access to the room. She said there were too many visitors, and that this did not allow for the restful environment that Dick needed. Vivek had taken time off from his rigorous residency program, and Sarah desperately wanted to see her dad.

I refused to accept Nurse Ratched's edict. I had read every word of the hospital literature and I marched down to request a patient advocate. I emphatically explained the situation and insisted that Sarah and her fiancé be allowed in to see her dad. A discussion between the advocate and the nursing staff ensued and they were finally given access. A decision was made to transfer Dick to a different unit and both the nursing staff and family were much relieved about the change.

During the first twenty-four hours, I had pushed aside my emotions and the enormity of the situation so that I could make the best decisions and focus on advocating for Dick. My social work training naturally kicked in and helped me to assess the situation and take one step at a time. My professional self took over when my personal self was too numb and scared to function.

Seth arrived from his base in Seattle, rattled and exhausted. When Sandra arrived, she was so upset that she backed into another car in the hospital parking garage. Once I made sure she was all right, I went back to the garage to examine the damage. I completely broke down to the parking lot attendant when I was trying to explain what happened. I couldn't control my sobbing.

"Can I help you?" a stranger asked.

Another asked, "What's wrong? Can I pay for you?"

Someone helped me over to a bench to sit down and sat with me while I told her, "I think my husband is going to die."

It was the first time I had said it aloud. There it was—the fear that I had not allowed myself to even consider in front of Dick and the kids because I had to be the strong one. I cried out my worst fear to this stranger.

I dumped all my troubles in that hospital garage and then quickly said, "I need to get back. My husband needs me."

We all felt tremendous relief as Dick continued to come out of the induced coma, talking like himself again and even more telling, asking questions about his case and wanting to read his own chart. He was worried about his patients. We reassured him that we had spoken to Michele, his office manager, who was calling his scheduled patients to cancel the next couple of days. He told me to make sure to tell our neighbor John that he would not be able to stop by to do a scheduled home visit for John's mom, as Michele wouldn't have that in her book.

I couldn't stop hugging Dick and telling him how much I loved him.

"I love you too, honey," he said. "Don't worry, we'll figure out what's wrong."

He then barraged me with questions about what happened, as he had no memory of the past two days. The immediate crisis was over, but we knew we were in for a long haul.

CHAPTER 3

Beginnings

Although Dick and I met in Cleveland, Ohio, and spent the first six years of our marriage there, we wanted to move closer to family when my father died in 1977 at the age of fifty-six. So in 1978, when Dick finished his medical residency in Cleveland, we returned home to Massachusetts, where we were both born and brought up.

Dick started his medical practice as an internist in Middleboro, a quaint, rural town in southeastern Massachusetts, where they desperately needed physicians. We rented a house in town and Dick rented an office in the Middleboro Professional Building. The office building was adjacent to St. Luke's Hospital in downtown Middleboro, just a five-minute drive from the house we rented.

We were delighted when our first child, Samantha, was born one year later. We were ready to start looking for a house of our own and we fell in love with a four-bedroom Tudor home in the adjacent town of Lakeville. Brilliant orange, native day lilies were blooming in abundance on the day we looked at the house and the magnificent garden is what won us over.

Dick was concerned that the house was too big and way over our budget. We intended to have a big family, and in the end, I convinced him that, one, we could afford it, and two, we would grow into it. Our daughter Sarah was born three years later, her sister Sandra in 1985, and our son Seth in 1988. We not only filled up all the bedrooms but also converted an attic room into an additional bedroom!

Whether I was working part-time or involved with the kids' activities, I always tried to be home for Dick's lunch break. I would make something simple, and if the weather was nice, we would sit in the backyard. We coveted that time together. My sister Priscilla used to joke that it was like back in the days of Ozzie and Harriet.

When the kids were older, I went back to work full-time. But by June 2011, I was unhappy with my job as Director of Social Services at a nursing home and I left. I was looking for the perfect job and I was not in a rush to go back to work. I loved the slower pace, taking photos in the backyard, and spending more time with Dick. I was able to continue our tradition of being home together at lunchtime, and we fell back into a comfortable, familiar pattern.

Seth left the house in March 2011, enlisting in the army. Our daughter Sandra had recently moved back home to save money to move out to Colorado. She was working in Dick's office as a nurse's assistant and Dick enjoyed coaching her. We had a short taste of being empty nesters and we were looking forward to that stage of our lives. We had always been so child focused that it was exciting to think about spending more time on our own passions and with each other.

In recent years we had taken photo workshops, invested in more sophisticated camera equipment, and become active members in the New Bedford Whaling City Camera Club. We also joined a nearby Photography Meet-up in Plymouth.

One weekend that summer, Dick set up his tripod in the backyard. We photographed the voracious hummingbirds as they batted their fragile wings up and down and dipped their beaks in the red bee balm and buddleia blooms.

I said to Dick, "This is exactly what I want to do in our retirement."

We agreed life was good and we had much to look forward to.

CHAPTER 4

Photography

With our love of photography, we had amassed thousands of photographs, and eventually I decided it was time to do something with them. We went to a one-day seminar in Boston sponsored by Adobe and were inspired by one of the speakers, Rafael Concepcion, who built his own photography website. Dick was a do-it-yourself kind of guy, so we bought Rafael's book, *Get Your Photography on the Web: The Fastest, Easiest Way to Show and Sell Your Work*. Following it to the letter, we accomplished the task of building our own website—www.backyardadventurephotos.com—and created galleries of landscapes, wildlife, butterflies, and flowers.

I never could have accomplished this feat without Dick. I can follow directions, but he knew how to read between the lines and take the steps that are often omitted. Dick was extremely bright and technical things came much easier to him. Although we had photographed in many parts of the world, it was our own backyard that provided the inspiration and subject matter for most of our photos.

I started a blog on the website with accompanying photographs. I wrote about our "backyard adventures"—raising monarch butterflies, the den of snakes that lived in our window well, and the raucous, nocturnal tree frog that lived by our pond. The blog gave me an avenue to combine my passions for photography, writing, and nature.

Dick and I complemented each other with our photography. I had a better eye, but Dick understood the mechanics of the aperture, shutter speed, and ISO. I had a feeling for what worked, and he knew why. He always assisted me on camera settings and post-processing techniques, and I helped him with creative seeing. He was my equipment guy. Together, we formed an excellent team and signed all our work *R&R Gross*.

Although I often got credit for being the creative one, Dick had a bit of the mad inventor in him and was highly creative in his own right. A few months before his sixtieth birthday, Dick started researching a new printer. He had his eye on an HP Z3100 large format printer that would allow him to print directly onto canvas, giving our photos a painterly effect. Although Dick spent hours looking at it online, he would never buy such an expensive gift for himself.

When I suggested buying it for him, he said quite emphatically, "I don't need it and we can't afford it."

When my daughter Samantha asked about a gift for her dad's birthday, I suggested we get the printer together, and the gift was set in motion.

Dick was astonished on his birthday when his research became a reality. He was like a little boy in a candy shop, and he definitely had a sweet tooth! We didn't see him the rest of the afternoon as he hooked up the printer, examined the parts, and played with the possibilities.

Dick printed out 20 x 30-inch photographs on canvas, put together stretcher bars, and gallery wrapped the photos himself. We eventually converted one of the kids' bedrooms into a storage area for the canvas photos. I took most of the photos and Dick put them into production. Over time, we learned from each other—I became more interested and skilled in post-processing and Dick took more time and interest in photographing.

Being home that year gave me the time to plan a special trip for our fortieth wedding anniversary, coming up in June. Dick saw an ad in an issue of *Outdoor Photographer* magazine for a photo trip to Monet's Garden in France and Keukenhof in the Netherlands for two weeks in April 2012 with photographer Charles Needle. We looked up both gardens online, and their unique displays of flowers in kaleidoscopic colors looked very inviting to our photographer's eyes. Monet's Garden was such a romantic place to celebrate our anniversary.

We were equally impressed with the Charles Needle Photography website, as he used a lot of innovative techniques to create painterly, impressionistic photos. Dick and I both loved that aesthetic and had already started experimenting with it ourselves. We committed to the trip with great anticipation.

CHAPTER 5

Medical Building

In 1986, most of the physicians had moved out of the Middleboro Professional Building to individual condo suites in the brand-new Southeast Health Center. Dick decided to stay where he was since he liked the convenience of being next door to the hospital, and he felt he was more accessible to many of his patients who lived within walking distance of his office.

Unfortunately, St. Luke's Hospital in Middleboro closed its doors in 1990 when Massachusetts implemented a plan to close many of the state's smaller hospitals. Dick applied for admitting privileges to Morton Hospital in Taunton and drove the thirty-minute commute every morning to make rounds on his inpatients.

Over the years, the medical building where Dick rented changed hands a few times. The most recent owner operated on a month-to-month lease, and right before leaving for Europe, Dick received an official letter saying that all tenants needed to vacate the building by July 1, 2012. That gave us only three months! We engaged a lawyer to attain an extension but were unsuccessful. We spent long nights discussing whether it made sense for Dick to invest in the cost of setting up a new office, as he would turn sixty-five in another year. It was clear, when we checked out available real estate and estimated the cost of renovating a suite, that this would be a very expensive proposition.

Would it be better to retire early? *Retirement* was a word that had only just begun to enter our vocabulary. It was hard for Dick to think about slowing down. He was a workaholic and he loved his job as an internist. However, changes occurring in the medical community would require major computerized modifications to his office by 2015. Dick felt strongly about maintaining independence in his medical practice and believed that the electronic medical record would be harmful to patients. He felt it was important to look at a patient face-to-face while taking a history and not be distracted by typing on a computer.

Another reason Dick considered early retirement was because his older brother, Sam, died of glioblastoma when he was sixty-five years of age. Like Dick, he was a hard worker, and was still employed as an engineer when he was diagnosed.

Despite his passion for his work, Dick was beginning to think about the next chapter of his life. He wanted to study, photograph, experiment, invent, and spend more time with me. We wanted to see the national parks, and we had always dreamed of walking the Appalachian Trail together.

We left for Europe with many unanswered questions. Despite the looming deadline, we tried to leave the stress behind and enjoy the present moment.

CHAPTER 6

Fortieth Anniversary Trip

We carefully went through the equipment list prepared by Charles and decided to buy another macro lens so that we would each have our own. I didn't regularly use a tripod, but we had a second, rather flimsy tripod that would serve its purpose for the trip. Luckily, we also paid attention to the clothing list and packed long underwear, fleeces, rain gear, hats, and gloves, all of which we wore on most days! We packed the beautiful Monet umbrella that Samantha and her husband, Adam, had given Dick for his birthday a few days earlier, and on April 12, 2012, we headed for Logan Airport.

I believe we were sent on that unforgettable trip for a reason. The amazing opportunity it provided for our photographic endeavors seems less significant than the relationships we made with our fellow travelers. The participants on our photography trip were not only our co-travelers in capturing the beauty of Keukenhof and Monet's

Garden, but would become our fellow travelers in the journey of life, death, healing, and renewal.

Dick and I arrived in Amsterdam, and at orientation later that day, we met the nine other participants in the group. We were asked to introduce ourselves, share our interests in photography, what drew us there, and our goals for the workshop. It was a mixed group in terms of age, geography, and photographic experience. Our leader, Charles, was in his late forties and had a genuine smile and piercing blue eyes. He had lived most of his life in Atlanta and had the accent to prove it. He had a warm, welcoming personality and made everyone feel comfortable. We were all affected by his poignant story of how he got into photography: suffering from chronic fatigue syndrome, he literally had to drag himself on his hands and knees to take a photo. But with his tenacity, brilliance, and keen eye, he not only healed his body but opened up a whole new world of seeing through his soul and became a master photographer.

Gena was an energetic, friendly, single woman in her early fifties who loved cycling. She was a retired corporate communications director and magazine editor. She had dark, wavy black hair, a beautiful smile, and a twinkle in her eye. I had no inkling at that first meeting that Gena herself was a widow and would become my guiding angel through the next few years. Gena and Charles both lived in Seattle.

Kirk and Wanda appeared to be in their fifties, and very much in love. This was the first photo trip that they had taken. Kirk was concerned about Wanda keeping up because she had longstanding health problems and moved at a slower pace. Wanda had one lung and had been through open-heart surgery more than once. Kirk confided he had almost lost her three times, and my heart went out to him. Dick later expressed his concern to me about Wanda as he recognized the seriousness of her condition. Kirk was always fiercely protective of Wanda and watched out for her at every step of the journey. Wanda used a small camera and enjoyed taking photos without all the fancy mechanics. She wore her thick, brown, waist-long hair in a braid. She was always adorned with beautiful scarves, her signature look. With Wanda as our teacher, the gals on the trip had fun learning various ways of tying scarves to achieve her sophisticated style.

Rene was there solo—her husband, Bruce, was still working and encouraged her to go on the trip without him. She had medium-length blonde hair and was one of those beautiful, ageless women with glowing skin who looked like a magazine ad even at six a.m. on a dark, rainy morning. Rene always had a ready smile and a phenomenal amount of knowledge about many things, photographic and otherwise.

John Craig was a reserved man who looked to be in his sixties. He was a retired print reporter and newspaper editor from Fargo, North Dakota. He had lost his wife a year prior to the trip, and this was one of his first forays out into the world since then. I sensed he was still grieving her loss. I remember thinking how brave it was of him to push himself out of his comfort zone to come on this trip. There were two men named John on the trip, so John Craig became known as John C. and John Hoskinson as John H. John H., who owned several businesses, including a camera shop, also came to the workshop without his spouse. As solo travelers, John C., John H., and Rene all became close.

Martha and Bob were a lovely retired couple in their eighties. Bob came along as a non-photographing spouse. He also enjoyed photography, but he was not well or as mobile as he used to be. Martha walked with the aid of a cane but managed to capture unique perspectives wherever she went. I was fascinated that she didn't develop an interest in photography until she was in her sixties, after a trip to Ghana. Prior to the trip, she purchased a Polaroid camera and loved seeing instantaneous results and sharing them with the people she met there.

Martha remarked, "I have been upgrading ever since."

She was very bright and had a wry sense of humor. When we shared photos from our first homework assignment, Martha's were my favorites. I always thought her background as an English literature professor contributed to her expressive, poetic style.

Lou was fairly new to photography, but he had a solid background in sound and technology, and it turned out, he was a natural. He was an audio engineer and a musician. He owned his own business in New York, and did the setup for many famous musicians and politicians. During our time together, he amused us with stories of the celebrities he had worked with when they came to New York to speak or perform.

There is always someone who is the life of the party, and on this trip, it was Lou. From a large Italian family, divorced, and in his mid-forties, Lou had an engaging personality. He and Dick took to each other right away and they had conversations about photography, physics, music, and many other topics that I often didn't follow (or understand). That was one special quality that Dick possessed—he could converse with people from all walks of life, on almost any subject, and he took a genuine interest in other people.

Pat was in his eighties and did not like using a tripod. His motto was, "At my age, if I don't want to, I shouldn't have to." Pat was a quiet gentleman who had lost his wife a few years before.

As I introduced myself, I shared that one of my goals was to be a more independent photographer. Although I had mastered the basics, I still relied on Dick for help in many technical aspects. I remember admiring both Gena and Rene, who were traveling by themselves. I couldn't imagine going on a photography trip without my photo buddy.

I noticed that many in the group were prior students and admirers of Charles' creative work. Hearing others talk about his positive encouragement and supportive teaching style, I recognized that Charles made strong personal connections and later found this to be so true.

Listening to everyone's stories, particularly those who had recent losses, made me realize how fortunate Dick and I were to be there together, celebrating our fortieth anniversary

CHAPTER 7

Keukenhof and Monet's Garden

We spent a week in Lisse, Holland, shooting every day at Keukenhof, said to be the most beautiful spring garden in the world. Even the camera lens couldn't capture the beauty of the boldly colored flowers and the incredible floral designs, which seemed like a well-orchestrated concert. There were water gardens with bridges, swans, and glittering reflections of the red and yellow tulips. The greenhouses held magnificent indoor displays with cultivars of unusual tulips. When we thought it couldn't possibly get any better, we came across a hidden woodland garden with masses of grape hyacinths flowing like a stream through the forest.

At midday, when it was too bright outside for good photography, we had classroom lectures, learning several macro and impressionistic techniques. Charles taught us different operations that involved moving the camera while taking a photo: rotating, zooming, tilting, and shaking. His ideas sparked our creativity and opened up many amazing possibilities. Charles would then demonstrate the new techniques in the field, and we had opportunities to try them out and experiment on our own.

Charles gave us homework assignments, and we would gather to see everyone's efforts and learn from his feedback. At first I was threatened by the idea of being critiqued in a group setting, but then I realized that the challenge made me pay attention, be more creative, and improve as a photographer.

We also spent time visiting and photographing unique venues like flower fields, windmills, and the Flora-Holland flower market and auction houses. It was fascinating to watch the trolleys jet in and out, moving the flowers that would be at a foreign destination within a day. The fast pace allowed for some fun slow-shutter photos that gave us a sense of the quick movement required for distribution.

After a fabulous week in Lisse, we traveled by van to Giverny, France. The trip had already exceeded our expectations, but we were anticipating the allure of Monet's Garden. It was a delight for the senses. The house gardens displayed a floral explosion of color with a spring palette. Where this garden exuded joy and energy, the water garden's mood was one of serenity and romance. Dick and I tended to drift to the water garden and never tired of photographing the famous green bridges, the captivating reflections in the late afternoon light, and all the secret vistas the gardens held.

Charles's arrangement with Monet's Garden gave our group exclusive use of the gardens in the mornings before the tourists arrived, and again in the late afternoons. During the interim hours, we traveled to local villages and photographed the marketplace at Vernon, Collegiate Notre Dame Church, Chateau et Jardins d'Ambleville, and a picturesque sixteenth-century farmhouse. We rarely took photos of each other, but Charles captured a shot of us with Dick holding his Monet's Garden umbrella over our heads as we walked down the street on a rainy outing in the village of Genainville.

Our group quickly bonded as we got to know one another on a more personal level. A few days into our stay at Giverny, we found out that Gena had been widowed when her husband died of colon cancer four years earlier. *She must have been so young*, I thought. I never would have suspected she had experienced such tragedy in her life. She always wore a dazzling smile, had a contagious laugh, and a cheerful demeanor. I vividly remember her focusing on the positive, saying that going through the dying process, she and her husband, Steve, had developed a more intense level of intimacy in their relationship than they might have under normal circumstances. I was in awe of Gena's strength and courage. I could not imagine what it would be like to lose Dick and have to go on living.

Charles planned a special dinner and entertainment for our last night together and we took a group photo outside our B&B. This was the only time we dressed up during the entire trip, barely recognizing each other without our layers of fleece, knee pads, and hats! Charles put all our favorite garden images and photos of each other into a slide show. We enjoyed the show immensely while we listened to a local musician and relaxed in the living room with a glass of wine.

We each shared what the trip had meant to us and how we had improved our photography skills. Everyone started with different levels of experience, so some became more comfortable with equipment, others improved their technical skills, and everyone learned new photo techniques. We all agreed we were fortunate to experience the glory of spring at Keukenhof, the quiet, early light of Monet's Garden, delectable French dinners and desserts, and traveling through the backroads and villages of France.

John C. went last in sharing his thoughts. He was fairly quiet during the trip, and I think he surprised us all when he got up, notes in hand, and addressed the group. I was so touched by his words that I've always remembered them.

"I saw Charles in Atlanta last year, about nine months after my wife passed away. I had a feeling he was trying to get me out the door and moving again. Anyway, it turns out he had a convincing argument why I should come along on this trip.

"I'm glad I did. I feel my walkabout is nearing its end. While I still have not arrived back to the point where I was before my wife's illness, where all three vital elements—heart, mind, and eye—come together when taking a photograph, I'm a lot closer than I was two weeks ago.

"During the past two weeks, I've seen beauty and strength, not only in Keukenhof and Monet's Garden, but in each of you."

As everyone shared their thoughts, the recurring theme was the camaraderie of the group and the relationships that were forged. After spending two weeks together, we had grown close and become like a family.

CHAPTER 8

Hospitalization

What a stark difference the stiff, white, hospital room was compared to the vibrant and colorful gardens we had just spent two weeks photographing. I relished the memories of that anniversary trip as I now sat by Dick's side in the hospital.

We were relieved that Dick came out of the coma and was acting like himself again, but there were more obstacles ahead of us. The MRI confirmed there was a glio tumor in the brain. Surgery was scheduled to biopsy the cancer and hopefully remove what they could. Three days after Dick was hospitalized at the Brigham, the biopsy was performed. During his week-long hospitalization, we had gracious offers from family and friends to stay overnight in Boston. We took turns staying the night at the hospital, so there were always two of us with Dick, while the others could get a good night's sleep in a real bed.

I took a break one night and stayed over with extended family. When I went to sleep that night, I was alone for the first time since the crisis. My thoughts wouldn't allow me to fall asleep. *Why did this have to happen to Dick? He was such a good person. Why couldn't it have been me? Dick had so much more to contribute to the world. It wasn't fair. I should have been the one.*

At the hospital I had been busy making and receiving phone calls, supporting family, communicating with Dick's office staff, and trying to keep Dick's spirits up, but in the stillness of that night I allowed my mind to think about the gravity of the situation and dwell on the future. I released the flood of emotions I'd kept inside of me and I cried for Dick, I cried for myself, I cried for my children and for my grandchildren. I cried for all the experiences we would never share. It was overwhelming to even contemplate the possibility of losing the most precious person in the world to me. How would I survive without him? We were a team. I could never go on by myself. Although it was my first night of uninterrupted sleep in a bed, I awoke the following morning drained and exhausted.

Samantha took the role of communicating with extended family and good friends. She quickly established a phone contact list and sent out group messages. Dick's sister, Cindy, flew in, and Samantha's husband, Adam, joined us at the hospital. Many Boston family and friends came to visit that week and our rabbi, Raphael Kanter, made the trip from New Bedford. In addition to our immediate family, there were two people who were there every day, all day—Dick's friend Bharani and Dick's cousin Lexie.

Bharani, a neurologist, was a great support, a fountain of information, and an advocate for Dick in the medical system. Lexie, a young professional, had a week-long interval between jobs, and she chose to spend it with us. She brought meals from the outside world when we tired of Panera. She transported family members to and from the airport, ran errands, and always provided a listening ear and a shoulder to cry on. I thought of Lexie recently when my watch battery died. I went to the jeweler to have it replaced and they informed me it had to be sent out. It would take two weeks and cost $150. When that same watch battery died while Dick was in the hospital, Lexie quietly took it and returned it to me the next day, fully functioning.

Dick was so pleased to have a visit from one of his office staff, Beth, who had worked for him for over twenty years. She had started out working from home as a transcriptionist. As her children grew, she began working in the office and later went back to school to become a nurse. At the time of her visit she was enrolled in a nurse practitioner program specializing in newborn infants. Dick was very proud of her accomplishments, and she was indebted to him for his support. Toward the end of the week, my niece Heather flew in from California and her presence gave us fresh, new spirit and energy.

On the day of the surgery, all of us, including Bharani, gathered in the family room on the first floor of the Brigham to wait. We tried to feign interest in reading books and magazines and helped ourselves to coffee. Somehow, we managed to pass the time with small talk and playing Scrabble. I slipped away to the quiet space of the chapel and said silent prayers for Dick's recovery.

We were familiar with the devastating disease of glioblastoma and its poor prognosis. The public was also more aware of the disease since Senator Ted Kennedy had been diagnosed and subsequently died in 2009. The bottom line was—no one got better from glioblastoma. Dick's surgeon, Dr. Mark Johnson, met with the family after surgery. We were all hanging on to the thread of hope that the tumor would be focused and they could remove much or all of it. However, Dr. Johnson confirmed that the cancer was widespread, and he could only remove enough tissue for the biopsy. He said the results of the biopsy would be available when we met with him for a follow-up appointment. We hugged and cried in sadness and anguish. Yet somehow it still felt unreal to me, like I was watching it all unfold in a movie of someone else's life and there would be, after all, a happy ending.

Ruth had been my best friend for many years as we raised our children and shared our innermost thoughts and feelings. But in recent years, Dick had become my new best friend. There was no one I would rather spend time with. We were both starting to think about all the exciting adventures we would have in retirement. We had even started thinking of downsizing in the future and had gone to look at homes in the nearby community of The Pinehills in Plymouth.

Just one year before Dick got sick, in 2011, I had heard on the news that an Iowa couple in their nineties had died one hour apart while holding hands on a gurney. I was so touched by the power of their love. I remember having a conversation with our rabbi about it. I had always thought Dick would have to die first because his love for me was so intense that I knew he could never survive emotionally without me. He enjoyed being with me all the time. I once went to a reunion in Israel for a week, and the kids said that he was heartsick and moped around the whole time I was gone. But, in more recent years, I had decided that *I* would have to die first, because I could never survive without Dick. Then, when I heard about the Iowa couple, I felt comforted in the thought that Dick and I would also die together in old age, because our love was so strong. I had held this image in my heart of us holding hands together. I wondered now why I had been thinking about such things a year before Dick became ill and if it was prophetic.

A few of us were in Dick's hospital room when he woke up after the biopsy. He recovered enough to start asking questions. I let my son-in-law Vivek take the lead, because he is a physician, but after his explanation, I was confused. He made it sound like the tumor had successfully been removed and we were done with the whole ordeal. It certainly wasn't the same message Dr. Johnson had given the family when he spoke to us after the surgery. I didn't know if it was because English was not Vivek's native language, he was trying to soften the blow, or whether I had misinterpreted what Dr. Johnson had said. I wasn't sure whether to speak up, and I regretted later that I hadn't.

"Finally, I catch a break," Dick said.

I went into the waiting room and conferred with family members and Bharani about what to do. They all felt I should let it go and let Dick believe what he heard for now. I had a horrible feeling in the pit of my stomach but decided to wait. I knew Dr. Johnson was coming in to talk to Dick himself and would clarify his findings. In the meantime, the hospital provided a celebration dinner after surgery. Samantha went one step further and ordered all Dick's favorite foods from Boston's finest restaurant.

Dr. Johnson and his team came into Dick's room and spoke to him about the result. Now Dick understood that he had not, in fact, caught a break. His celebration dinner arrived and remained mostly untouched.

CHAPTER 9

Diagnosis

When we returned home from the hospital, I checked in on the cardinal's nest, but the birds were gone and the nest abandoned. *Had a hawk attacked? Had the babies fledged and flown off on their own? Would they survive?* It made me think about the fragility of life and that one day I may also be pushed out of my comfortable, nurturing nest.

A week later, we headed back to the Brigham for a follow-up appointment with Dr. Johnson. Our son, Seth, had already returned to base, but the girls and Bharani accompanied us. There was a long, anxious wait. When the nurse finally called us in, everyone rose to follow.

Dick said to the girls, "You wait here. I only want Mom and Bharani to go in."

You could see they were crestfallen, but I let Dick make that decision.

The way the visit went was fascinating to me. Dr. Johnson started talking about glios and went right into all the treatment options available. Dick and Bharani seemed to be following the doctor's discussion. I was trying to make sense of the direction Dr. Johnson was taking. I finally interrupted and said, "Wait, can you back up? I think I missed something. I thought you were going tell us the biopsy result and what stage the disease was in."

Dr. Johnson responded, "Dick has Glioblastoma Multiforme, Stage IV," and continued on with his discussion as if there had been no interruption. He also shared that there was new research to support the idea that some types of glioblastoma were genetic.

I later asked Dick why the doctor didn't initially go over the diagnosis and the fact that it was stage IV.

He replied, "He didn't have to."

With their medical training, Dick and Bharani had known the diagnosis all along.

We discussed Dick's family history of his first cousin Fred and his brother Sam, living eight and ten months, respectively, with glioblastoma. Dr. Johnson, when pressured by me for a time frame, said he estimated Dick had eight to ten months to live.

I looked at Dick with a heavy heart. He looked strong and courageous. I did not see a man who had just been given a death sentence.

As we reentered the waiting room, the children knew it was a dire diagnosis from our expressions and my tears. They had a flood of questions and none of the answers were satisfactory.

"What did he say? What stage is it? Can they treat it?"

Unfortunately the only question that was relevant was, "How long?"

I was immediately brought back to a similar scene thirty-five years before when my dad had an aneurism. When I heard the news, I got on the next available plane to Boston. My mother and three siblings were at Logan Airport to greet me. One look at them and I knew I was too late.

There was such a display of emotion that I remember people at the airport kept coming up to us to ask, "Are you alright? Is there anything we can do?"

My four children were just a little older than my siblings and I had been. In both cases, there was nothing anyone could say or do to make it better.

On our drive home, we hit rush hour traffic at its worst. Since Dick's first seizure activity, I had been doing all the driving, and I hated highway driving. Everyone was moody because of the terrible news. Although no one really had much of an appetite, we decided to stop for dinner till the traffic eased up.

A bubbly young waitress approached us with "Good afternoon, how are you all today?"

I somehow managed to mutter, "Okay," but I wanted to shout out to her and the whole world, "Terrible! My husband is going to die!"

Our hopes had been crushed. Glioblastoma, Stage IV—the worst news. Dick explained to the kids what Dr. Johnson said—that there was new research indicating that some types of glioblastoma can be genetically linked.

It sounded to me like Dick was using his best patient-teaching voice. I was amazed that he could remain so calm. We were all worried about what this meant for our family and for future generations. But most of all, I was scared about losing my husband and they were scared about losing their dad. Dick directed the conversation back in a more positive direction and started talking about treatment strategies and breakthrough research protocols. By the time he finished, we all thought the same thing—*if anyone can beat this thing, he can.*

Despite the intense conversation, what kept coming back to me about that dinner was the waitress's innocent greeting. Later, I spoke to Dick about how awkward that interaction was for me. I remarked how the waitress, with her cheery disposition, could never have imagined the trauma we had been through that day. It was so hard for me to project normalcy. He said something very profound that will stay with me always.

"Robin, you don't know what troubles the waitress may have been hiding and how difficult it might have been for her to project that cheery smile. Everyone is fighting a battle we know nothing about."

CHAPTER 10

Submerged in Feelings

The children went home; they had to get back to their own lives. Samantha had left her two children for more than a week's time. Sandra, who had been working in Dick's office, started job hunting nearby—suddenly, Colorado seemed much too far away. A few weeks later she found a job in Boston and moved to an apartment there, although she came home to visit often.

Dick confessed one night, "I don't think I was a good enough dad." Before coming to the rescue, I listened to him as he shared his feelings about not being home enough and not having the influence on the kids that he would have liked.

I said, "You know, parents always wish they could have done more. That's natural. Parenting isn't easy, especially when your kids are different than you are."

He had been a studious type of kid who always followed the rules and never misbehaved. Our children all had minds of their own and could often be challenging.

Dick had tried hard to be home as much as he could. He never missed the important things. He was at every birthday party, although many times he pulled in from the hospital at the last minute. I have pictures of him at petting zoo birthday parties, still wearing his suit.

I reminded him of his dedication and told him, "The important thing is the kids knew you loved them, and as they got older, they understood how important your work was and how dedicated you were to your patients. You were a good example and you taught them a lot through your hard work and diligence."

"I know you did most of the child-rearing," Dick said. "I wish I could have helped you more."

I wished so too, but I didn't focus on the rough days. I focused on the times he was there for them.

"You did so much for the kids. You took time off to be co-teacher for Samantha's nursery school co-op—you taught the class the official way to wash hands. The teacher thought you would lose the three- and four-year-olds when you taught them about Salvador Dali and Gandhi, but you didn't. They understood exactly what you were trying to get across."

I reminded him how he spent his Wednesday afternoons off coaching Sarah's *Destination Imagination* team with me. And the times he stayed up all night holding Sandra as a baby, when she had difficulty breathing. I recounted how he supported Seth through his participation in Cub Scouts and helped him build winning Pinewood Derby cars.

I ended my trip down memory lane by saying, "You always encouraged the kids to try new things. They are proud of you and I am proud of you too. You are a wonderful father."

Dick hugged me. "Thank you Robin, you always turn things around for me and make me feel better."

On Memorial Day weekend, our first weekend home, a number of our closest friends called to see if they could come by. I thought it would be good for Dick's morale. We had always enjoyed entertaining company, especially in the summer months. It was a warm, balmy day and we sat out by the pool, which remained unopened for the season. Friends brought drinks and snacks and we settled into a comfortable afternoon. One of the friends who came by was Dr. Bob Friedman. Bob arrived in town a year after Dick and they entered an office sharing and on-call coverage agreement.

When we first moved to town, I was naively under the impression that Dick's job as a private practitioner would be a breeze after all those years of working long, intense hours as an intern and resident. I could not have been more wrong! Dick had purposely chosen to go to a place that was underserved for primary healthcare. I barely saw him that first year before Bob arrived, and Dick was quite relieved to be joined by a well-trained, board-certified internist.

Eventually, Bob got his own office, but they continued to share coverage until 1990, when St. Luke's Hospital closed. Then Bob associated with Cardinal Cushing Hospital in Brockton while Dick associated with Morton Hospital in Taunton. Some of the physicians in the Middleboro area belonged to the Massachusetts Medical Society, Plymouth District and some to the Bristol North District. Again, Bob and Dick fell into two separate camps. Bob was Dick's physician and although their association changed through the years, they always remained good friends and Dick was thrilled to see Bob that afternoon.

On Bob's arrival, our friend Sandy called out to him. "Congratulations on being named this year's recipient of the Community Physician of the Year Award! You're quite a celebrity."

It was the first time Dick and I had heard this news. The award was given annually by the Massachusetts Medical Society (MMS) to recognize a physician who stood out as a leading caregiver from each of the society's twenty districts—Bob was being honored by the Bristol North District. Dick shook Bob's hand and heartily congratulated him, and I managed to mumble something appropriate.

Although I knew it was a well-deserved honor, I could only think of it from a personal perspective. Dick had been very active in the MMS, serving as president of the Plymouth District in 1974 and as a member of the House of Delegates for many years. I wished Dick had been nominated for that award. This would have been his last chance and he deserved it! His patients loved him. I was frustrated that my husband's contributions to his patients would not be recognized. Dick never expressed any feelings of regret or bitterness about the award, but I felt enough for both of us. It didn't even occur to me at the time that Dick wasn't eligible as he was not a member of the Bristol North District.

Socializing with friends was a welcome distraction from the reality of the previous ten days. However, as our friend Sandy was leaving, I heard him say, "I just want to congratulate you again, Bob, on such a wonderful honor."

His words felt like a knife in my back. I just wanted to punch Sandy. Punch Sandy—of all people! Sandy, who was one of our closest friends, the nicest guy, who would do anything for us. This is what it had come to—I was directing all of my grief, fear, and anger toward Dick's illness on poor, undeserving Sandy!

Suddenly, I didn't want any company. I wanted them all to go away. I wanted everything to go away—the brain tumor, the dismal prognosis, and all of our unrealized dreams.

Office Practice

After receiving the diagnosis, one thing became clear—we needed to close Dick's practice. Although Dick recognized he could not go back to work, the fact that he was forced to close his practice was devastating to him. This was his life's work. It was so much a part of his being.

I made the first call to Michele from the Brigham Emergency Room and told her to cancel Dick's appointments for the following day. That followed with a phone call to cancel the next week, and by mid-week it became evident that Dick would not be able to return to work at all. Michele contacted other physicians, who were more than willing to provide coverage and anything else they could do. In the time lag before his diagnosis was confirmed and we could make a definitive statement, patients were calling and stopping by the office. Michele had the overwhelming task of managing their inquiries and mixed emotions.

Michele was struggling with her own emotions of shock, fear, and grief. She was also losing her livelihood. She told me later that Dick had not only been her boss for fifteen years, but also her counselor, investment advisor, teacher, and friend. When Michele was finally cleared to communicate Dick's diagnosis, his patient community was overwhelmed, and Michele did her share of grief counseling.

Aggravating the whole situation was the fact that Dick was still under pressure to leave the premises by July 1, as the building where he rented his office was being sold. I contacted the lawyer Dick had previously hired to see if he could get an extension on the eviction. Despite the change in our circumstances, the lawyer representing the office building stood fast and would not give us any leeway. Ironically, three years later, the medical building in downtown Middleboro still stood empty.

I was nervous about handling the business end of dissolving the practice because Dick had always handled those matters. But after a lot of research, I chose a lawyer whose specialty was transitioning medical practices and hired her that first week while we were still in the hospital. I also consulted with a good friend and member of our chavurah (Jewish study and fellowship group), Stu, who had retired as the administrator of a large community health center. In his retirement he had been working as a consultant for synagogues that were closing or merging with other synagogues. I thought his expertise might be helpful in the dissolution of Dick's practice, but his offer to work with Michele and the lawyer in overseeing the closing of the practice was more than I ever expected. Stu would not hear of taking any compensation for his work.

Stu was in the office every day at eight a.m. and worked hard with Michele to let the staff go, organize records, dispose of the contents of the office, and, along with the lawyer, facilitate the sale of the medical practice to Porter Health Care. He helped set up a timeline for patients to pick up their records from the Middleboro office. All other records would be taken over and stored by Porter Health Care.

Dissolving the business was traumatic for Dick. He was terribly worried about his patients, frequently asking about their follow-up care and what arrangements were being made for them. His emotions leaked out as anger. He was furious with the lawyer I hired to negotiate with Porter Health Care.

"She's charging way too much! That's ridiculous that she says the practice is not worth much without a practicing physician. I have over eighteen hundred active patients. I built that practice. I know it's worth more than that. She doesn't know what she's talking about. There will be nothing left for you after her fees."

He also got increasingly agitated with Porter Health Care. We had several go-rounds with the contract for the sale of his practice, including office hardware. Dick felt he was giving his practice away.

At a later date, when the sale was complete, Dick found out from former patients how much Porter was charging his patients to retrieve their records. He was so upset that he called the Porter representative and screamed at him, "I heard from one of my patients how much you charged them to get their medical records. That is inexcusable. You can't charge my patients that much to get their *own* medical records."

The Porter Health representative explained they needed to house the records at an external site and retrieve them from there. But Dick would have none of their excuses.

"You will be in trouble with the state. That's against the law."

His face was red and contorted in anger. I had rarely seen him so incensed. They finally agreed to reduce the fee, but Dick feared many patients had already suffered the higher cost.

Dick had infinite patience with Michele, Stu, and me, but his anger over his diagnosis and the loss of his practice and his livelihood, came out against the strangers in his midst—the lawyer and Porter Health Care. He found fault over every detail. He was sure they were trying to trick him and cheat him. His disease was beginning to show.

There were a lot of bumps in the road, and it took patience and perseverance from all parties to reach an equitable agreement. Dick was eager to send out a formal communication to his patients but needed to wait until the contract was negotiated. Porter came up with a letter they wanted to send out with their signature. Dick flatly rejected it. He wanted to write his own personal communication to his patients, signed by him, which would accompany the letter from Porter. After several revisions and much angst, the following letter was agreed upon by both parties.

June 14, 2012
Dear Patients,

I have enjoyed treating and taking care of you over the last thirty-five years. I have been fortunate to get to know you and your families. Regretfully, I need to close my medical practice at this time. I have been diagnosed with a particularly aggressive and invasive cancer of the brain called glioblastoma. I am sorry that I was unable to give you more notice and that I did not have an opportunity to personally say goodbye. I very much appreciate all your kind notes and cards.

The letter went on to say that Porter Medical Group would be taking over the practice and there was an enclosed letter from Porter detailing information regarding patient referrals, records, and continuity of care. Dick also shared that he had retained Michele to be in the office through June 30 to assist with the transition.

He closed with these words:

Thank you again for the privilege of serving you.
Best Regards,
Richard Gross, M.D.

Although thirty-four years had passed, it felt like yesterday when we had moved to town and enthusiastically set up Dick's office space in the basement floor of the medical building. Years later, as Dick's practice grew, he moved upstairs to a larger, first-floor office.

I felt heartbroken as I took down our canvas photos that decorated the walls of Dick's waiting and exam rooms. I remembered how proud we were when we replaced the original artwork with our own photography. Rotating his photography through the office allowed Dick to share his hobby with his patients, and he always appreciated their generous comments. It was gratifying to him to give each of his office staff their favorite photograph. Although most of his equipment and furniture had been updated, reupholstered, or replaced, it turned out the items we had so carefully picked out when he established his office were basically worthless now.

Dick had always taken the time to talk with each patient. He would ask about their parents, siblings, children, and grandchildren. He remembered what they did for a living and where they traveled; he knew their strengths and their weaknesses. Many patients had multiple charts because they were with Dick for so long.

Dick rarely shared stories about work, but he once told me about making an unusual diagnosis he was proud of. He had a young patient who was having difficulty breathing and was confused—he even got lost on his way to Dick's office. In taking a thorough history, Dick found out that his patient had just returned from a scuba-diving vacation and had flown shortly after diving. Dick figured out that his patient had the bends (decompression sickness), not a common diagnosis in a small-town practice. Dick stabilized him and quickly made arrangements to get his patient to the nearest hyperbaric chamber for recompression, and he made a full recovery.

Closing his office was agonizing for Dick. Each chart represented a real, important person to him. It was a crushing blow to see his life's work being filtered down by Porter Health to the monetary value of a chart.

CHAPTER 12

Treatment Strategies

We met with neuro-oncologist Dr. David Reardon at the Dana-Farber Cancer Institute to discuss treatment options. We handpicked Dr. Reardon, who had trained at Duke University and climbed the ranks there before moving to Boston. He was knowledgeable about all the recent advances in glioblastoma research. He was a bright, young, personable physician who made us all feel comfortable. He took the time to answer everyone's questions, so we never felt rushed in making such a daunting decision.

Dick's sister, Cindy, researched studies and consulted with other professionals in preparation for the meeting and flew in to join us. Cindy was a PhD biostatistician, a professor at the University of Minnesota Schools of Pharmacy and Nursing, who had wide experience in the field of health research and had presented papers around the world. Over the next few weeks, whenever Dick had an opportunity (whether it was appropriate or not), he always threw in his sister's background and credentials; he was so proud of her.

He did the same for his uncle Dr. Samuel Gross, who had recently passed away and was renowned in the field of pediatric hematology. Dick told everyone who would listen that his uncle had written a hematology textbook used in medical schools and had won the Lasker Award, a prestigious award honoring physicians and scientists for medical research and achievement. Dick never showed off about himself or his accomplishments, but he was quick to praise others.

Bharani also joined us as we reviewed treatment options. Since his diagnosis, Dick had spent a great deal of time studying glioblastoma statistics and research. After much discussion about trials, medications, vaccines, and treatment protocols, we honed in on what we thought were the best alternatives that had proven benefits to prolong life with glioblastoma. Dick did not want to take any chances of being part of a randomized or blind study. He would begin a course of chemotherapies with daily oral therapy and a weekly infusion, and he would begin a course of targeted radiation. By making this choice, we understood that he would not be eligible for any trials.

We had an initial meeting with Dr. Brian Alexander, the radiation oncologist at the Brigham, and they made a mold for Dick's radiation mask. Dr. Alexander explained that Dick would require six weeks of radiation, five days a week.

Dick responded, "We live in Lakeville, about an hour from here and that's with no traffic. I would prefer to go to St. Anne's Hospital Cancer Care Center in Fall River. I know it is an accredited Cancer Center that recently affiliated with Dana-Farber. I don't want to spend my limited time on the road."

Dr. Alexander replied, "The radiation involved with the brain is so specialized that they can't do it at the satellite locations. I want you to come here to the Brigham, where you can get the advanced radiation therapy you need, and we can monitor you every day."

Dick agreed that he would if he had to, but he wasn't happy about it.

On one of our very first trips to Boston, Dick had a gleam in his eye as he said to me, "We have an important stop to make on our way home today."

He was secretive about it but very determined. I wondered where he wanted to go, as I knew he was usually exhausted and anxious to get home. He directed me to drive to 520 Commonwealth Avenue, which turned out to be the Boston location of Hunt's Camera Store.

He instructed the salesman, "My wife needs a really sturdy tripod that isn't too heavy."

"I want to get you one like Lou had on our trip," he told me.

When we had reviewed our photos from the trip to Monet's Garden, Dick noticed that mine were not nearly as sharp as his, and he decided that I needed a new tripod.

After reviewing different models, Dick carefully chose a top of the line tripod that would also be light enough for travel. Despite his exhaustion from a day of medical appointments, Dick was smiling broadly, so pleased about his purchase for me.

I was surprised that with everything going on, Dick prioritized buying me a tripod. It was definitely not on my radar. But I later realized it was part of Dick's extensive plan to take care of me today and far into the future.

Dick started radiation treatment at various times of day, until a regular time slot became available. He was taking two types of oral chemotherapy that also contributed to his fatigue, poor appetite, and forgetfulness. One week into treatment, Dick questioned whether to continue.

He was lying on the bed after a long, arduous day at the Brigham and complained, "If I have only limited time, I don't want to spend it in traffic. My whole day is traveling back and forth to Boston, having radiation, and then feeling so tired I collapse into bed. This is not living. I want to spend time with you. I need to fix the jacuzzi. Who's going to open the pool and mow the lawn? I need to take care of everything. I'm too tired now to do anything else when I get home."

I panicked at the thought that he might not want to continue treatment. This was not the Dick I knew, who would never give up and would fight until the end for his patients.

I tried to remain calm as I responded, "I realize it's frustrating and hard on you, honey. If you really want to stop treatment you can, but it is only for a limited time. You've made it through the first week. We've had lots of extra appointments, so the upcoming weeks will be a little easier. They are trying to get you into that ten a.m. time slot on a regular basis, which will make the traffic much easier. Why don't we wait another week and see how you feel?"

"I wish I could have gone to Fall River."

"I know. But you have the best doctors and the best treatment team. You are so used to taking care of everything and everybody that it's hard for you to focus on yourself. Think of this as your job. It's full time. It takes a lot out of you. But you don't have to worry about anything else right now.

"I can take care of everything. The kids can help me open the pool. I know what to do—I've been doing it with you for over thirty years. I just didn't prioritize it. I can call a repairman for the jacuzzi.

You don't have to do everything yourself. Our neighbor John came over and mowed the lawn the week you were in the hospital, and Seth mowed it when he was home. I will help you with whatever you need. I love you so much."

"I love you too," he responded.

I curled up on the bed next to him, kissed him goodnight, and positioned my head securely in the crook of his arm where my body naturally fit against the curve of his. As he drifted off to sleep, I could hear his steady breathing, but he could not hear my weeping.

CHAPTER 13

Finding Purpose

Dick wasn't used to being a patient. He liked to stay active and was frustrated at not being able to work or have the energy to do anything when he got home from treatment. He was tired, grouchy, and depressed. I was appreciative when his friend and colleague, Dr. Julia Edelman, called to see if she could come by for a visit. Dr. Edelman was the current president of the Massachusetts Medical Society, Bristol North District, and a published author. She asked Dick if he would read and review her just-released eBook on sleep disorders on Amazon, and he was honored to do so.

Julia shared two things that day that would have a huge positive impact on our lives. The first was an idea she offered.

She told Dick, "You are an excellent physician, especially known for your ability to communicate well with patients. Many doctors could learn from you. Would you be interested in co-authoring a book with me that would be a guide for physicians on doctor/patient relationships?"

I fought tears as I realized she was giving Dick a lifeline—something to give him purpose.

Although Dick didn't commit, I could see he was quite pleased with the offer. Julia suggested he write down some ideas and send them to her. In the following weeks, Dick faced a grueling chemotherapy regimen and radiation schedule. He was physically exhausted and sometimes disheartened but didn't often let it show. He ordered a dictation software program for his computer, recognizing that he was starting to lose some of his skills. It remained unused and he never did any writing.

I occasionally reminded him of Julia's idea and suggested he might like to work on the project. I'm not sure if it was because he was so preoccupied with his treatment and just staying alive, or because how he dealt with patients came so naturally to him that he could not define it in text, but he never followed through.

It didn't matter, however, because the offer was the important part.

The second thing Julia shared was that the Massachusetts Medical Society Bristol North District had chosen Dick to be the Community Clinician of the Year for the following year, 2013. The award would be presented in the fall of 2012 on a local level and in the spring of 2013 on the state level. Although Dick was not a member of the Bristol North group, he worked with colleagues and clinicians in that district. I felt tremendous relief and gratefulness that Dick would receive the recognition he deserved. We all knew why Dr. Edelman had arranged to have the local presentation in the fall. I prayed Dick would still be alive to receive the award the following spring.

"Thank you, Julia. I am so honored to be chosen by my colleagues," Dick said.

Dick's blue eyes had come alive and his face wore a spirited expression, a look I hadn't seen in weeks. Julia's visit had aroused his will to live, and I intended to build on it.

CHAPTER 14

Acceptance

The indecision Dick had expressed about continuing treatment was brief, and he never mentioned it again. With the love and support of his family, friends, patients, and colleagues, Dick developed a positive outlook and was driven to do everything in his power to live as long as possible.

Dick asked Dr. Reardon for a prescription for modafinil, a drug that would help him stay awake. He wanted to be as fully present as possible. Dr. Reardon was agreeable, however, the insurance denied the request as the drug was typically used for patients with narcolepsy. Luckily, Dr. Reardon was able to make a persuasive argument in his appeal and Dick began taking modafinil to help him get the most out of each day.

Early on, we met with Dr. Reardon's whole team, including neuro-psychiatrist Dr. Halyna Vitigliano. Because her name was long and hard to pronounce, we referred to her as Dr. V.

Dick was offered a meeting with the team social worker to receive therapy, but he refused. He was not one who talked much about feelings. Dick was an honest, caring, empathic man, but he was not prone to introspection. He was more of a scientific thinker who looked at the facts. He researched and then acted on the best information possible. He felt more comfortable with a physician, so with my encouragement, he scheduled a follow-up appointment with Dr. V. I requested to join Dick during their first session but Dr. V said she would like to meet with him privately, and I was invited in for the last ten minutes.

Once she recognized how hard it was for Dick to share his feelings, it seemed to provide a good balance to have me take part in the sessions, and that became our continued mode of treatment. I had my own private therapist to share the depths of my grief, and I couldn't imagine how I could contain my feelings without her. I asked Dick on occasion if he wanted time alone with Dr. V, but he always said no, and he tried to put on a good show in his sessions of how wonderful everything was.

We met with Dr. V on a monthly basis, and part of her routine was to do a mental status exam. I remember the first time Dr. V stated, "Name all the words you can think of that begin with the letter '*G*.'"

I was amazed with the substantial list Dick came up with, including many three syllable words: *grass, governor, geothermal, glioblastoma, garage, gaiter, gopher*. . . . He seemed to go on and on. Dr. V was also quite impressed and actually had to stop him, because he seemed poised to recite words indefinitely.

Although Dick had already noticed some brain fog, he could still subtract from 100 by sevens faster than I could. He was able to recall all the words Dr. V had asked him to remember ten minutes earlier.

He drew the abstract shapes and filled in the clock as directed with no flaws. Over the following months, his skills dropped off quickly, but he always put in a pretty good showing on the task of words that began with a particular letter.

Being part of the sessions allowed me to highlight some of the ups and downs Dick was experiencing. This provided an entry point for Dr. V to address more sensitive issues. She discussed the pros and cons of taking an anti-depressant, and Dick finally agreed to start on a low dose. Although he didn't verbally express anger over his diagnosis, Dick felt it. In one of our early sessions, I told Dr. V that Dick had ordered a thirty cubic yard construction container from our disposal company and started throwing things out. He attacked the basement first. That was his territory.

Whenever life had gotten complicated in the past, Dick had always "cleaned" the basement, which seemed to help him feel more in control. It made me sad when I saw Dick throw out all the miscellaneous wood, bricks, pipes, electronic parts, etc., I had seen him use to fashion a cage for our peacocks, make a swing set, or help the kids build a science project. He tossed his high school yearbook in the cavernous bin. I knew, in a sense, he was also "cleaning house" for me. As upset as I was, I knew Dick was even more angry. He was throwing away his memories.

My brother, Neal, came to pick up Dick's moped from our early student days and some tools which Dick wanted to give him. He also gave Neal his prized wooden shoeshine kit, but weeks later, when he was feeling more confident, he asked for it back.

As I walked my brother out through the garage that day, we started talking about the memorial breakfast in memory of my dad, which we had hosted in our hometown of Fall River, just one month before Dick got sick. We had a discussion about if and how we would continue the scholarship program we had held for the last thirty-five years. The Sam Kaplan Memorial breakfast event was sponsored through the Jewish War Veterans' Fall River Post 168, who participated in the statewide JWV "Classmates Today—Neighbors Tomorrow" scholarship program. Our family gave an annual scholarship in my dad's memory to a B.M.C. Durfee High School senior. It gave us an opportunity every year to gather with family, friends, and JWV members to remember and honor my father. But the Fall River chapter of the JWV was dissolving that year and we had to make a decision about how to go forward.

In the back of my mind, I knew right then that someday I would carry on this tradition for my husband. His two grandchildren and future grandchildren would hear about his character and values, just as my children had learned about the grandfather they never knew.

CHAPTER 15

Lotsa Helping Hands

Just days after Dick was diagnosed, Samantha established an account on a website called Lotsa Helping Hands. She named the site community "We Love Dr. Richard Gross."

"Mom," Samantha enthusiastically explained, "people can sign up to help you and Dad with driving, yard work, cooking, or whatever you need. It will give you guys more time to spend with each other. I can update everyone on Dad's condition. You won't have to be on the phone all the time, answering everyone's individual calls."

I was feeling overwhelmed and was less than enthusiastic about taking on something additional. Computer skills were not my forte; Dick was the expert in that area. But I gave in, thinking it probably wouldn't pan out anyway. I gave Samantha permission to add friends from my email list but told her I needed to focus my attention on Dick. She agreed to be the administrator of the site so I wouldn't have to take responsibility.

Samantha introduced the site to Dick and asked him to write an initial letter. She entitled it *Letter from Dad* and posted it one week after he entered the hospital.

Dear Wonderful Family and Friends,

Thank you for your loving calls and visits. I deeply appreciate them and feel so fortunate to have family and friends who are so incredibly kind!

I regret this condition has started with a vengeance, and it has given me problems with confusion, short-term memory, seizures, and fatigue. I am doing everything I can to fight back and am receiving excellent medical care.

In news of my medical practice, I have decided to retire early. I'm working rapidly to transfer my practice to some of the best young doctors I know.

My family has rallied from all over the country and I am deeply heartened to hear of your thoughtful prayers and good wishes. Let it be known that I have a hearty appetite and I am getting time to enjoy my photography.

I wish you all a happy and productive summer, and I look forward to seeing you!

Love,

Dick

The Lotsa Helping Hands site states, "private communities empower a caregiver's 'circles of community' to come together to provide support and help to the caregiver and family."

Thank goodness we had lots of "circles of community"—our neighbors, camera club, synagogue, chavurah, co-workers, bootcampers, garden club, gourmet group, patients, friends, and family. The community grew every day and we had 222 members in total.

Samantha had been right. Lotsa Helping Hands became a godsend, and I quickly learned how to manage it myself. I later became co-administrator, started accepting new members, and writing updates on Dick's progress and setbacks. I thought it would be an additional task, but in fact, I found writing about our journey very therapeutic. Friends from near and far responded to my updates with reassuring notes filled with love and support, and they were a big part of my staying sane through our journey. Dick and I felt enveloped by this community of love.

Once a month, I put a request up on Helping Hands for drivers for four of the five days a week for the six-week schedule of radiation. It was at least a four-hour commitment on beautiful summer days, yet the calendar miraculously filled up. Later on, I would request volunteers for driving to physical therapy, occupational therapy, cognitive therapy, and the LIVESTRONG program at the YMCA. At a later stage I asked for help so I could keep my own appointments and for respite. Whatever the request, volunteers were always at the ready. It was so reassuring to know we could count on our Helping Hands family.

Bharani, who lived in Brookline, met Dick every day at his radiation appointment at the Brigham. When Dick went in for treatment, Bharani sat in the waiting room with the Helping Hands volunteers and got to know many of our friends. Dick really enjoyed being accompanied by friends, neighbors, and patients. Whenever I mentioned this to volunteers, they always told me it was they who were honored to have the opportunity to be with him.

Although I loved spending time with Dick, this gave us a break from each other. I joked at the time that he was getting sick of my company. As is often the case, it is safest to show those we love our deepest emotions. Dick got agitated more easily now and sometimes it was hard for us to hold each other up. He really perked up with friends and always had a story or adventure to tell me when he returned.

While Dick was gone, I spent time arranging appointments, dealing with insurance and prescription issues, managing Lotsa Helping Hands, monitoring the closing of his business, and other everyday tasks that didn't halt because cancer had invaded our lives. I don't know how I would have accomplished these responsibilities without that dedicated time and the generosity of volunteers.

One of my first projects when Dick was not home was to contact the local weekly paper, the *Middleboro Gazette*. I suggested the *Gazette* write an article about Dick and his sudden retirement after thirty-four years of practice. I thought it would be a good way of reaching the larger community and lifting Dick's morale, so I was persistent when the newspaper dragged its feet.

From day one, Dick received letters in the mail from patients expressing their sorrow and well wishes. I cannot tell you how meaningful those heartfelt messages were to him. With permission from a few patients, I shared their names and phone numbers with John Tessier, the *Gazette* correspondent who was eventually assigned to write the article.

When Dick came home, I told him, "The *Middleboro Gazette* called and wants to write an article on you."

He agreed to provide an interview. The article was published on July 12, 2012.

In part, the article read:

Dr. Gross explained that he regrets not being able to give his patients more of an opportunity to seek other doctors, but there was no time as it has all happened so fast.

Since patients began hearing about their doctor's condition, they have been getting in touch to express their appreciation and support. Former patient Brianne Kessimian's sentiments are typical.

"I am very sad that he has to retire," she said. "He's been such a fabulous doctor; he doesn't just treat you like a patient, but as a person. You can tell he really cares about you. He always takes the time to ask about my family."

It was a well-written article communicating how Dick's illness and the loss of his practice were a blow to the community. But Dick was upset about one statement. The article said he "suffered" from glioblastoma.

Dick told me, "That is not true. I am not in pain. I am not suffering. I feel uplifted by the love and kindness of my family, friends, and patients."

A flood of letters from Dick's patients followed the *Gazette* article. These letters and email responses on Lotsa Helping Hands had a powerful effect on Dick's mood. They reinforced for him that his life's work had made a difference. He realized that the care and consideration he had shown to others was admired and appreciated. He had saved lives. He knew that he had filled an important role on this earth.

CHAPTER 16

Gena's Letter

A few weeks after we got home from the hospital, I emailed our devastating news to the friends we had made on our recent photography trip.

Charles and many of the participants became members of Lotsa Helping Hands. Although they did not live close enough to help physically, they read my updates on the site and their support was immeasurable. Rene had been on a trip to Africa when I contacted her but called me as soon as she returned.

"Your message just sucked the air right out of me," she said. "I always felt like the four of us had so much in common. You know, Bruce and I had some serious discussions about retirement after my trip to Europe. When I came home, I told him about the three group members who had lost their spouses. I talked about Wanda's fragile condition and Martha's husband, Bob's failing health. It forced us to discuss the future and recognize that we wanted to be able to enjoy retirement while we could still be active and travel together." Rene continued, "Then, with the tragic news of Dick's diagnosis, Bruce and I got serious about our plans. He is easing out of his job, and he will fully retire in 2014."

As I listened to Rene, I thought again what a significant impact the people on that trip had on each other. I believe God was looking out for all of us.

* * *

After Gena received my email, we had a heartfelt phone conversation. A two-page, emotional letter arrived in the mail a few days later, telling me how sorry she was to hear about Dick and how she had survived her husband, Steve's, diagnosis. I did not have any friends who had been widowed so I was grateful to Gena for her support and advice. Gena wrote: *When my husband was diagnosed with Stage IV colon cancer, I remember the incredible shock, devastation, and despair I felt. I would wake up after a night's sleep without that knowledge in my brain and then suddenly remember that our lives were forever changed in one brief moment of discovery. The thought of losing him, the loss of our future plans together, and the fear of what lay ahead, left me paralyzed, terrified, and overwhelmed with grief and other emotions.*

I identified with everything Gena said. She reminded us to treasure every moment and make the most of every day—to spend quality time with family and friends. She talked about how she and Steve had gotten support through their church and through cancer support groups. They had created a "bucket list" of things Steve wanted to do, and Gena did everything possible to make those happen. One of them was to drive all of Route 66, which they did. Steve wrote cards to his nieces and nephews on the occasion of future milestones. They celebrated an early Christmas and Steve told everyone around him that he loved them. They went on bucket list getaways as Steve's health allowed and talked about his wishes for Gena in the future. Most important, Gena's letter reminded me that we still had each other and could talk about our lives together, share our love, experiences, and memories, and comfort one another through this difficult journey.

She ended her letter with: *I know the next few days, weeks, months and years, will be a terrible, immensely painful, sad journey for both of you. I also know that there will be moments of joy, intense love, sharing, and amazing intimacy. Somehow it is possible to live, love and cherish each other for the time you have left.*

With Love,

Gena

We read the letter from Gena together and hugged each other as my tears ran onto Dick's cheeks.

"Don't cry," Dick said. "I don't want you to cry. I love you so much. I want you to be happy. We are so blessed to have experienced that incredible photo trip to Monet's Garden and Keukenhof to celebrate our fortieth anniversary! It was fortuitous that we met Gena and so many wonderful new friends."

"I know, I know," I said. "I think God sent us on that trip for a reason. Gena is so amazing and so strong. But I don't think I can be that strong. I love you so much. I can't imagine ever being without you."

"Please don't cry. We're here together. We've had such a wonderful life and we still have a lot of living to do."

"You're right. I'm so glad that we met early and that I let you talk me into getting married when I was still just a kid!"

We smiled and laughed as we renewed the early days of our romance.

Gena's letter became our bible throughout our journey. We reread it many times during different stages of Dick's illness. Once in a while I called Gena, or she checked in with me, and I knew I could rage or sob and it would be okay. Gena instinctively knew when I needed that extra boost and I looked to her for that special understanding we shared. Dick also enjoyed talking with Gena, but it was a different sort of conversation. They might talk about camera gear, our trip to Monet's Garden, or the weather in Seattle.

CHAPTER 17

Our Real Fortieth Anniversary

June 18 was our fortieth anniversary. We had a tradition of looking through our wedding album each year and chuckling at how young and thin we looked. This year the memories were even more poignant.

Samantha posted a beautiful Happy Anniversary announcement on Lotsa Helping Hands:

Today is Robin & Richard's FORTIETH WEDDING ANNIVERSARY!!!! They are romantic, madly-in-love, gentle with each other, and truly each other's soul mates.

They met when my Mom was only eighteen and Dad was in his first year of medical school. Just kids! Dad says she was captivating at first sight, wearing her aunt's long, beaver fur coat and her brother-in-law's combat boots. They began to date and after just a short time, Dad asked Mom to marry him.

Samantha went on to say we met at the Case Western Reserve University Hillel library. I spotted this tall, good-looking guy with beautiful blue eyes, masked by geeky-looking glasses that pointed up at the ends. We were the only ones in the library. I watched him studying as he occasionally stole glances in my direction. While I was trying to get up the courage to say something, he shyly came over to talk to me. We talked and talked as though we were old friends seeing each other again after years had passed.

The question of how and when Dick asked me to marry him was always a mystery. There were so many different versions. The problem was there was no conclusive time or place. I seem to remember Dick *always* asking me to marry him. I knew he was "the one" but I was just a college freshman. He was persistent, but I told him I was too young to get married. We were both students. How would we support ourselves? I had spent the year after high school in Israel and had my heart set on going back for my junior year abroad.

I remember one of our first dates—we walked across campus to the Stosacker Auditorium to see the movie *Gypsy*. It was a bitter cold winter day and Dick was wearing gloves from the army/navy surplus store. They had a soft mitten liner and a large army green glove shell with a trigger finger. He took my hand in his and held it as we walked and I felt so warm and protected.

Dick was very smart and he had a keen, dry sense of humor. He was the kindest, most generous person I had ever known. Through the Hillel organization, I was collecting donations for the United Jewish Appeal. Most students were on a very tight budget and if they donated, it was generally five dollars, occasionally ten. Dick donated twenty-five dollars.

I had a work-study job for fifteen hours a week at a residential facility for children with severe developmental disabilities. I used to share stories with Dick about the children's intensive needs and the agency's limited resources. It meant a lot to me when he independently donated to this facility; I knew he denied himself any extras. He would often include my roommate in our outings and bring us both fun little gifts like a chocolate bar or a kite.

We loved going to the University Circle Wade Lagoon to study, although lying on the grass together, we quickly forgot our good intentions. We roamed through the dreamy, romantic gardens at the Cleveland Botanical Gardens and the impressive galleries of the Cleveland Museum of Art. Our favorite room in the museum was the atrium, which had lush gardens and benches to sit and relax. Admission was free and we took advantage of this opportunity to make frequent visits. Dick's favorite painting was *Cupid and Psyche* by Jacques-Louis David, of two young lovers, which he said reminded him of us.

Dick was head over heels in love with me and I knew I wanted to spend the rest of my life with him. He was the first and only man I ever made love to. My all-female dormitory had a strict sign-in policy, with a dorm mother who supervised guests leaving at nine p.m. on weekdays and eleven p.m. on weekends, although we somehow managed to get around that. I put my name into a lottery for my sophomore year to be part of an experimental inter-racial program where the students would be housed on a co-ed floor in the graduate dorms, and luckily, I was chosen. Dick convinced me to "just go look" at engagement rings and that became one of our pastimes.

That summer we returned home to Massachusetts and met each other's families. They were both in the needle trades, active in their synagogue communities, and kept kosher homes. They each valued hard work, education, and family.

When we headed back to Cleveland in the fall of my sophomore year, Dick said,

"I know you really want to go back to Israel for your junior year abroad, but if you marry me, I promise I will take you to Israel when I graduate from medical school."

This meant a lot coming from someone who had no extra money and had never been out of the country. There was no question in my mind that he would keep his promise. I also had hatched an idea for graduating college in three years, which I was later able to accomplish.

Dick was ecstatic when I finally responded, "I do."

But I had one condition: we were going home in October for my younger sister Priscilla's bat mitzvah and I did not want to steal the thunder from her special occasion, so I told Dick we couldn't tell our parents until after the bat mitzvah.

"And," I told him, "I am holding you to your promise to take me to Israel!"

It was exciting to keep our secret, and this time, when we went shopping for engagement rings, it was for real. Dick formally asked my dad for my hand in marriage, and when we announced our engagement, our families were thrilled. Our parents agreed to continue to help us out while we were in school, and a June 1972 wedding was planned.

Samantha's Lotsa Helping Hands entry ended,

They've been through it all together: school, graduation, residency, my Mom becoming a social worker, my Dad becoming a doctor, moving back to MA, parenting four children (I'm especially thankful for that!), traveling the world, building a home, gardening together, discovering their love of photography, and, of course, the million other beautiful things that make up a great marriage and life together.

Happy 40th wedding anniversary!

Please join me in congratulating them on building an everlasting love.

Samantha shared our email and phone numbers but warned people that they might not get to speak with us, as we had three doctors' appointments in Boston that day. I was determined to do something special to celebrate our anniversary, so I made arrangements to stay overnight in Boston and got tickets for the Cirque du Soleil performance. I distinctly remember the day I called for the reservation at the Hilton Hotel downtown. I had a hard time controlling my emotions as I explained to the reservation clerk that we were celebrating our fortieth anniversary, and I understood we could get a discount because my husband was a patient at Dana-Farber. I ended up telling her much more than she needed to know as I broke down in tears.

After a long day, we left the Dana around 4 p.m. and hit terrible traffic en route to the Hilton. Dick was tired and impatient, and I regretted making the decision to stay in Boston. However, once we arrived at our destination, we were treated like royalty and quickly forgot all our woes. We were surprised and delighted as the valet led us to the penthouse suite! It was elegant and enormous. I just kept going from room to room, shouting, "Dick, come see this view," or "Come look—there's another bedroom and a sitting room." A complimentary bottle of champagne and a dish of truffles awaited us. They had upgraded us to the best room in the house! I gave a silent prayer of thanks to that kind reservation agent who had a big heart.

Attending the Cirque du Soleil performance did not turn out as well, as Dick was cold, tired, and the music was too loud for him. He had developed increased sensitivities and we were both still learning his limitations. But our posh hotel suite more than made up for it and we spent a night feeling like a king and queen.

When we returned home from Boston we were welcomed by another surprise, a magnificent arrangement of flowers surrounded with rose petals in the shape of a heart, sent by our children.

Our friend Charles Needle remembered that although we celebrated our anniversary on the trip with him in April, our actual anniversary was in June. We were touched by the meaningful gift he sent—a book, *Photography and the Creative Life*—written by his dear friend Nancy Rotenberg. Nancy had recently passed away from cancer.

I told Dick, "I remember Charles talking about what a special person Nancy was. You are like Nancy. You touched so many lives. You are living life every day with courage. I am so proud of you. I love how you greet each day with an open heart and that beautiful smile. . . . Maybe that's because you don't have to wake up at 4:45 a.m. any more for bootcamp!"

Dick laughed, and responded, "Every day is a vacation now. I love waking up and fooling around with you in bed. And that's just what I want to do right now!"

"Happy anniversary," he said, as he took my hand and led me upstairs to our bedroom.

CHAPTER 18

Our Backyard

B y the time we bought our Lakeville home, I already knew that Dick's work would dictate our lifestyle and that this house had everything we needed to make it work. In the years to come, I found it was easier to swim in the backyard pool than drag four kids to the beach on my own. Dick built a swing set for the kids with the help of his dad. He added on his own invention of a zip line as the kids grew older. I remember the inaugural run where Sarah banged her leg into the tree. After that, Dick perfected it by covering the tree at the point of impact with a thick carpet.

We nurtured vegetable, flower, herb, butterfly, and wildflower gardens. The kids helped in the garden, but harvesting was their favorite activity. They loved picking the sweet, tender peas that Dick had set up on makeshift trellises made with old wire netting. The peas never made it into the house—the kids devoured them straight from the garden. At one end of the yard was a hammock where Dick often napped after being on call all night, so he could still be with the family.

On a typical weekend Dick was up early to do rounds on his patients in the hospital and didn't arrive home till around noon, both Saturdays and Sundays. If it was his weekend on call, which was every other weekend in the early days, he might get home mid-afternoon and likely be called back later in the day and again during the night. He always carried a beeper and received frequent calls from the nursing staff, which always took top priority. He was also responsible to go in for patients who were admitted through the emergency room. There were no hospitalists in those days.

We rarely fought in our marriage, but when we did it was almost always over his working too many hours and not spending enough time with the family. When Dick returned from rounds on the weekends, we sometimes made plans to go out as a family. He would often say, "Let me just rest for a few minutes," and you can imagine what happened next. So I put my energy into building our lives around our backyard.

When our second daughter Sarah was five and Sandra was three, we attended a Lakeville Library preschool program about the life cycle of the monarch butterfly, and they were hooked. Instead of swimming in the pool that summer, we could often be found on a hot summer day in the fields of Lakeville searching amongst the milkweed plants for eggs and caterpillars.

We grew a variety of butterfly-nectaring flowers that attracted several species of butterflies. We acquired a library of books about butterfly gardening and participated in field trips with the Massachusetts Butterfly Club. As we became more knowledgeable, we grew larval plants that would attract certain types of butterflies, and we were able to watch the whole life cycle right in our own backyard.

Dick was not pleased when I introduced roadside milkweed into the garden, but he forgave me when he saw how exciting it was for the whole family to watch the monarchs lay eggs on the milkweed and transition into caterpillars. We brought the caterpillars inside as they matured and raised them in big fish tanks. The kids fed them daily with new milkweed leaves (although they weren't as studious about removing the poop!). The caterpillars sought higher ground when they were ready to form a chrysalis. We kept them on our dining room buffet, and they climbed up to the underside of the hutch, which created the perfect spot for them to attach their chrysalis. The kids' friends all knew that it was not unusual to see chrysalises or caterpillars hanging upside down in the shape of a J on our dining room hutch.

Over time we gave up the butterfly nets for cameras, and thus was born my passion for photographing butterflies.

We also had a pet chicken before it was popular. Because the kids held her in their laps when she was a chick, Lox was very placid and provided endless hours of entertainment for the children. They built nests for her, but the only nest she ever owned was the one she discovered herself. We had a built-in grill on the back of the house that was protected on three sides, and Lox hopped up there every night. Each morning, we found a fresh egg on the grill!

When the kids were a little older, Dick came up with the idea of getting pet peacocks. I researched the possibility and found a bird farm just twenty minutes from our home, where we picked out a pair of baby Blue India peacocks. Dick built a luxurious peacock house out of lumber and some materials he had in the basement, including an old glass door. Joe, the gentleman who sold us the peacocks, came to visit a few weeks later.

He said to Dick, "You did a great job. It's fine for now but peacocks grow fast. When their wingspan gets bigger, they'll never fit in that little 'cottage.'" The kids had outgrown the swing set by then so down it came. Dick used two sides of the fence that bordered the yard and added a third to make a huge triangular enclosure for the peacocks. His dad helped him cover it with netting. The peacocks still had their original "cottage" to seek shelter in at night.

The peacocks were a big hit in early spring when they went through their mating ritual. The male peacock had a distinctive rustling sound when he danced and shook his glorious feathers, and we never tired of watching this elaborate show. We got used to the peacock's earth-shattering shrieks, and the neighbors put up with them. Over time we let them have free rein in the yard. They looked majestic walking through the flower gardens and were great photography subjects.

Around four p.m. we usually penned the peacocks up for the night. Over time they caught on to the routine, and at five minutes to four they flew up to the roof, where they liked to roost on hot summer nights. Their mating call was piercing from the backyard, but when they broadcast off the roof, it echoed throughout the neighborhood. One Sunday morning, the peacocks shrieked at 6 a.m. and a neighbor called to ask us to quiet them down. Unfortunately, we couldn't ask the peacocks to "keep it down," so, after five years, we decided it was time to give them up and returned them to our friend Joe.

For our twenty-fifth anniversary we put in a small pond that lent itself to the natural outcropping of rocks in the backyard. Within a few years the surrounding plants and bushes grew in and the pond looked like it had always been there. When Dick came home for lunch, he loved feeding the fish and enjoying quiet moments in the serenity of the garden. It was our little oasis.

Dick was talented in a lot of areas, including building and fixing things. He also had some Yankee ingenuity in him and believed in doing everything himself. He saved pieces of lumber, mechanical parts, and other leftover materials in his basement workshop and usually found a use for them later in one of his projects. On his days off, Dick loved tinkering in his workshop and working on the house and garden.

Winberg's True Value Hardware store, around the corner from our house, was his favorite place to shop. The owner, Paul Winberg, always exchanged a friendly hello and helped Dick choose supplies for his latest project. Dick even got me a few birthday presents from Winberg's (until I got smart after receiving a shower head one year and started buying my own presents for him to give me!). A Polaroid surplus store opened up on Route 28 in Raynham, and Dick loved to stop there en route from the hospital on Wednesday afternoons. He couldn't wait to show off his latest finds when he got home.

Another project that turned out to be a great success was the solar heater Dick invented for our swimming pool, using the south-facing roof by the pool. We had converted the upstairs attic into a bedroom for Sandra, which was very hot in the summer. Dick thought of a way to cool the room and heat the pool at the same time.

He ran hosing across the top of the roof like a drip irrigation system. He connected the hose to a pipe that drew the cold water up to the roof using the power of the pool pump. The water dripped down the hot roof into the gutter and collected into a pipe that ran the warm water back into the swimming pool. Keeping it simple, he put a sock on the end of the pipe so it collected all the pine needles and acted like a filter. Every week we changed the filter with an orphan sock. The kids loved to swim over to the deep end of the pool where the hot water streamed in on a sunny day. After two successful summers, Dick made the system permanent by digging the pipes underground.

Dick was not afraid of physical labor. He always seemed to be digging ditches for something. There was a drainage ditch on the other side of our fence that diverted runoff water from the golf course. When it became ineffective over years of buildup from leaves, Dick dug it deeper. Our in-ground swimming pool was not designed well. The pump house was uphill, and the pipes were all buried underground. One year he dug up much of the lawn to locate and repair an underground leak.

At my insistence, he hired a pool company to make repairs when it sprang a leak years later, and the following summer it happened again. Dick was angry that the pool company hadn't buried the pipes past the freeze line and just threw the earth in so that rocks lodged against the pipes. It was one of those *I told you so* moments where I had to admit he was right. He dug trenches again and made the repair himself. Although I was always trying to save him extra work, Dick preferred to do things himself rather than hire someone.

Because it was so hard to get adequate help when you needed it for seasonal repairs, Dick learned to replace the pool pump, motor, and pipes himself. I always told him he was the best swimming pool mechanic in Southeastern MA. He would be out there working on repairs late at night with the outdoor lights on, dirty, sweaty, with a swarm of mosquitoes buzzing around him, but he felt good that he had fixed it himself.

Although there were times when Dick swore that he would cement in the pool, it gave him pleasure to know that the kids, their neighborhood friends, and I, enjoyed the pool during the day. When the kids were young, they would perform elaborate water ballets for us. Samantha, at about ten years of age, would choreograph and direct the younger kids in their roles. They would dive in on her command and do synchronized swim moves. And later, in their high school years, the kids were on the swim team and became certified lifeguards.

One year, after I took an herb class, Dick dug out a sunny portion of the yard to make me an herb garden. It smelled as enticing as it looked. We created a shade wildflower garden under the pine trees where there were native lady slippers, wild roses, and ferns. We added trilliums, jack-in-the-pulpits, Solomon seal, and several varieties of wildflower plants that thrived in that environment.

We encircled the wildflower garden with rhododendron bushes, which we bought from Dick's patient who owned a rhododendron farm in Lakeville. Around Memorial Day the wildflower garden was in its full glory and the highlight of our yard. For Mother's Day one year, Dick dug trenches around the wildflower garden in the shape of a heart and filled them with shiny white pebbles. It was our first garden to bloom in the spring, and after the barren New England winters we always looked forward to those welcome dog tooth violets.

CHAPTER 19

Taking Care of Business

When we returned from the hospital after Dick's diagnosis, he was driven to take care of business while he could still think clearly. We arranged a meeting with our family lawyer, who quickly updated and revised our wills and trust.

I had always paid the bills and balanced the checkbook, and Dick had overseen savings and investments. In recent years he had been using a financial advisor from a Boston firm. I explained to Dick that I preferred working with a New Bedford firm we had previously used. I felt like I had a personal connection with their team and I could trust them. We immediately made an appointment, looked over the big picture, and received reassurance that they could work with us in transitioning our investments. I was grateful for all the years that Dick was so careful to limit our spending and make savings a priority.

Father's Day was approaching and Dick surprised us all by asking for a gift—a Sony 500 ml fixed lens, perfect for birding. Asking for anything for himself was uncharacteristic of Dick, so the children were thrilled to oblige.

Everyone except Seth was able to come home for Father's Day, and we had a beautiful weekend hanging out in the backyard with the kids and grandchildren. The day lilies seemed especially lush that year, the flowers more fragrant, and the birds and butterflies more numerous.

Dick thoroughly enjoyed playing with Aerin, age four, and Jacob, age two. He never really played much with our own kids—Dick was always more of a "let's do a project" kind of dad. I remember when Samantha was two years old, he carried her down to his workshop in the basement, sat her up on the work shelf, and made a step stool with her, which all the kids used in future years. She was so excited to watch her dad hammer the wood and to help him sand and paint. Dick had mellowed in recent years and was able to relax and enjoy the grandkids more.

On this Father's Day, Dick swam with the grandchildren, swung them in the hammock, and showed them a bird's nest he had discovered. The grandkids always enjoyed trying to catch frogs in the pond. Unlike our kids, who would have held them and played frog and toad stories, when the grandkids were successful, they screeched in glee and fear as they dropped their nets and ran. They were New York born and bred, after all. Our son-in-law, Adam, manned the grill so Dick could relax. Our family had shared so many glorious memories in that backyard and we savored that Father's Day together.

Dick set up the camera and tripod with the new lens and said to me, "Why don't you try it out?"

"It's your new lens, you should use it," I responded.

"I just want to make sure you like it."

It was not a heavy lens but did a remarkable job. I could see the farthest birdhouse on that side of the yard in minute detail. I took some shots and later that night we saw that they came out crisp and sharp. Dick was once again thinking ahead and taking care of me. He only used that lens once, but I have used it countless times to photograph the birds and the butterflies.

CHAPTER 20

New Medication

Dick signed up to participate in research studies on glioblastoma, although he was very disappointed that he was not accepted for one study, which was looking for a link to an inherited risk for brain cancer. The study required live tissue from two family members, and we discovered there was no live tissue saved at the time of his brother's death. This prompted Dick to make arrangements to bank his DNA with a private company.

While his mind was still sharp, Dick spent a lot of time researching glioblastoma. He studied his particular numbers as soon as the pathology report came in and discovered he had a high epithelial growth factor. The drug category of kinases, which inhibit epithelial growth factors, are useful for a number of cancers. He researched a Phase II study in California that used one such drug, Tarceva (also called erlotinib), to treat lung cancer, and he concluded that erlotinib would be beneficial for his specific case.

During his research, Dick saw a citation in an article that proposed such treatment by Dr. David Reardon, his own neuro-oncologist. He discussed his theory with Dr. Reardon who agreed Dick's idea had merit and supported him in trying the drug in addition to his regular medications. Dr. Reardon wrote the prescription and made a plea to our insurance company on Dick's behalf. Unfortunately, they would not approve paying for this costly drug because it was not routinely used to treat glioblastoma.

In July 2012, Dr. Reardon filed an appeal with Blue Cross Blue Shield, explaining the potential benefits, but the appeal was rejected. It stated erlotinib was not considered the standard of care for glioblastoma. Although Dick was dismayed, he had anticipated the rejection because he understood how insurance companies worked. Recognizing his cognitive decline, Dick believed it was imperative to start treatment immediately, so we purchased the first month's supply ourselves at a local pharmacy at a cost of five thousand dollars.

We heard erlotinib was available in Israel at a lower cost. Dick's sister contacted a colleague at Tel Aviv University who was able to arrange for a neuro-oncologist to review his case and agreed to write a prescription. I contacted my cousin Oren, a physician in Israel, who also assisted us with the logistics. He found out it would be $3,500 for a thirty-day supply. If you bought three packs, you got the fourth one free. However, Oren also found out the drug was not manufactured in Israel. It was shipped there from Switzerland and the drug representative could not ascertain where it was manufactured. Because of all the scams with drugs being sold overseas, we were very cautious. There had been recent incidents in the news of counterfeit medicine being sold in Canada and Turkey.

Our friend Bharani found out that erlotinib could be purchased in India at a fraction of the cost we paid here. It would be eight hundred dollars for a thirty-day supply. With the help of his parents, who lived in India, Bharani started working on a plan to obtain the erlotinib. We knew Bharani's parents from their visits to the States and they were rooting for Dick as well.

They found a factory in India with high standards and a reliable reputation. Three months of drugs were allowed to be brought into the country at a time. Bharani took care of all the details. His dad picked up the drug himself at the factory. He then transferred it to a friend of his who was traveling to the States. Bharani prepared a medical letter of explanation in case his friend was questioned by customs. Bharani then drove to New York to meet his friend and hand delivered a three-month supply of erlotinib to us the next day.

We were so grateful to have such a dedicated friend. Dick had side effects of irritated red skin and itching from the drug, but he rarely complained. I believe one reason Dick fared as well as he did in the course of his illness was because of his own initial research, starting on the erlotinib treatment, and everyone who assisted us in making it a reality.

CHAPTER 21

In the Dark of the Night

We always ended our day with an automatic "Goodnight, I love you," but those words now held more intensity. In the sanctity of our bedroom, we would hold each other tightly and make passionate love like it was the last time.

My emotions often crept to the surface at night and Dick would wipe away my tears and say, "Don't cry, we're going to be okay." It was hard for him to see me so bereft, so I tried to control my tears or to turn over and cry silently.

Dick was the practical type who rarely talked about his emotions. I had only seen him break down once—when our daughter Sarah had been in the hospital near death, with an inconclusive diagnosis.

It was easier to share our intimate thoughts in the dark. We talked about Gena's letter. We talked about how grateful we were that we had these precious days, how fortunate we were that we had married young and had so many wondrous years together.

Mostly we talked about the past and the present.

"Remember how I used to sneak into your freshman dorm and tiptoe around so the housemother wouldn't hear us?"

"You did not tiptoe! I was always scared she would hear you. I remember sophomore year when you used to stay over in the Clark Tower dorm. I would warn you to be really quiet when I made the weekly call to my parents on Sunday mornings. I swear you moved around and made noise on purpose!"

Even in the dim light, I could see Dick's clear blue eyes crinkling with laughter.

The first two years of medical school, the students had every afternoon off to study, so we spent lots of time together.

"Remember how we explored every library within thirty miles of Cleveland?"

"I sure do. I took six courses and got all A's that semester!" I responded. "Yeah, you tricked me those first two years. We spent so much time together and had so much fun. Then you talked me into getting married and I had no idea that when clerkships started in the third year of med school, I would never see you again!"

"I can't believe we have been married for forty years. They've been the best years of my life. I'm so glad I robbed the cradle. I feel like we grew up together. I love you so much," Dick said.

"I love you too," I said as we hugged each other and became eighteen and twenty-one again.

Some nights we talked about all the trips and adventures we'd been on. We laughed at the misadventures.

"Remember when we got lost in the White Mountains?" Dick said.

"That was so scary!" I said.

In preparation for a climb up Mount Kilimanjaro in Africa for our thirtieth anniversary, we spent a week's vacation in New Hampshire climbing mountains.

We headed off at seven a.m. one day for our most ambitious mountain climb yet. We saw a few people at a waterfall early on and only spotted one lone climber the rest of the day. We had a picnic and took some photos at the summit. We were still descending at around seven p.m. We began to get anxious that we had taken a wrong turn as the terrain didn't look familiar. We hadn't reached the falls yet, which we should have seen by then. We backtracked and had no success. We got more nervous as darkness approached. We were exhausted, clasped hands, and walked slowly to avoid falling.

We were getting short with each other.

I said, "It's too dark to keep going. I think we should call for help."

Dick had resisted until now but finally agreed it wasn't safe to continue.

"Okay, maybe someone can direct us down," Dick said.

Luckily our cell phones were within range and Dick called the local park ranger.

The ranger responded, "Is anyone hurt?"

"No, we are okay," Dick assured him.

"Do you have a light?"

"Yes, we do."

Dick was an old Boy Scout and even though we never thought we would need them for a day hike, he had packed matches and a flashlight.

"Do you have water?"

"Yes."

"Okay then, it's a mild night. Hunker down and find your way out in the morning. Just follow the water downstream."

We laughed about the ranger's casual response to "hunker down" and figured we weren't the first ones in this predicament. We castigated ourselves for not starting out earlier in the morning. We spread out our fleeces, laid down in a bed of leaves, and finally fell asleep. At early daylight we followed the stream down. We had been going in the right direction before we backtracked but had not anticipated how much further we had to go. Apparently our pace had been too slow, and we had miscalculated how long it would take us to climb. It took us another two hours to reach the falls that morning and shortly after, we arrived at the trailhead. We were so embarrassed about our escapade we snuck back into our B&B and swore we would never tell anyone what happened!

As we reminisced about that day, we laughed until tears ran down our cheeks over the ranger's suggestion to "hunker down and find your way out in the morning!"

Although we spent many hours talking about the past, it was more painful to talk about the future. Dick talked about being grateful that he was able to see his four children grow up to become independent. He was thrilled that he had gotten to know his two beautiful, healthy grandchildren. If it were me, I would have been thinking how I wanted to see my younger three children walk down the aisle at their weddings. I would be distraught that I would not see my grandchildren's bar and bat mitzvah's and weddings.

But Dick never mentioned those things. He focused on people and experiences in his life that he was grateful for. He told me how much he appreciated all his patients' sentiments. He told me over and over again how much he loved me.

We had conversations about dying, but it was more often the practical rather than the spiritual.

One night I asked Dick, "Is there anything important I should know, that you want to tell me?"

He responded with absolute seriousness, "Always remember— righty tighty, lefty loosey."

CHAPTER 22

Our New Normal

Dick and I had been part of the sunrise bootcamp class at the local YMCA for years. Three times a week we attended the 5:30 a.m. class. April through September or October we met outdoors at a variety of sites including the Y camp, the field behind the old Middleboro Memorial Junior High School, and Massasoit State Park. I am not an early morning person but Dick and I supported each other to get up at 4:45 a.m. and get going.

Once we were there, we enjoyed the camaraderie of the gang and, believe it or not, felt better after the strenuous workout. It was invigorating to be outside surrounded by nature, running through the tree-lined paths and seeing the majestic sunrise over the pond at the camp. Our dynamic instructors, Jen and Gretchen, kept the class lively and the workout was never the same twice. Dick got such a kick out of trying to outrun all the thirty- and forty-year old women!

We were by far the oldest participants, but over time we got into a rhythm where we kept up pretty well.

After Dick's diagnosis, I racked my brain to think if I had missed any early clues or signs that something was wrong. The only incident I questioned was one day on our way home from bootcamp. We were in the car at the stoplight at Routes 28 and 105 when Dick told me he was worried he got tired easily and couldn't keep up as well as he used to. I reassured him that he was competing with a much younger group and that at almost sixty-four years of age, he was very fit and looked great. We often joked about how jealous I was since we started bootcamp—Dick lost weight and toned up but I stayed the same! There were a few mornings when Dick slept in and I went to bootcamp on my own. I just thought he needed more sleep. *Should I have taken his concerns more seriously?*

We had a short gap after returning home from the hospital and before Dick started radiation. He really missed exercising and wanted to keep up his strength as long as possible. One of the bootcamp regulars, Brenda, offered to come to our house to work out with Dick. She did gentle stretching, as Dick's physician had recommended. Brenda was a thirty-something, stunning blonde who had two school-age children. She always had a smile on her face at the 5:30 a.m. bootcamp class and a pleasant word for everyone. Many of us could barely speak at that hour. Brenda worked part-time, had just started a master's program in social work, and had a son with significant medical problems, but she managed to fit in working with Dick to her busy schedule. He was thrilled to be exercising with one of his favorite bootcampers who just happened to look like a starlet!

Susan, a dear friend of mine since childhood and an accomplished hypnotherapist, also volunteered to work with Dick during those early weeks. He thought the hypnotherapy would be a helpful tool to keep his mind focused for as long as possible. Susan had many strengths and could have been a master therapist. I think just spending time with her was the greatest benefit. I suspected, and Susan verified much later, that their time together gave Dick a chance to talk about his own fears and his concerns for me. More than once, the Dana-Farber team had offered to provide a social worker, but Dick refused. He didn't think he needed a therapist. He had Susan.

We had signed up for the annual New England Camera Club Convention in Amherst, Massachusetts, before Dick's diagnosis. We discussed whether we should still go to the three-day weekend in July and decided we would. We wanted to do as much as possible for as long as we could. It took some maneuvering, as we had to arrange Dick's radiation treatment in Boston very early that Friday and leave directly for Amherst from there. We had been to the convention previously, so we knew the routine, and it was great to see friends from our camera club and photography meet-up groups. Getting around was slow. We took afternoon breaks and didn't feel obligated to go to every session. I realized then that even a short weekend away was not easy on us. The radiation was definitely taking its toll on Dick.

CHAPTER 23

Retirement Party

I decided to have a retirement party for Dick, primarily to give his patients an opportunity to say good-bye to him in person. At first, Dick was not open to the idea because he did not feel like partying. I honored his decision but a few weeks later, when he was feeling better, I asked again. He wasn't enthusiastic, but did not outright refuse, so I went ahead and planned it.

I put an open invitation in the *Middleboro Gazette* article as well as on the Lotsa Helping Hands site. It stated all were welcome to attend a Retirement Party Open House at the local Riverside Restaurant to wish Dr. Gross well. There was no RSVP, so we had no idea how many people to expect. The number of people who came surpassed my wildest expectations. Dick's sister, Cindy, brother-in-law Pete, and our daughter Sarah greeted people as they came in the front door of the restaurant and provided them with name tags to fill out. This was not for Dick's benefit, because he remembered every patient's name, but for mine. We went through 500 labels!

I positioned myself right by the doorway as people entered the function room and introduced myself to guests.

In ones and twos patients greeted me with expressions of grief and gratitude.

"We've been seeing the doc for twenty-five years. He's like part of the family."

"He never rushed us. It felt like he had all the time in the world."

"He saved my husband's life. If there is anything we can do, please let us know."

"You look too young to be Dr. Gross's wife!"

"Thank you for giving us this opportunity to see Dr. Gross again. He took care of my whole extended family. We'll never be able to find another doctor like him."

Several patients mentioned how upset Dick was when I had an accident five years prior. We were on vacation in Mexico with extended family at an all-inclusive resort. The adventurer in us couldn't resist going on the free side trip for a horseback ride. They took us to an area where they were building a road with large machinery and the horses got spooked. I was thrown from my horse at high speed and dragged. I should have been leery when assigned to the horse named Machete! I broke several ribs, had a spinal burst fracture, broken foot, broken nose, and pneumothorax.

On the third day, when I was stabilized, I was airlifted from Mexico to Massachusetts General Hospital in Boston. Dick accompanied me on the flight. I remember being beside myself when Dick told me he had to go back to work while I was still an inpatient at Mass General. His patients gave me a much better appreciation of how worried he was about me and how difficult it was for him to leave me to go back to work.

I had definitely done my share of complaining through the years when Dick didn't get home because he had to accompany a patient on the ambulance ride to Boston or because he had to stop and make a home visit. It was a humbling experience to put names and faces to real patients who were so grateful that Dick had been there for them. I understood better now why Dick had to sacrifice some time with me and the family for his work. I always thought I knew Dick inside and out, but I felt like I learned a lot about him from his patients that day.

It was a hot, steamy day in July. The slow-moving line chained through the hallway and continued halfway across the room where Dick greeted everyone with a hug or a handshake and spent time talking with each guest. Although the restaurant was air conditioned, the narrow hallway was hot and crowded. At one point, I encouraged everyone to come into the room where it was cooler and more spacious.

They doggedly refused, saying, "No, we want to wait in line to see Dr. Gross."

After close to two hours, we tore Dick away from greeting people to take a rest, sit down, and have some refreshments. People came and went all afternoon but after his break, Dick addressed the group who were there.

He began by saying, "I'm sorry you had to wait so long to see me today. I'm pretty sure you never had to wait this long to see me in the office!" He had not lost his sense of humor.

"Thank you for coming to my retirement party. I have truly appreciated your friendship and am overwhelmed by your kindness. It has been a fabulous source of healing to live and work among such wonderful people and to have such a loving family.

"I had the great fortune to follow some remarkable doctors. I was also privileged to practice with the greatest doctors right up until my retirement. I have enjoyed learning from them and working with them all.

"I will let you in on a little secret. Several years ago there was an article published in the New England Journal of Medicine. The recovery rate in intensive care units at that time was not related to the fame or skill of the individual star physicians, but rather to the ability of the whole staff to work together. We had great local hospitals and we miss them dearly. It was a privilege to work at them.

"I am astounded by how many of you have gone out of your way to support and help me with your meaningful cards, delicious meals, lovely flowers, donations in my honor, and rides to radiation and chemotherapy. It has been especially wonderful to be comforted by a couple of you who have received your chemotherapy right next to me.

"I have crossed over from being the doctor to the patient and you have all been healing me. I love you all, and you have made what might have been a sad time, a time of inspiration, reaffirmation, and comfort."

Many people left cards and gifts, and we opened them slowly over the next week and savored each message. Both Dick and I were astonished by the generosity of his patients. They shared beautiful thank-you notes and sentiments that spoke from their hearts and clung to ours. Those letters had a profound impact on Dick, who recognized how much he meant to so many people. He felt good knowing that his life's work had a deep impact on so many lives.

One of Dick's patients presented him with this beautiful framed poem she wrote, as she said, "representing the sentiment of his many local patients."

Always, The Gentle Spirit

Always patient, always kind.
He has been there for us, year after year.
Giving us reassurance, comfort, care,
Taking his time to draw us near.

Always seeking knowledge within his field,
He shared the latest trends,
Giving his best medical advice
To his patients and friends.

Always, when he listened,
We knew we had been heard.
We left with much confidence
In his treatment, in his word.

Always, Dr. Gross, as we express our Love and Thanks
For all the times you tried to give us a sense
Of a better way to treat ourselves.
Your gentle Spirit has made all the difference!
Written by Pam Bailey
On behalf of many others!
2012

He received thoughtful gifts including multiple gift certificates to restaurants, movie theaters, bookstores, and nurseries and donations in his honor to the Dana-Farber Cancer Institute. Among the hundreds of cards and letters Dick received, the overriding theme was the same—you are an excellent doctor and I also consider you my very good friend. I was so impressed by this acclamation of the special relationship Dick had with his patients.

I will never forget the note that accompanied a ten-dollar cash gift.

"Dear Dr. Gross,

Thank you for taking care of my family and me for so many years. I can't begin to tell you how sad I am that you have been dealt this cruel blow. May God bless you and may he be kind to you. Enclosed is a little gift. I know that money means nothing to you now, but it is the only means I know to let you know I care."

Many patients wanted to give back and they did—and more.

The letters Dick received also affected me deeply but in a different way. I had always arranged our social calendar, and as a couple, we participated in many social events in the medical community, our synagogue, and other local activities. Together with our closest friends, we were part of a gourmet group for over thirty years. Because Dick was working so many long hours in the early years, I developed a wide circle of female friends and belonged to groups such as the Lakeville Mothers' Club and the Garden Club. I looked forward to nights out on my own at club meetings and with friends. Through the years I had often asked Dick if he didn't miss going out with the guys, playing sports, or poker, like some of his friends did.

He would always say, "No, I talk to people all day long!"

I never thought much of it until then, when I realized that his patients were his friends. Each and every one of them.

CHAPTER 24

Letter from Dr. Friedman

Dr. Bob Friedman could not be at the retirement party because he was participating in the second day of the Pan-Mass Challenge (PMC)—an annual bike-a-thon that raises money for cancer research. That was Bob's twelfth year participating in the challenge, which benefits the Dana-Farber Cancer Institute and the Jimmy Fund. The ride covers 190 miles from Sturbridge to Provincetown. Dick was so proud that Bob was biking in his honor. Bob had already raised over twenty thousand dollars that year. The hospital medical staff donated a large sum in Dick's honor to support Dr. Friedman's ride.

Dr. Friedman sent the following letter, which I read at the retirement party on his behalf:

In the years after our medical school training, Dick and I both had internships and residency training where we were generally up all night and had to think on our feet and make important decisions during the day. Federal regulations have now made these types of programs illegal due to the hardship and stress that they caused, but Dick and I benefited from those years. They prepared us well for our early experiences in Middleboro. Starting in 1978, Dick was on call every night, and I have no idea how he did that. After I arrived in 1979, at least the schedule changed to every other night and weekend. By then the word was out that when anyone in the community was sick or when there was a sick surgical or emergency room patient, the order went out to "call one of the boys." And that meant Dick and me.

We not only shared the same office, we also shared the same desk. That was a bit of a problem as I tend to be a little neater than Dick, but we managed that. The person who was on call at night would straggle into the office usually with little sleep and see patients until about 2:30 in the afternoon and then the other one of us would take over until 8 p.m. and then be on call all night. We were both always in the hospital a lot when on call. In the early years, there was very little backup. We had no cardiologist, no neurologist, and we were pretty much on our own with very sick patients. We frequently found ourselves doing spinal taps, chest taps, bone marrow aspirations, and we often had to insert temporary pacemakers in cardiac emergencies.

We did the best we could, but if patients were too sick, we would arrange for them to go to Brockton or Boston. In those days the EMT system had not yet started and we would frequently ride in the ambulance monitoring our patient en route. I remember one night not only watching over a patient in the ambulance, but having to give directions to the driver on how to get to the Boston hospital! I know Dick had many similar experiences and when we got back to town, there was plenty of work waiting for us.

When St. Luke's Hospital in Middleboro closed in 1990, Dick and I went our separate ways, but we have remained friends. I am honored to be Dick's physician. He has always been in great health and I can only hope, along with everyone else, that he will meet this current challenge. He is doing well now with the excellent care he is getting at Dana-Farber. I am proud to be a part of the fundraising for this institution through the Pan-Mass Challenge and to play a role in finding cutting edge treatments for people just like Dick.

We are all behind you Dick.
Your friend and colleague,
Bob

I posted this letter and Dick's speech on Lotsa Helping Hands and received many responses including this note from Rosanne, who was a patient of Dick's and a friend of ours.

Loved reading this letter . . . paints a true picture of how hard doctors worked and many still do . . . and more insight into Dick's early years. Dick's illness has brought about the opportunity for so many of us . . . family and friends . . . most importantly for Dick himself . . . to remember, to express, to appreciate . . . to love. Most of us do not experience this in our lifetimes. Maybe a few words spoken at a milestone party, a quick toast once a year or a short note from an old friend but not like this—Sayre and I admire both of you from afar.

Feel free to call us when you want to get together. Keep in touch. We care about you.

Love,
Rosanne

CHAPTER 25

Summer 2012

Each mental status exam with Dr. V became more disconcerting. On our appointment of July 6, 2012, Dick had difficulty recalling some of the words.

Dr. V would share the words of the day. "Remember: *bed, cow, green,* and *foot.* Repeat them please."

I found myself repeating them in my head.

"Bed, cow, green, foot," Dick would quickly repeat.

"Good, now I will ask you to repeat those words in about five minutes."

After another part of the exam, Dr. V would say, "Now, can you repeat those words that I told you earlier?"

Dick's responses were much slower now.

"Green . . . cow . . ."

Foot, bed, I thought and wanted to blurt them out. I was silently rooting for him. *Remember. Come on, you can do it!* I could feel my whole body tense up and my back start to ache as we waited.

He went past the allotted time.

"One was a piece of furniture," Dr. V reminded him.

"Oh yes, a bed!"

"Do you remember the word that was a part of the body?"

Dick mulled it over. "Foot!"

"Good."

I knew you could do it, I thought, as I relaxed back in my seat.

Dick no longer rattled off the answers like he did a month earlier. Now when he counted backwards by sevens, I could keep up with him! He still gave a pretty good showing of words that began with a letter of the alphabet, although Dr. V no longer had to stop him in his tracks. Now he might hesitate to think of the next one and she would say, "That's enough for today."

During the six weeks of radiation, Helping Hands volunteers came from as far as southern Rhode Island, South Dartmouth, New Bedford, and Westport. Many signed up for multiple trips.

One of Dick's greatest joys was presenting each volunteer with a canvas photo. Luckily, we had a huge stock. When he returned home from an appointment, I always had three or four photos laid out for the volunteer of the day to choose from, and Dick would tell them stories of when and where the photos were taken or how he had enhanced or adapted the photo with software. Dick beamed as volunteers selected a photo they liked.

Our rabbi took Dick to radiation treatment one day. Upon their return, Dick suggested he might like the canvas photo of the lotus and the bee, which had won Dick the award of Photo of the Year from our camera club. He told the rabbi the story behind the photo.

"Robin was chanting the haftorah (selections from the Prophets read on Shabbat following the reading of the Torah) in memory of her father's yahrzeit (anniversary of loved one's passing) one Shabbat morning last July. Her mother was here and we were all ready to leave for the synagogue. The lotus in our water garden had bloomed that morning and the bloom only lasts for two days. Just two days out of the whole summer! I was so glad it fell on a weekend. I was out in the garden taking photos when Robin came to get me."

I interrupted, "Dick was all dressed in his suit and tie. I asked him if he would like to stay home and photograph the lotus instead of coming with me to services. I convinced him it was fine because he had heard me many times and my mom was coming with me.

He was still there patiently taking photos when we returned home four hours later. He got every angle of the flower, every change of light, and multiple bugs and bees alighting on the lotus blossom."

Rabbi Kanter laughed as he told Dick, "I think you made the best decision to skip services that day!"

Most weekends that summer, members of Dick's extended family visited from all over the country and Dick was thrilled to see them. His sister, Cindy, was in Maine for the summer so she made multiple visits. Many of my immediate and extended family made the trip as well. Dick got to meet his new great-niece, Hannah, from Atlanta and enjoy a day with my three-year-old twin great-nephews from California.

When we finally closed Dick's office on July 1, I had some time to devote to other aspects of our lives, and I called our friends Brent and Marty Young in Cleveland, Ohio, to let them know about Dick's diagnosis. They were our best friends during our Cleveland days. We had lived in a duplex house together, shared many treasured memories, and had kept in touch through the years.

The next day, Brent and Marty drove straight through from Cleveland to Massachusetts, and we spent a few fabulous days together. We reminisced about our Cleveland adventures, including the Thanksgiving when we took a walk to let the turkey cool and their dog Taylor jumped up on the table and helped himself to turkey dinner!

Brent is a professional glass blower and Dick was fascinated to see and hear about some of the new work Brent was creating. Dick was very proud of our own collection of Brent's glass, most of which we acquired in the early stages of Brent's career. Brent now had his glass displayed in permanent collections in many museums throughout the country, including the Museum of Fine Arts in Boston.

Brent and Marty accompanied Dick to radiation treatment and got to meet our friend Bharani. We all went to the Museum of Fine Arts in Boston to see Brent's work. Dick had always wanted to give Bharani a gift to thank him, but Bharani wouldn't accept any money. That day, when Dick saw how much Bharani admired Brent's work, he knew the perfect gift. He chose one of his prized glass vases that Brent had created and presented it to Bharani, who was delighted with the gift.

Despite the grueling radiation regimen, we tried to keep up some of our regular activities. Our gourmet group had been getting together for thirty-three years. We started out having elaborate themed dinners at each other's homes with everybody contributing various courses. Over the past ten years the group had evolved to going out to restaurants. We participated in gourmet group when we could that summer although Dick had a poor appetite and going out at night required pre-planning with a heavy dose of afternoon naps.

Since he started treatment Dick had been experiencing symptoms of brain fog, poor memory, and fatigue. His follow-up MRI showed the tumor was shrinking and the combination of radiation, chemotherapies, and, I believe, prayers from all denominations, was working. So I didn't understand why Dick was still having so much difficulty with short-term memory. Dr. Reardon explained that some of the symptoms might be caused by inflammation from the radiation as well as the disease process. He also warned us that symptoms might continue for up to six weeks after the radiation stopped.

On August 2, Dick completed his radiation treatments and was so grateful that he wouldn't have that daily grind to Boston. We discussed next steps with Dr. Reardon. Dick would get infusions every two weeks.

"I'd like to get the infusions from Dr. McNamee, an oncologist in Taunton," Dick requested. "Mac is my friend and colleague and it would be a much shorter ride to Taunton."

Dr. Reardon agreed that Dick could get every other infusion locally. He explained that Dick would also begin a higher dose chemo drug that he would take five days in a row out of each month for twelve cycles.

At the next monthly visit, Dick's mental status exam was disappointing. He made math errors and was less precise in copying shapes. I could see he was frustrated at not being able to accomplish these simple tasks.

"You got two words," Dr. V encouraged. "Do you remember the others?"

Silence.

"One was a piece of furniture."

The silence felt like that long pause between musical sets at the orchestra when you are anxiously waiting for the next sequence to begin. But it never came.

I was glad Dick could not see my face from my position next to him. My whole body was stiff from crunching my muscles hard, reciting the words over and over again in my head, hoping that Dick would remember them.

When he couldn't recall the words with the hint of a category, Dr. V gave him three choices.

"Was it a bed, chair, or table?"

"A table," he remembered.

My body relaxed, but I left there with a headache that day.

CHAPTER 26

Travel

One of the best things about moving back to Massachusetts in 1978 was that we didn't have to spend all our vacations going home to visit family! In March 1979, my sister and brother-in-law invited us on a one-week vacation to Jamaica. We had never been to the Caribbean. We were married seven years and I was seven months pregnant with our first child, so we decided it would be a good opportunity to take some time for ourselves.

I discovered a few things about Dick on that vacation. He was not a "lie on the beach" type of guy. He had to keep moving. His sweet tooth equaled my own. He could sit in the shade and read a book and still get a better tan than I did when I sat in the sun for hours. And, he never stopped worrying about his patients—by day five of vacation he was anxious to get back to work. That information would color my future vacation planning.

We took a snorkeling trip and I discovered that it was not easy for a seven-month-pregnant woman to climb back on board. It took a little pushing from Dick and a strong arm from the boat hand. But we got hooked on snorkeling! We eventually became certified scuba divers and probably logged over fifty dives. We both enjoyed the alluring colors of the tropical fish, the dazzling coral, and the challenge of the dive.

I decided it would be important for our marriage to take a one-week vacation every year for just the two of us. It was always a struggle to get Dick to agree, but I persisted. Eventually, I figured out that most of the doctors in Dick's coverage group took four to six weeks of vacation a year.

"It doesn't seem fair to me that you have to cover so many nights for other doctors who are taking more vacation time than you are," I complained.

"It's different. They don't have a solo practice. I still have to pay the staff and the overhead when I am away. I can't afford to take more time off. We also have to save for the kids' college funds and for our future."

"What about Berger? He has a solo practice and they take extensive vacation time."

"He is a gastroenterologist and specialists make a lot more money than internists do."

I could never understand why internists worked the hardest and got paid the least but realized I was never going to win that argument.

I also knew that Dick was worried about leaving his seriously ill patients in the hospital under other practitioners' care. He knew his patients the best and he worked long, extra hours to manage them when they were hospitalized. Although Dick was an excellent doctor, he still had to worry about lawsuits. He was always confident he had done the best possible for his patients, but the suits, which could sometimes drag on for years, gnawed at him and made him extra vigilant.

We also took a one-week vacation every summer with the kids. In the early years, when the kids were young, we stayed pretty close to home. Sometimes we went tent camping in the local state parks, where Dick's beeper was still in range and he was driving distance from the hospital.

As the kids got older and Dick's coverage group widened, we became a little more adventurous. We went white water rafting on the Kennebec River in Maine when Seth was eight, the minimum age and weight for the class IV rapids. We had a frightening experience at the part of the river named "Hell Hole" where we watched as Seth was sprung by the churning rapids out of the raft, into the air, and underwater.

We were so relieved to see him finally surface far on the other side of the river where he was rescued by one of the staff and proclaimed "Hero of the Day." The award was given on each rafting trip and Seth certainly deserved it after that harrowing experience.

For our twentieth anniversary, I desperately wanted to take Dick to Europe, as he had never been. He was insistent that he could only take one week off, so I found a trip that included three days in London and three days in Paris and booked it. As we developed our interest in photography, Dick became more enthusiastic about travel. For our twenty-fifth anniversary we planned a ten-day safari in Africa. This was before the era of digital cameras, and we shared our DSLR Minolta on that trip. We got some excellent photos, and Dick was hooked.

We befriended a couple on our trip who were climbing Mount Kilimanjaro after the safari. It was then that I set my goal to climb

Kilimanjaro for my fiftieth birthday and our thirtieth anniversary. Four years later I put my goal into reality and we made plans to climb Kili and take a safari in Tanzania. As usual, Dick went along with my offbeat whims.

We started preparing a year ahead. Anticipating and getting ready for the trip was part of the excitement. We broke in our sturdy, new, hiking boots and tried out our waterproof jackets and all the hiking gear specified on the list. We stepped up our workout routine. In the sunroom, where we rode the exercise bike, Dick built a shelf for a small TV so the time would go faster. We climbed Mount Washington in New Hampshire with our daughter Samantha. In the summer of 2000, Dick and I took a weeklong vacation in the White Mountains and hiked a different mountain every day.

The last hike we took before our trip was in the fall with Dick's nephew Paul, an experienced hiker. We were climbing Mount Adams in New Hampshire when it began snowing pretty heavily. We kept seeing signs which got harder to read as we ascended, saying, "If this sign is covered, take precautions. It may be too dangerous to proceed any further."

I got pretty nervous as the signs became almost illegible, covered with a thick layer of glistening snow. Paul and Dick seemed to be forging ahead and I had no extra breath for conversation, so I plowed forward after them. After we left the safety of the tree line, we had to don our ski goggles, as we were being pelted with sharp, biting shards of ice on our faces. Now I knew why goggles were on the packing list for Kili. We wore gloves with liners, but my hands were still wet and cold.

Finally, I said I needed to go down. I felt guilty because I knew Paul kept a lifetime record of the mountains he had conquered—we were so close—and now he could not mark this one off his list. But

I didn't feel safe and I knew I had to descend. Dick was also relieved to be heading back and we slipped and slid our way down to firm ground. The unfulfilled hike had a purpose though—we learned that our gloves were not adequate. Paul advised us that we needed a third layer of water-resistant mittens that would stretch up to mid arm to keep our gloves dry. That was our last purchase before the big climb, and a necessary one.

Right before our trip to Africa, I bought Dick the book *A Walk in the Woods* by Bill Bryson. We both had plenty of time to read it on our long journey.

"I think we should hike the Appalachian Trail in our retirement," I concluded after reading the book.

"You just won't give me a minute's rest, will you?" Dick said with a laugh.

But I was already thinking of all the exciting adventures we would have in retirement.

Climbing Kili was an extraordinary experience. There were twelve participants who started out and seven of us who made it. The trip was much more difficult than we had anticipated.

We ditched the cameras from our backpacks after day one and stowed them in our duffle bags for the Sherpas to carry. Too much extra weight. I was always anxious to grab my camera when we hit camp to take a few shots documenting the changes in terrain from rain forest to moorland and alpine desert to glacier.

Dick would promptly yell out, "Put the camera away! I need your help. We have to get the sleeping bags in our tents, set up for the night, and purify our water for tomorrow before it gets dark!"

We unexpectedly encountered rainy weather, which made the trip very challenging. The most valuable item on the mountain became the resealable plastic bag. We were told to pack all our clothing in different size plastic bags and luckily Dick and I had followed the equipment list and packing instructions to the letter, so we still had dry underwear and socks, a rare commodity, on day five.

Around day four, every couple on the trip had a slightly different version of the same conversation. It started off with the agitated voice of the partner who went along with the spouse who initiated the trip.

"What could you possibly have been thinking when you planned this trip? Didn't you realize how dangerous it is? Did you see that headstone back there?"

"You're doing great. I know it's rough. We've just had exceptionally terrible weather. But we're almost there. We'll get through it. Just remember, one step at a time."

"Do you realize for the same money we could have gone on a trip to Hawaii or a relaxing cruise?"

But the people in this group were not cruise types, and two days later, when we reached the summit, everyone was smiling and cheering.

Dick also felt great purpose, because he saved a life on the mountain. Our Sherpas came upon one of their own who had been abandoned by his group in a frigid rain. He had had asthma as a child and was having difficulty breathing. By this time our leaders knew Dick had helped out on several occasions with medical issues and had a comprehensive medical bag. They sought him out while we were all eating in the dining tent.

Dick tended to the porter with the supplies he had. Then he came back to the tent with a serious expression and explained the situation.

"The porter will not make it through the night unless he has oxygen. He's just a young boy. Our group only carries an oxygen supply for emergencies, for us—the tourists. I advised our leaders that the porter needs it, but they don't want to give it to him. I am asking for your permission to use the oxygen on his behalf."

There were overwhelming expressions of support by each and every person to save the porter. With that firm commitment, Dick was able to persuade the leaders to let him use the oxygen to treat the porter. One of our leaders assisted the porter down the mountain the following day, accompanied by two of our group participants, who, with this life and death scare added to previous challenges, decided to curtail their climb.

When hospitalists became the norm in the last ten years of Dick's practice, he became more at ease about going on vacation and leaving for a two-week period. He generally fulfilled his continuing education credits in Boston, where there was excellent training, and he could save money by commuting from home. But one day he came home and said, "How would you like to climb Machu Picchu?"

"You know the answer to that. I would love to!"

I was genuinely surprised because I had always been the one to initiate and plan vacations.

"What made you think about that?"

He showed me a brochure he had received at the office from Wilderness Travel. There was a sixteen-hour conference course on wilderness medicine where they covered topics like hyperthermia, lightning, and surviving the unexpected night out. It combined a twelve-day trip to Peru including a four-day trek on the Inca Trail to Machu Picchu and three days in the Amazon rain forest.

I was so excited that I threw my arms around him. "That sounds fabulous."

Then I started worrying. "But I'm so out of shape since my accident. Do you think I can do the climb? How hard is it? And I don't know if I can get time off from work."

"I think you can do it. We have time to get ready. We'll practice together. We already have all the gear we need. Your Sony camera is light enough to take and I'm sure there will be incredible photo opportunities. If you want, I bet you could sit in on the talks. They're just simple first aid."

"Ok, I'm sold."

In the next week, I arranged time off from work, booked the trip, and signed us both up for bootcamp at the local Y.

During Dick's illness, especially toward the end, we found solace looking through picture albums and reliving all our precious memories. I was meticulous in taking photos of every life event and putting them in albums, until digital photography took over. We had accumulated sixty-three albums marking every birth, holiday, vacation, Cub Scout and school event, birthday, graduation, and more.

As we were perusing albums one night, Dick said, "You know if it was up to me, I would have been content to stay home most of the time. I'm so glad we didn't wait till retirement to travel. You were so smart. I know sometimes you had to drag me, but I loved every minute of it—even climbing Kilimanjaro!"

Dick gave me a big hug and said, "Thank you, honey, for bringing so much joy and adventure into my life."

CHAPTER 27

Community Clinician
of the Year

In August, Dick was notified by the president of the Massachusetts Medical Society (MMS), Plymouth District, that he was selected as their 2013 recipient of the Community Clinician of the Year award. He was still basking in delight over being chosen for this honor by the Bristol North District. A representative from the MMS interviewed Dick and they put out a press release stating this was the first time a physician was ever honored by two district societies since the award's inception in 1998.

In September, Dick was feted by both MMS Districts with a dinner and award presentation at a local restaurant. In addition to the MMS members, Dick was pleased that he could invite physician friends and immediate family as guests.

Dr. Julia Edelman shared many of Dick's accomplishments, including his service as president of the MMS Plymouth District from 2003–2004, member of the House of Delegates, the District Leadership Council, and the Committee on Public Health and Geriatrics. She quoted one of Dick's patients who said he was a credit to the medical profession and would be sorely missed by his patients.

What I remember the most about Dr. Edelman's speech is the example she gave of how Dick used his creativity and compassion in his work. She shared that he had a patient who was worried that her memory was starting to fail. Dick and his patient came up with the idea that she would send him her annual Christmas letter with news of the family and this would supplement his check-in with her.

Dick was thrilled to be surrounded by his colleagues that night, many of whom he had not seen over the last several months. They greeted him at the reception with open arms. Part of me was surprised that it was conversation as usual. There was no emotional, *I'm so sorry to hear you have glioblastoma.* I think there were a few reasons for that: the nature of most physicians to hold their emotions in, the formality of the setting, and the uplifting atmosphere of the event. Also, that would be the way Dick wanted it and his friends probably knew that.

Dick delivered a speech that night, primarily focusing on the outstanding work ethic of his predecessors and of the new, young doctors who had come into the area. I smiled to myself as I heard him, because that was so much like Dick.

The following is an excerpt from his speech:

When I finished my chief residency at a big city hospital, I thought I could do the most good by practicing medicine in an underserved area. That turned out to be true. What I never anticipated was how emotionally rewarding this would also be for me. Thirty-five years later,

I find my colleagues and my patients are helping me, and I must say, the turnabout is gratifying.

Having this glioblastoma is challenging. The emotional pain of seeing so many wonderful friends and considering that it might be a while before I get to see you again is sad. I realize, however, all that we have accomplished together, and I find that very rewarding—and so should you.

When I completed my training and we moved to Middleboro in 1978, Robin and I found a welcoming community, clean, efficient hospitals, and an area that was evolving from blue collar to red cross and blue shield.

Dick chuckled as he said this.

I had proofread Dick's speech ahead of time and questioned the blue collar to red cross and blue shield.

"Is that really what you want to say?"

He laughed as he said, "I think it's fine to be a little mixed up. They all know I have brain cancer."

He continued: *I thought small town medical life would be a piece of cake, but when I started my private practice, I found that was definitely not the case! When done right, community medicine is just as demanding and difficult as academic medicine. My colleagues and I had to work seventy hours a week just to keep up. I felt like an intern all over again! Fortunately, I had a rugged immune system and a great wife.*

Dick looked up at me, smiling proudly. I got teary eyed at the mention of his sadness that he might not see his colleagues again, but when he talked about me, the tears flowed freely.

Most of you, like me, learned the pleasure of practicing in a small town where everybody knows you and most everyone is your friend. I have been honored by my patients, who have sent many cards and offers

127

of assistance. Most of our patients understand that doctors are people, that no one is perfect, and that medicine is a craft that relies as much on compassion as abstract knowledge.

I realized then that this was the crux of the book Dr. Edelman wanted Dick to write but he never did.

I am humbled to accept this award and I want to thank you from the bottom of my heart.

I remember the bitterness I felt in the spring when I found out that Dr. Friedman had received the 2012 Community Clinician of the Year award. Now I felt tremendous reassurance and joy that Dick had received the honor and appreciation he deserved. One of the Plymouth members came over to me and shared that Dick had been nominated for the award prior to his illness. Traditionally this announcement and event were held in the spring. I was very grateful to Dr. Edelman and the MMS officers for having moved up the schedule to recognize Dick in the fall of 2012, when he could still understand and appreciate the honor.

CHAPTER 28

Two Phone Calls

We got a sobering phone call from our son Seth at the end of the summer.

"My unit is being deployed to Afghanistan in the next few months. You don't have to worry; I won't be involved in direct combat."

My first thought was, *he won't have to go because of his dad's terminal illness,* and I suggested this.

"I need to go with my unit. I want to go," Seth said emphatically.

Dick supported Seth's decision. "We knew this might happen. He needs to go and do his duty."

I felt a lump in my throat and a migraine brewing. Terrible thoughts crowded my brain—*What if Seth didn't make it back before his dad died? What if something happened to Seth?*

Seth was granted two weeks' vacation in early September. He would be deployed in December for his ten-month tour of duty in Afghanistan.

Seth's visit home was less stressful than his last visit, which was precipitated by Dick's initial hospitalization. Seth had matured in the army and we were proud of him. Dick often wore the army cap he bought when we went to Seth's basic training graduation ceremony in South Carolina. Against the khaki camouflage design, shone the words "Proud to Have an Army Son."

While Seth was home, he helped out by mowing the lawn, closing the pool, and doing many chores Dick was itching to do himself, like cleaning the gutters. The two weeks went by quickly with family visits from his three sisters and spending time at his favorite haunts around town.

I overheard Dick talking to Seth when he said good-bye.

"I admire your decision to join the army and to serve your country. I boast to everyone that my son is in the Army Corps of Engineers. The most important thing is to work hard at whatever job you do. Remember that. My dad taught me that lesson. You've been very successful in the army and I am very proud of you. I love you."

"I love you too, Dad."

I held Dick close that night and told him, "I just know Seth is going to be safe. I also know that you will be here when he returns. I feel it so strongly in my heart and soul." I tried to project a strong exterior, but my voice was quivering.

"You know what I think about sometimes?" I asked Dick. "I think we're doing everything we can to take the best care of you. You have the best doctors, the best possible treatments, and everyone is praying for you. Even though I know glioblastoma is terminal, sometimes I think you will survive. I believe there will be a miracle. Do you ever think that?"

He looked directly into my questioning eyes.

"I love you so much but that's not the way it works, honey. It's a fatal disease. I hope someday there will be a cure. That's why I'm participating in the glioblastoma research study. But I am fortunate in so many ways. I am not in any pain. The tumor is not growing. We still have each other. We have incredible family and friends. You are wonderful at helping me make the most of every day. And, we're still having adventures."

I could barely get the words out, "We'll keep going and having adventures as long as we can. I love you so much."

He gently wiped away my tears. "I love you too."

* * *

The next day, Dick was getting ready to go to an appointment with his volunteer Jamie, a former patient. He was excited to see Jamie and hear about her daughter's progress in her first year of medical school. All of a sudden, Dick felt hot and started to slump. As an RN, Jamie immediately noticed the signs of an oncoming seizure and knew what to do. Over time, I became comfortable with following the protocol for seizures, but Dick had only one prior petit mal seizure at this point and it was still a frightening experience for me. I was so fortunate that Bharani was with us the first time and that now, once again, a trained medical professional was right there. I think God was looking out for us.

An hour later, when Dick was stabilized and receiving IV Ativan at the ER, I called the children to alert them of his status. When Samantha called back, she said urgently, "I need to speak to Dad. I have something important to tell him."

I nervously handed the phone to Dick, as he laid on a gurney, but my anxiety was short-lived.

"I'm pregnant," Samantha shouted so loudly that I could hear her. "We're going to have another baby."

Despite his condition, Dick grinned, "Congratulations, that's fabulous."

"I wasn't going to tell you yet," Samantha confessed. "We just found out. I haven't even been to the doctor. But when Mom said you were in the hospital, I wanted to let you know right away. You're going to be a grandfather again!"

"I couldn't think of anything more wonderful," Dick said. His mind was clearing and he was alert and animated.

I was standing very close, practically jumping up and down, ready to grab the phone.

"Can I speak to Samantha?" I asked.

Dick passed the phone to me.

"Samantha, I'm so excited! I know you talked about possibly having another baby but I didn't expect it so soon."

"We moved up our timetable. I wanted Dad to be able to see and hold our third child."

Tears started to flow but they were tears of triumph and hope. Suddenly the seizure seemed less significant. The announcement of a new baby coming was so thrilling. A new life, part of a new generation to carry on family values and traditions. Another genetic link to Dick. It was awe-inspiring to think about. The grandchildren brought us such joy, and now the gift of another one!

Throughout Dick's illness, Samantha brought the grandchildren from New York to visit as often as possible. Her in-laws generously gave us every holiday. Aerin and Jacob were precocious, fun-loving children. Dick joined them swimming in the pool, feeding the fish in the pond, and swinging on the glider in the backyard. Whenever they saw their Zayde (Yiddish for grandfather) they brought over their toys or projects that were broken or they needed help with. They had graduated from saying, "Fix it, fix it, Zayde," when they were younger to asking in more sophisticated language. It was getting harder for Dick to comply, and sometimes he had to pass the project off to their dad, Adam. They also went to their Zayde for all their ailments. They knew he was a doctor and if they bruised a knee or an elbow, they ran to him. He was usually able to fix them up with a Band-Aid, sympathetic words, and a lap to sit on till they forgot they were hurt and quickly jumped off to play again, as kids do.

Dick felt sad that he was often tired and had to give in to napping. But the grandchildren still took afternoon naps, so Dick took that opportunity to lay down next to them.

Samantha would say, "Jacob's taking a nap and he needs a Zayde to lie down with him."

Dick was happy to comply.

And the reverse was true as well. When I explained to Aerin one day that Zayde's illness made him tired and he had gone to take a nap, she asked, "Can I lie down next to Zayde?"

She melted my heart.

We thoroughly enjoyed spending precious time with our grandchildren. It made us proud to see them growing up to be such caring and sensitive little souls.

Over the next ten months, I held on to three beliefs—Seth would return home safely, Dick would be there upon his return, and Dick would greet his new grandbaby in March 2013—because that's what I needed to do.

CHAPTER 29

An Unexpected Honor

We attended an informative daylong seminar at Dana-Farber titled "Living with Glioblastoma." They encouraged a regular exercise program, so when Dick's radiation was complete, we registered for a stretch class at the Y.

As we entered the gym, we heard, "Dr. Gross, it's so good to see you!"

Dick's former patient, Tim, came up to Dick and gave him a firm handshake. As the class proceeded, Tim observed that Dick's balance and coordination were compromised. He didn't say a word—he just pulled his mat and chair over next to Dick's and assisted him with all the moves.

"There you go, Doc. That's it. Great job."

I participated in the class as well. I felt like I'd been demoted from bootcamp, and I imagine Dick must have felt the same way. But Dick and Tim became a regular team, and I think their camaraderie made it easier for Dick to swallow the idea that the most he could do was a "stretch" class. It felt good to get some exercise and when Tim was there, I was "off duty." Between the rhythmic breathing, movement, and not worrying about Dick falling, I was able to relax.

One day in August Dick received a phone call from State Representative Keiko Orrall.

I listened intently to one side of the conversation as Dick repeated some statements for my benefit because he knew his memory was poor.

Two of Dick's loyal patients, Bob and Marilyn Guthrie, wanted to recognize his hard work and dedication over the past thirty-five years and approached Representative Orrall, who brought Dick's accomplishments to the attention of the Massachusetts House of Representatives. Representative Orrall informed Dick that he was the recipient of a commendation by the State House and she would come to our home on September 6 to personally present him with the plaque.

Dick rarely had occasion to wear a suit anymore, but he dressed in his best one in anticipation of Representative Orrall's arrival. She was accompanied by her aide Jeanine and the Guthries. Our friend Bharani joined us as well.

Representative Orrall presented Dick with the honorary citation, which read, in part: *Be it hereby known to all that: The Massachusetts House of Representatives offers its sincerest congratulations to Dr. Richard Gross in recognition of his many years of commitment and dedicated service to his community.*

The proclamation was signed on August 30, 2012, by the Speaker of the House and State Representatives Orrall, Calter, and Straus, with the entire membership extending their best wishes.

Dick was so honored that he glowed like a candle. He was elated to see the Guthries, and I was so pleased to meet them. Representative Orrall was not rushed as I expected she might be. She spent time getting to know Dick, and we had a relaxed, pleasant afternoon. Dick was excited to show everyone our backyard, which still boasted colorful blooms and butterflies. The *Middleboro Gazette* later ran a story accompanied by one of the photos we took that day. Dick thanked Representative Orrall and presented her with a canvas photograph of one of our backyard birds. We sincerely thanked Bob and Marilyn, who gave me their phone number and offered to help in any way they could.

For Dick, it wasn't the citation, the Community Clinician of the Year award, or the recognition from the newspaper article that made the difference. It was the people. People like Bob and Marilyn Guthrie. People like Tim. People like Dr. Bharani, Dr. Edelman, and Dr. Friedman. The heartfelt letters he received from patients and friends, the support he got through Helping Hands volunteers—all these lifted his spirits and made every day a gift.

CHAPTER 30

Move Ahead

I looked forward to bedtime and I didn't. At this stage it was a time when we could hold our bodies close, rest our heads gently on each other, and share our deepest thoughts. Many nights Dick quickly dropped off to sleep in exhaustion. Although I had started taking a prescription sleeping pill our first week home from the hospital, I still had difficulty falling asleep and often lay awake for what seemed like hours. It was the time of night when my fears, doubts, and overwhelming sadness came to the surface and sometimes plagued me through the night in fragmented, frightening dreams.

One night, Dick totally surprised me when he said, "I think we should sell the house and move to a smaller place."

It took me a moment to respond while I was trying to comprehend what he was saying.

"Are you serious? I could never leave this house! I love this house. I could never leave my backyard."

"I'm thinking of your future. You know I love you so much," he said, as he took me in his arms. "I only want the best for you. It's too much for you to maintain this house alone. You won't need such a big house when you're on your own. I think a condo would be the best choice. Then you wouldn't have to worry about the lawn, snow removal, and all the house maintenance."

Dick was right—between the pool, hot tub, and backyard pond, there always seemed to be a leak somewhere or something in the house that needed fixing. Dick had always done most of these repairs himself.

I tried to keep the anger out of my voice. "I know you're thinking of me, but I can't imagine trying to make a move right now. I want to focus one hundred percent of my attention on you. Moving is a huge job. I want to put all our energy and efforts into doing everything we can for you right now."

"But that is what will make me feel better—knowing you are taken care of after I'm gone. I don't want you to have to move out of this house on your own someday. I want to help you while I can."

I hugged Dick close. "You are the best husband in the world. You're facing the worst time of your life and you're thinking about me first. But I'll have plenty of time to move when I'm on my own. I can do it myself."

"I feel really strongly about this," he said. "I don't want you to have to do it yourself. I want to help you."

I sat upright now, still shaken by the bomb Dick dropped.

"We've been in this house thirty-four years," I said. "We've accumulated so much stuff. The kids' rooms are still full. You know how we joke all the time about this cancer business being a full-time job for both of us? Well, it's true. I just can't imagine adding in the extra stress of a move."

Dick responded, "I always told you to clear stuff out. You save too much. The kids should take what they want, and we'll have to get rid of the rest."

"I love Lakeville," I said. "Everybody here knows us. Most of Middleboro knows you too. It's not a good time to lose our support system."

"We won't lose our support system. Our friends will remain our friends, wherever we are. We can look close by. Remember when we looked at The Pinehills in Plymouth? You liked it there."

"Let's give it some thought," I said.

"We don't have much time, honey. We need to think about it now."

I suggested we talk to Dr. V about it at our upcoming session and Dick agreed. Even my sleeping pill didn't help that night as memories of my beloved home and garden drifted through my consciousness.

The following Wednesday we talked with Dr. V about the pros and cons of a move. She helped me to realize how important this was for Dick. He needed to see me settled and taken care of before he died. I knew what I had to do. Dr. V suggested that if we were going to make a move, we should do it as soon as possible as Dick would have more and more trouble with short-term memory and adapting to change.

We started looking at condo properties around the South Shore. I was very discouraged because you cannot work the land at a condo property, and my garden was so much a part of my life. I thought this would never work.

We had been introduced to The Pinehills community in Plymouth a few years earlier when my sister and brother-in-law had visited friends of theirs who lived there. We had gone back to The Pinehills a few times to look at properties and get to know the area, not really with any intention of buying, but just as a pleasant afternoon diversion. Retirement had seemed so far off at the time.

Now we went back to look at The Pinehills through more serious eyes. It had a quaint village green with a post office, hair salon, doctors' offices, a grocery store, gas station, and other shops and services. There was even a coffee shop where they had outdoor seating, reminiscent of a European café. We sat there to take a break one sunny afternoon and chatted with local residents who were open and friendly.

"You know what this reminds me of?" Dick joked. "The Stepford Wives! Everybody is always smiling and so exuberant about life at The Pinehills, it almost seems artificial."

He had me laughing as I agreed.

We stopped at the Stonebridge Club where the clubs and activities center boasted about fifty clubs, including everything from tennis and bridge to painting and Great Works courses.

Once we started looking in earnest, The Pinehills quickly moved to the top of our list. This time we only looked at condo townhouse properties. We fell in love with the Fresco model 3, which had an inner courtyard and pathway where we could design and care for a garden ourselves. The model unit had a stone fireplace in the beautifully landscaped courtyard. I could envision how our own courtyard would look filled with flowers and butterflies. For the first time since thinking about a move, I felt excited.

Maybe we could do this. Maybe a new place wouldn't be so bad.

They were building the Frescos in two areas and asked if we preferred the more expensive units on the golf course or the units in the Rebecca's Landing neighborhood on the pond. It was no contest.

140

We could imagine photographing the pond and surrounding woods. We also loved the idea that The Pinehills community had walking trails throughout and was committed to remaining eighty percent green.

In December 2012 we bought a unit that would be built and ready by July 2013. We signed papers, they snapped a photo, and it was official. We consulted with Dick's medical team at the Dana and they confirmed Dick's thought that we should have the unit built handicapped accessible. We made accommodations to have wider doorways, no lip on the shower floor, and added grab bars in the bathroom. When the design team was having difficulty with the logistics in widening the study room door, Dick commented that it didn't matter. He said if he was at the stage where he needed a wheelchair, then he wouldn't be using the computer anyway, and he ended up being right.

Our new home was built by The Green Company. A week later we were surprised to receive a phone call from Mr. Green congratulating us on our purchase and welcoming us to the community. Dick was so reassured by this personal phone call and felt confident we had made a wise decision.

CHAPTER 31

Road Trip

In the fall, we received an invitation to a surprise sixty-fifth birthday party for our dear friend Brent in Cleveland and decided to take this opportunity to visit our old stomping grounds.

We discussed the medical risks of the trip with Bharani. He offered to drive us to Cleveland so that he would be alert to any medical problems and we could stop and get help if needed. Bharani had enjoyed Brent and Marty's recent visit and said he would love to see them again. We all agreed it would be a fun road trip.

"We would be so grateful," Dick said. "What could be better than traveling with our own physician? We'd be happy to pay your expenses. Are you sure you can take the time?"

"Yes, it would be my pleasure to take you."

I suggested we could stop and visit Sarah and Vivek in Buffalo on our way back and Bharani said he'd be happy to do that.

Dick's physicians agreed it was doable and I tackled the project. It took a lot of precise planning to arrange the trip between infusions, medication deliveries, appointments, and getting blood work done en route, but it was well worth it. Cleveland is where our romance blossomed and we fell in love. We lived there for the first six years of our marriage. So, although Cleveland may not seem like the most romantic city, it was for us.

In the process of researching hotels in the University Circle area, I discovered that Dick's old graduate dorm, where he lived when I met him, had been converted into a hotel—the Tudor Arms Doubletree. I could imagine it as a stately hotel. It was quite ornate when it was originally built as a private men's athletic club in the thirties. I didn't have to look any further.

When we checked in to the Doubletree, Dick said with a glimmer in his eye, "I don't even have to sneak you into my room this time!"

Dick told the manager that he lived in this building in 1970 when it was used as a dormitory for the CWRU professional schools, and the manager was eager to take us on a private tour of the building, at our convenience. I think from Dick's balding head, prominent scar, and shuffling gait, he understood that this was a special trip.

After Dick was well rested the following day, we toured right from the bowels of the building, where the old bowling alley and squash courts had been, to the rooftop. We surveyed the shell of the old swimming pool on a floor that was not yet open to guests. Our hearts melted when we got to the final room on the tour—the grand ballroom.

"I remember when we danced in each other's arms in this room," Dick said. "You had on that short, orange velvet dress with the mirrors that you got in Israel, and you looked ravishing."

He reached out his hands to draw me in, kissed me on the lips, led me in a few dance steps, and twirled me around. I felt like I was eighteen again, falling in love with this handsome medical student.

Dick's Uncle Sam, Aunt Ina, and their four children had been our surrogate family during the years we lived in Cleveland. Sam was a pediatric oncologist at Children's Hospital and had always been a mentor to Dick. Their daughter Abby and her family, who still reside in Cleveland, were our personal tour guides on this trip. We visited the Ronald McDonald House, which had been established in 1980 through Uncle Sam's efforts. It was one of the first in the nation, and we were proud to see Sam's portrait on a dedication plaque gracing the entrance wall.

Brent was totally blown away by his surprise party and couldn't believe that Dick and I had made the trip. We also got to join Brent and Marty at the opening reception the next evening of Brent's glass exhibit at the Akron Art Museum. We enjoyed visiting many of our old favorites—the Wade Park Lagoon, the Botanical Gardens, the Cleveland Museum of Art, and attended a performance of the Cleveland Orchestra. There were days when Dick didn't feel well, but he soldiered through and rarely complained, as he was thoroughly enjoying connecting with people, places, and memories.

We saw old friends, including Marty and Suzi Mandel. Marty had been a resident a few years senior to Dick. Suzi had become a music therapist and gave us some ideas about the important role music can play in managing illness. We had a wonderful reunion and they later became frequent contributors to Lotsa Helping Hands. After I wrote an update, there were members who always wrote back with encouraging responses, and Suzi became one of the regulars. I would share these comments with Dick, and they would help keep our spirits up.

We visited our old dorms, including the Steiner International House where Dick had lived for a year as the American representative. The door was locked but we managed to get the attention of one of the current students who let us in. He was from Korea and we chatted about what Steiner House had been like then and now.

Dick was the dorm president when he lived there in 1971. "It was always such a struggle to get everyone to do their jobs," he said.

"Nothing much has changed in that respect," the student chuckled.

As he graciously toured us around, we discovered on the living room wall a framed photograph of Dick and his housemates from 1971.

We went by the basement apartment we lived in when we were first married.

"Remember how we painted the whole place in rainbow colors with contrasting colors on the exposed pipes? I loved that apartment," I said.

"Yeah, until we got a mouse in the house."

"Oh my God, you're right! I was petrified the first time it scurried across the living room while you were at work! I'm surprised you didn't hear my scream at the hospital. I couldn't wait till you got home."

Dick had set up a mousetrap, but we couldn't catch him. The Spagnuolos, our wonderful Italian landlords who lived on the third floor, gave us some advice, "This is an American mouse, not an Italian one. Don't use cheese in the trap; try a peanut butter cup."

First try with the peanut butter cup—success!

"That's when we got our cat, Dusty," Dick recalled. "He was all gray, so we figured he'd infiltrate the mice."

We were both students and didn't have any money when we set up house, so we went furniture hunting in Shaker Heights on garbage day. We picked up a ratty, dilapidated chair and re-covered it ourselves in some blue material. Our best find was a rusty old glider that Dick stripped, primed and painted. After we replaced the cushions, it looked brand new. The glider moved along with us to Massachusetts and our grandchildren now played on it.

"We sure started out with nothing. I remember when we made a hamper out of a cardboard box," Dick said.

Bharani took a photo of the two of us in front of our old apartment—yet another memory preserved.

* * *

We drove on to visit Sarah and Vivek for two days before heading home. We got Dick's blood work done at the Buffalo hospital where Vivek worked. With lots of advance planning, it all went smoothly. We were so grateful to Bharani for driving and accompanying us on the trip. It was comforting to know he was there for us whenever we needed him. It was a big help having an extra set of hands to keep track of keys, pills, and belongings. Dick was having more and more difficulty with these skills, and it was especially challenging when traveling. Our friends and family enjoyed Bharani's company, and we were fortunate to be traveling with not only our own physician, but our own personal photographer as well!

All in all, it was a very nostalgic trip, a romantic jaunt back in time.

CHAPTER 32

LIVESTRONG

It was getting more and more difficult to fit in at our own Y. We occasionally attended the "Zumba Gold" class where Dick got a kick out of being one of the only men in the class. Over time, balance was becoming more difficult for him, but he insisted on going with me. At one class, the instructor became increasingly concerned about Dick's safety. She invited him to use a chair, but he would have no part of that. He was having so much fun dancing and was oblivious to the risks. I had trouble redirecting him, so she stopped the music and asked us to leave. It was an awful experience and soured us on returning to exercise.

I was angry with the Y staff but even angrier at myself. I knew Dick was getting to the stage where he might be unsafe, but I had only been thinking of myself. Dancing, singing, and yelling was a great tension release, and I felt like I needed it that day.

The Dana-Farber staff later informed us of the LIVESTRONG program, a physical activity and well-being program for cancer patients and survivors provided by the YMCA in partnership with the LIVESTRONG Foundation. LIVESTRONG had not yet been implemented at our own Y but the program director informed us that the East Bridgewater Y had just completed their first trial session and another one was starting soon.

"Why don't you take it there?" she suggested. "When we get our program rolling, you can always participate again here."

Dick began the twelve-week LIVESTRONG program at the East Bridgewater Y in late November 2012. We attended an orientation for the twelve participants and their partners where everyone introduced themselves and got to know each other. They had cards displayed on a table with pictures of everything from fall leaves and a person walking in the woods to a family having a picnic. Each participant chose a card and shared what it made them think or feel. Dick chose one of a boy on a swing.

"I love the feeling you get while riding through the air on a swing. I experience that joy through the comfort, help, and love I'm getting from family and friends. I'm looking forward to flying through the air with all of you!" he shared with the group.

Some participants took the card exercise very literally. Some gave profound, thoughtful responses and all were accepted with equal enthusiasm.

There was no cost to the group participants, as the LIVESTRONG Foundation covered the program. Caregivers or volunteer drivers could use the pool and gym facility during the hour and a half class. I put up a request for drivers twice a week over the next twelve weeks on the Lotsa Helping Hands calendar and the dates quickly filled.

I was so grateful for that time twice a week to run errands and take care of business. There were a lot of insurance issues to iron out, as our COBRA plan from my employment ended that November. I filled out endless forms for our new individual Blue Cross Blue Shield plan and dealt with the inevitable problems that came with changing insurance and pharmacies. We had finally gotten into a routine and then all the rules changed. Updating the new insurance information with all the providers also proved to be time consuming.

We needed more erlotinib, and our dear friend Bharani came through for us again and was able to get a new three-month supply from India. Managing day-to-day life in general was becoming more challenging. Everything was taking Dick more time as he tried to stay organized to make up for his poor short-term memory. He was forever misplacing his glasses, wallet, and phone. His wedding ring tended to slip right off his finger now due to his huge weight loss, but he refused to take it off.

Shortly after he returned home from LIVESTRONG one day, Dick suddenly cried out, "Oh my God, my ring—my wedding ring!"

"What's wrong?" I asked as I ran to him.

"My wedding ring is gone!" Dick yelled as he slid his fingers up and down over his ring finger. He was beside himself with anxiety.

"Don't worry, honey, we'll find it," I told him.

We had matching gold wedding bands with the inscription "I am my beloved's and my beloved is mine," from the Song of Songs, engraved in Hebrew. Bharani had been his driver that day and was still visiting when Dick realized the ring was missing. He ran out to check his car and the pathway to the driveway. We called the East Bridgewater Y and they carefully searched the building, inside and out. No luck.

I tried to reassure Dick, "It will probably turn up, and if it doesn't, we'll replace it. The ring is just a symbol. Our love is still strong—stronger every day," I told him as I looked into his anxious blue eyes, holding his face in my hands.

Two weeks later, Bharani was scheduled to transport Dick again. I opened the front door as I heard them returning from LIVESTRONG. Dick threw his arms around me in a bear hug.

"Yay!! We found the ring!" he yelled excitedly.

I cried tears of relief and joy and hugged Dick tightly.

As Bharani had gone to help Dick put on his seat belt, he spotted the ring where it had fallen into a crevice of the seat belt mechanism. When Dick put his ring on again, it literally slid right off his finger, so we made it a priority to go to the jewelers and have it resized the next day.

The group of participants at LIVESTRONG had a strong camaraderie. Dick became known for his good humor and trying to be a bit of a "showoff." I think he was trying to live up to his bootcamp days.

The staff were so caring and always there to assist Dick with his balance. He formed a special bond with them, particularly Lauren, as they bantered back and forth. He always came home with a smile and a story or two.

Pearl, a member of our synagogue, picked Dick up one Tuesday morning to drive him to LIVESTRONG. We were appreciative of her time as she was fitting in volunteering between her job and being a mother of school-age children.

Something didn't feel right that day when they arrived home. Dick seemed very subdued. The tipoff was when he did not immediately go into the living room to give Pearl a photo. He was always so proud and excited to present an assortment of canvas photos for his volunteers to choose from.

"Are you okay?" I asked Dick.

He replied with an expressionless, "Yes."

I quickly recognized the symptoms. I took a deep breath.

"I think Dick had a seizure," I said. "Did you notice anything on the way home?" I asked Pearl.

Her answer confirmed my suspicions. "Dick was talkative and engaging on the ride to East Bridgewater but barely spoke on the way back. I thought he was just tired."

I called the LIVESTRONG staff who told me they thought Dick was just having an off day, or that he wasn't feeling well. Petit-mal seizures were hard to recognize. I explained his typical seizure symptoms and reminded them Dick carried an Ativan pill in his wallet. Before hanging up, I told them to call me if anything ever happened or if they had any question and I would come right away. I also advised them to call 911 if Dick was having a seizure and the professionals could assess whether he needed to be hospitalized.

I gave Dick his pill, called his doctor and helped him upstairs to lie down on our bed. I crawled in next to him and held onto him. I tried to stay awake in case he had another seizure, but I was emotionally exhausted from the scare and fell asleep beside him.

I was surprised that the staff had not recognized Dick's change in behavior as seizure activity. But I realized they were not medically trained, and I did not blame them. They loved Dick and would never allow harm to come to him if they could help it. The next day I typed up a list of signs and symptoms of seizures and what to do in case of a seizure, including how to position his head, what to do if he vomits, and how to give him the Ativan pill if his teeth were clenched. I gave the list to the LIVESTRONG staff and put it on Lotsa Helping Hands for future volunteers.

I spoke with Pearl the following day and reassured her that Dick was feeling better. I admitted I felt guilty I hadn't been with Dick during the episode because I would have recognized the seizure activity. She reminded me I couldn't always be there, I was doing an admirable job, and I needed to take care of myself also. Pearl, an accomplished Ph.D. psychologist, came up with an excellent suggestion; she expressed uneasiness about driving Dick again but offered to visit with me while Dick was at medical appointments so we could talk. No one had offered to do that before, and I had never recognized I needed it.

In February 2013, my daughter Sarah, her close friend Kristen, Bharani, and I attended Dick's LIVESTRONG graduation. It was a heartening afternoon with the staff giving out special awards for everyone and sharing a little about each person's goals. Although Dick had actually regressed in his physical abilities over the twelve-week period, you would never know it, as the staff focused on his strengths and we were all so proud of him. He won the "Best Dressed Award" as one day he showed up wearing two different socks! They repeated the same "choose a card" exercise that they had done at the orientation and this time Dick chose a photo of a group of people who were having a party.

"I picked this card because they are having fun together," he said with a grin. My heart skipped a beat as I waited for him to elaborate and to draw the parallel with the relationships he had made in the program. I was willing him to say more but as I looked around, I realized he didn't have to. Everyone understood exactly what he meant.

The LIVESTRONG staff announced they would have a reunion in six months for all LIVESTRONG graduates and welcomed everyone to return. It was bittersweet, of course, because we didn't know whether Dick would ever see his LIVESTRONG community again.

CHAPTER 33

Sharing My Husband

In 2010 Dick built his Windows computer with our son, Seth. Two years later, with the onset of the brain cancer, he felt exasperated when he couldn't make the computer do what he wanted. He tried to fix it but the more he tried, the more it became a tangled jumble. Unfortunately, I was no help, as Dick had always taken care of all the electronic equipment. I used email and Microsoft Word, but I didn't understand the inner workings of the computer.

I would try to lure Dick away from the frustrations of the computer with the distraction of a walk in the garden or a ride to the coffee shop.

Dick's response was predictable.

"No, I want to get some work done."

It was hard for him to relax and enjoy leisure time. That's something he had never done well. He always liked to have a goal, to be productive.

I asked if he needed help or if I could call a friend to help him.

"No, I don't need any help. I *built* this computer. I *know* how it works."

It got to the point one day in February when the computer wasn't functioning at all. It was a frustrating situation for me also as I couldn't get onto the Lotsa Helping Hands site. I called our friend Josh Goldman, as I knew I could count on him to get it running again. It was awkward because I knew Dick felt like I "called Josh on him," but I didn't know what else to do.

Josh and his wife, Marcia, came down from Somerville and we enjoyed an afternoon filled with stories and laughter. Marcia had been my college roommate my sophomore year, so Dick, Marcia, and I went way back. Josh was very diplomatic in helping to get the computer functional.

One of the members of our Camera Club, Mike, was scheduled to pick Dick up later that week. He called the day before to say he had read on Helping Hands that Dick had a seizure and wanted to know if he could bring his son-in-law, KC, with him, who was a trained EMT. I thanked him and welcomed KC.

When Dick returned that day, he was excited to tell me about the time he spent with Mike and KC.

"Mike is such an interesting person. I'm so glad I had the chance to get to know him better outside of the camera club. Did you know that Mike is a chemist? I can't believe he took time off from work today to drive me. And KC came with him after working the night shift.

"Mike and I have so much in common! You know the scientific glassblowing I did at the lab at RPI?" Dick was referring to Rensselaer Polytechnic Institute, where he attended college.

154

"Of course," I responded, "We still have the yellow glass apple that you made there."

"Well, Mike also did scientific glassblowing early in his career. I was telling him about my chemistry professor, Dr. Robert Reeves, who was one of my role models. We talked about Gandhi, Mandela, Einstein, and other people we both admired. Mike is such a caring, interesting man."

A few days later I received a letter in the mail from Mike.

Dear Robin,

I want to thank you and Richard for the opportunity to spend a delightful day with a person with a wonderful mind and a warm heart. What I learned about his early career as a Man of Science, first as a physicist/chemist and then as a Doctor of Medicine just left me even more impressed at the couple so willing to share their enthusiasm for the quest for learning no matter the subject.

I am bemused by Richard's apparent feeling that he was not "smart enough" to pursue his Physicist/Chemist career path. What I see is a great mind/human being, redirecting his energy to make the most positive impact in this world. From all independent accounts that I have been able to assess, this is exactly what he did.

I was also fascinated with our discussion of role models. He is one of mine.

Thank you,
Mike

I sometimes doubted my decision to rely on volunteers, feeling guilty that I was not doing it all myself. Receiving that letter made me feel validated. I felt like I was sharing my husband with others. Dick and I knew each other's histories and stories. I doubt Mike had known that Dick was a physician, because in camera club, our commonality was our love of photography, and what we did outside the club wasn't important.

I could never have provided Dick with a stimulating discussion on chemistry or physics. Dick had an amazing ability to speak to people on all levels, on any topic. He still had a lot to offer people even though he wasn't practicing as a physician. I was pretty sure he didn't realize that. He usually measured things through work or accomplishments.

I shared Mike's letter with him. "Do you know that so many of your volunteers tell me how honored they are to spend time with you? When I thank them, they always say they should be thanking me. They admire you and they learn from you. Mike says you are one of his role models! I'm so proud of you."

Dick didn't say much but I think he heard me.

I kissed him on the cheek. He shrugged his shoulders and said, "I don't know why Mike thinks that, but I had such a good time with him."

In October 2016, a memory popped up on Mike's Facebook account and he wrote this:

I still have no idea how Facebook notes from five years ago are now appearing, what I do know is I have been blessed knowing the Gross's. It is rare to see a couple so in love, so giving to the outside world, so talented, so able to bring out the talent in others.

I was reminded how some people just come into your lives when you need them. I have not seen or heard from many of the volunteers who were there for us at the time. They just appeared like angels. I hope I can do the same for others some day.

CHAPTER 34

Dana-Farber Cancer Institute

O n our monthly trip to Dana-Farber, a typical day began with check-in at the Yawkey Center and then lab work at 7:30 a.m., which meant we had to leave Lakeville around 5:45 a.m. We often listened to books on tape to ease the tension while we were stuck in traffic and to take our minds off tumors and treatments. We then headed over to the Dana Building for an MRI. I filled out the two-page form for Dick, checking with him about any changes in symptoms. Bharani was there to meet us if he hadn't made it to the lab earlier.

Dick liked to carry the notebook we had compiled. It was a blue binder with brightly colored sections I labeled for him including upcoming appointments, consent forms, resources, previous appointments, and miscellaneous/parking. In the front inside pocket were brochures from the National Brain Tumor Society, including

"Understanding Glioblastoma," which I encouraged volunteers to take a look at while they were waiting for Dick.

"So good to see you, my friend. How are you doing this morning?" Bharani would greet Dick, and I could see Dick's face light up with the security of knowing Bharani had arrived. Bharani and I often grabbed a coffee and muffin while Dick was having his MRI, choosing an appealing one with gooey chocolate for Dick, although we both knew he would take only a few bites.

We then headed back to the eighth floor of the Yawkey Center for our appointment with Dr. V, the neuropsychiatrist. This was the only appointment Bharani sat out on. After the ongoing cognitive testing, we talked about how Dick was handling the new struggles he came up against each month. But Dick didn't usually see them as challenges. He always saw the silver lining.

"How are you doing?" Dr. V inquired.

"I'm excellent," Dick would most often answer with a smile.

I remember one particular visit when Dr. V brought up the topic of Dick closing his practice and the loss of his ability to do the work he loved. Dick responded, "Robin had a wonderful party for me and all my patients came. I was so honored. I am so fortunate to be blessed with such wonderful people in my life. Some of my patients are coming to take me to my appointments." He tried to gloss over the tough stuff.

Dr. V called me at home only once during the two-year period she worked with us. She wanted to know if Dick was experiencing some kind of euphoria or if this was his normal personality. I assured her it was just who he was. He certainly understood the reality of his terminal illness, but he was not going to waste time getting angry or depressed over it. He wanted to live life. He wanted to enjoy the good times. He saw the best in everyone and everything. He was truly grateful for every day.

We headed down to the cafeteria for lunch and then back to the neuro floor for our appointment with Dr. Reardon. By that time the labs and MRI test results were available. Dr. Reardon always let us view the results, and Dick and Bharani pored over the films. We could see how the radiation had attacked the tumor. So far, every month, we heard those incredible words "no new tumor growth." We were always thrilled to hear this positive news that gave us the courage and faith to keep going forward.

Dr. Reardon patiently addressed whatever questions Dick, Bharani, or I brought in. As I listened, I always felt like it was more of a case conference discussion between the three doctors, as Bharani and Dick offered their suggestions and interpretations. Dr. Reardon was the perfect balance of friendly and approachable, yet professional, always greeting each of us with direct eye contact and a warm handshake.

Every other month we saw Dr. Reardon's nurse practitioner, Jennifer Stefanik (Rifenburg). She was a beautiful, young woman with an engaging personality. You could just tell that she had a special fondness for "Dr. Gross," and we felt the same way about her. She was a good listener and always spent a lot of time with us. She was invested in Dick's progress. If we had a problem between appointments, I knew I could email Jenn and she would promptly respond. She sent regular emails when we were going through difficult times.

We talked about life beyond the cancer with Jenn.

"I'm planning on running the Boston Marathon," she shared one day. "Dr. Gross, I bet you were a pretty good runner."

Dick had boasted about his bootcamp days before he got sick.

159

"Well, I did the best I could to keep ahead of all those young girls chasing after me!" he joked. "Did I ever tell you Robin and I climbed Kilimanjaro ten years ago?"

"Dr. Gross, you never cease to amaze me. It's fortunate that you were in such good shape going into this. I believe it has helped you to do as well as you have."

I always felt like Jenn knew what we were going through. Sometime later, Jenn told me in confidence that she had lost her husband to cancer, and it was then that I understood our strong bond.

After Dick's office visit, I went to the checkout desk to make appointments for the following month. It was not easy for the scheduling team; they had to coordinate all the appointments in a certain order. Sometimes we had to make our appointment extra early or have a mid-day gap. I then went to pick up a hard copy of the MRI, while Bharani accompanied Dick to the infusion waiting room. There was always a long wait, as they did not make up the chemo solution until you checked in. Dick's infusion nurse set him up and if he didn't fall asleep in that comfortable chair, we used that time to make phone calls to family.

If we had a break during the day, we liked to go to the Healing Garden, a soothing, two-story, glass-walled space filled with plants, shrubs, and seasonal flowers. It was a meditative sanctuary in the midst of the bustling activity around us. I relaxed on the cushioned benches with Dick's arm around me. We were surrounded by the changing array of greens and annual blossoms, with a view of the Boston skyline in the distance.

Bharani snapped a photo of the two of us.

"You look beautiful," Dick told me.

"You're silly," I responded. "I've gained a lot of weight, I'm wearing my comfort clothes, and I did not put on any makeup at five a.m. this morning!"

"I don't know why you think you need makeup. You look just as beautiful as the day I met you."

I leaned my head on his shoulder as we sat for a while longer in silence.

Dana-Farber has excellent programs for both patients and caregivers. The Zakim Center offers alternative therapies, crafts, exercise, and support groups. Once Dick started his course of daily radiation, we knew extra trips to Boston would not work for us. The one program we considered participating in was a support group for glioblastoma patients. However, it was the third Friday of the month from one-thirty to three p.m., not ideal for the traffic flow.

Twice during our time at Dana-Farber we took advantage of programming. Once was a qigong class that happened to fall on a rare day when we were not scheduled for an MRI and had a break between appointments. We were unfamiliar with the practice, but the instructor led us through the class with gentle guidance. We lost ourselves in the movement and in the moment. It was a relaxing break in an otherwise hectic day. I left there promising myself we would try to attend again, but we never managed it.

The other time was on my birthday. I remembered they had an eight a.m. yoga class on Wednesdays, so I planned ahead and made a reservation to participate. Bharani arrived early that day and escorted Dick to his first appointment so I could attend. I was out of shape and hadn't had much experience with yoga, but it didn't matter. It felt so good to stretch even if I couldn't attain the perfect pose. I was so focused on my breathing and positioning that my mind was clear of everything else. The forty-five minutes went by quickly and I left feeling energized and refreshed. It felt good to carve out a little time and treat myself on my birthday.

The staff at Dana-Farber, without exception, were kind, gracious, and respectful. From the receptionists to the nurses, they did everything in their power to make a difficult time as pleasant as possible. The patients also treated each other with knowing kindness. Our day often ended between four and five p.m., sometimes later. We parted with Bharani and headed toward the highway at rush hour traffic.

It was a long day and we were both exhausted, but we knew Dick had received the best care possible. He was always appreciative of his doctors and more than once, asked me to help him in writing letters of thanks. He also gave them gifts of his canvas photos. Even through his illness, Dick continued to touch the lives of those around him.

CHAPTER 35

New York Reunion

In November, we received an invitation to a photography exhibit from our friend Lou Mannarino, one of the participants from our Monet's Garden trip. The reception and exhibit would take place in December in Staten Island, New York. Lou held an annual photography show and donated one hundred percent of the funds from his sales to charity.

Dick and Lou really hit it off in France. They were both creative thinkers and do-it-yourselfers. Dick had explained to Lou the process of printing and gallery wrapping his photos and Lou had invested in his own printer when he returned home.

"What do you think? Are you up for another trip?" I asked Dick.

"I would love to go and support Lou. It would be nice to see the kids and our cousins. Maybe we can even see a Broadway play."

I suggested we donate one of our canvas prints for the show and Dick thought that was a great idea.

We checked the calendar to make sure the date didn't conflict with any doctors' appointments. Since Dick had completed radiation, in addition to his regular chemo regiment, he took a very high dose of a chemo drug, Temodar, five days of the month. The medication made him feel sick and fatigued so we tried to limit our activity that week. The weekend of the exhibit fell exactly in the middle of those five days, so I discouraged Dick from taking the trip.

"I want to go," Dick said. "I don't want to hold back on living life. I can manage okay."

"Then we'll go! We'll try to do as much as possible. It will be great fun. I'm sure our cousins will understand if we can't see them or need to change plans last minute."

We were excited to hear that Gena, our close friend from the photo trip, was planning to come from Seattle. That sealed the deal. Gena had been our anchor these last seven months, giving us immeasurable support through our journey. We often looked back over the letter Gena sent us at the beginning of Dick's diagnosis and reexamined where we were and our approach toward life.

Lou was the owner of L&M Sound & Light, which created audio and lighting design for musical artists, theaters, and special events. He had worked with prestigious celebrities such as Bon Jovi, Whoopi Goldberg, and the New York Philharmonic. The exhibit took place at his studio. There was a lovely reception on the first floor and then the doors were opened to the exhibit hall upstairs.

We immediately heard comments from the crowd.

"It looks just like a painting!"

"That's the bridge in Monet's Garden. It looks just like an original Monet."

There was a magnificent display of photographs, the majority of which were taken on our trip to Monet's Garden and Keukenhof. Sold stickers quickly appeared on many of my favorites. One impressionistic photo of fall trees that Lou had taken on a photo trip to the Adirondack Mountains stood out to both of us.

"See how Lou used the panning technique that Charles taught us, of moving the camera down over the subject at a slow shutter speed?" Dick said.

"Yes, I remember. It works well here."

"I'd love to buy this photo. All the proceeds are going to charity. What do you think?" Dick asked.

We'd been together so long that our tastes were as one. We were always attracted to the same paintings, furniture, and museum exhibits.

"I think it's a wonderful idea. We'll own an original Lou Mannarino! I'll let one of the runners know before it's sold out from under us."

Dick was so energized by the exhibit that he suggested we should have another exhibit of our work. He hadn't had the energy or motivation to work on photos over recent months, so I was thrilled that Lou's show inspired him.

"We should have more time now that you're done with the radiation. We'll start printing out more photos from our trip and see how it goes," I said.

It was a sell-out show that evening. Lou made an announcement toward the end of the evening, "This year's proceeds will be given to a fund that furthers research in glioblastoma and supports patients and their families affected by the disease."

Dick later told Lou how much that gesture meant to him, and Lou responded with a big Italian hug. We had the opportunity to meet all the family members Lou had talked about on our trip—his dad, his children, and his girlfriend, Lindsey. We brought our daughter Samantha and son-in-law Adam, who had heard stories of the friends we'd made on our anniversary trip; they were thrilled to meet Lou and Gena.

The chemo took its toll on Dick, and he felt nauseous and fatigued that weekend. We didn't get to do everything we intended. But we did the important things—we visited with friends and family. We enjoyed an evening out with our cousins from New Jersey. We were even able to enjoy brunch the next day with Lou, Lindsey, and Gena, and reminisce about our days in Monet's Garden.

When we parted, there were generous hugs and tears as I felt overwhelmed with the awareness that Dick might never see Lou and Gena again.

CHAPTER 36

Fall 2012

Dr. Reardon and Dr. V asked Dick if he would be willing to have neuro-psychological testing to assess his current cognitive status, help with research, and see if he would be a good candidate for cognitive therapy. Dick agreed to set up yet another appointment. It involved several hours of testing, so we had to break it up into two separate visits. We reviewed the data a few weeks later with Dr. V.

Dick wasn't surprised that his scores fell in the low-average range on most items as he felt he was losing ground every day. I was shocked, however, as his functional ability was so much better than his testing revealed. He could still have an intelligent conversation on almost any subject.

Dr. V and the medical team recommended cognitive therapy with a speech therapist to help Dick with memory skills. We arranged it through Braintree Rehab in Taunton. The speech therapist, Roseann, worked with Dick on memory strategies and ways to stay organized. For example, if he couldn't remember what he was looking for, he could take something with him to remind him, like taking his notebook if he was looking for a pen. She advised him to try Luminosity, an online brain training site. Roseann gave him a notebook with suggestions and homework assignments for each session. Yet another notebook to keep track of.

Dick started teaching me the memory tricks and cues he learned from his therapist.

"Try associating someone's name with something that starts with the first letter of their name, maybe a characteristic or a hobby of theirs," Dick would repeat to me.

"Or associate a visual image with someone, like picturing a rose sticking out of my therapist Roseann's head."

We would then try making up silly names and images for people we knew, and we would end up laughing hysterically.

Once again, we had ample Helping Hands volunteers to drive Dick to his twice-weekly appointments and we were very grateful.

Despite any cognitive deficits, Dick tried hard to stay on top of his own treatments and medications and contributed to his own care plan with thoughtful suggestions. He wrote the following letter to his physician on December 5, 2012:

Dear Dr. Reardon,

Overall, I am doing well but I have some concerns, which I would like to address with you. I have lost thirty-five pounds in total. At today's infusion appointment they noted a five-pound drop since my last visit. I have met with the Dana-Farber dietitians. It is difficult for me to eat because I do not feel hungry. I feel that I am at the stage where I could benefit from an appetite stimulant like testosterone, Marinol, Deca-Durabolin, Atarax, or even Megace, and I would certainly appreciate it if you could prescribe any of the non-sedating appetite stimulants.

Twice a day I develop extreme fatigue. As I have increased the dosage of the Lamictal, could we try again to reduce the Keppra? I would like to make this change as soon as possible.

I have recently read of consideration of kinases in the treatment of glioblastoma that work on three EGF isomers. If one of those is available and you feel it is appropriate and just as safe or safer than erlotinib, which I am presently taking, then I would like you to consider me for it. If need be, I would be willing to travel abroad to try it.

At my initial visit with you, you presented the option of taking part in a vaccine study. I could not participate because I chose to take Avastin. Is there any new or additional treatment that you might recommend now that I could take advantage of while taking my current therapies?

Thank you for your excellent, thoughtful and attentive care.
Sincerely,
Richard Gross, M.D. (Retired)

CHAPTER 37

Winter 2012/2013

During the winter months, when we weren't tied down with daily radiation appointments, we enjoyed our forced retirement as much as we could. We celebrated our granddaughter Aerin's fifth birthday and had a heartwarming Thanksgiving at my brother and sister-in-law's. We enjoyed a lovely night out with our Y "bootcamp gang," whom we missed seeing on a regular basis. Although Dick was no longer interested in food, he did enjoy socializing, so we made as many of our monthly get-togethers with our gourmet group as possible.

We saw our good friend Charles Needle in Boston one afternoon, when he was en route to a photo workshop in Maine. Although we had met for the first time in April when he led our trip to Europe, we felt like we'd known him forever. We had visits from Dick's cousins from Colorado and Israel, and Dick enjoyed catching up on family, reminiscing, and going over the family tree.

We attended the beautiful country wedding of our friends' son in Hudson, New York. Dick had become quite sensitive to the cold, and we had no idea how challenging this would be both at the bed & breakfast and at the wedding, which took place on a charming, rustic farm. Dick had to forego the outdoor reception and wait inside the barn by a heating unit where the sit-down dinner would take place. A wedding guest had an extra blanket in her car, which we put to good use. We were thrilled to be able to celebrate with our friends, but nothing was easy anymore.

Dick came with me for routine errands to the grocery or drug store. He loved running into friends and patients when we were out and about. He told me one day, "When I decided to practice medicine in a small town, I remember other medical professionals warning me about missing academic medicine and giving up my privacy. I don't see it that way at all—I love being greeted by my patients all around town. It's one of my greatest joys!"

One evening in December we went to an opening reception for a friend's photography exhibit. We enjoyed seeing many familiar faces, including our friend Linda Fuller from our photo meetup group. We had met Linda on a photo trip to Acadia National Park and kept up through Facebook. Linda was an expert, dedicated, nature photographer whose specialty was wildlife. She mentioned that she had had good success that winter photographing the snowy owl and invited us to join her the next day.

Dick was very excited about the prospect of photographing the snowy owl. The idea of being retired and able to take a spontaneous field trip was still new to us, and we loved jumping headlong into enjoying the moment. This was our new philosophy of life. Although there were often challenges, we didn't waste time worrying about the elements and the logistics. We just said yes.

We headed to Duxbury Beach where the snowy owl was frequently seen. When we spotted the owl, Linda and I dragged our butts along the beach with our cameras, long lenses, and tripods in tow, so that we would stay low and not scare the owl. Dick was probably the smarter one who kept a dry bottom and stayed warm in the car.

When the owl took off, we continued driving down the beach and were fortunate to spot another snowy as it flew to the chimney of a building at the end of the beach. We all got out and took some shots, although Dick tired before the snowy did. We considered it quite a successful day, observing and photographing a few snowy owls. As we were heading home, Linda checked one more location right by the beach exit. There was a stately snowy owl hiding behind a rock right at the fence line. He was so close, Linda could practically drive right up to him. We rolled the windows down slowly and Dick was able to photograph the snowy owl right from the car window. It was like the snowy owl had just been waiting for him.

I was thrilled to have my camera in hand and be out on the hunt again. I didn't realize how much I missed it. I had always admired Linda from afar. When I would see her Facebook posts with fabulous wildlife photos, I would think—*that's what I want to do someday when I retire. I want to be like Linda Fuller.* I often thought of her over the next year and she helped me keep my goal in mind.

In life, it often seemed like time and opportunity wouldn't align, which frustrated me. When Dick and I started out and had more time, we didn't have much money for things like travel. When we had enough money, we didn't have the time. When we had the time, we didn't have our health. I had a glorious setting to photograph in my lush backyard, but I was at work all day or taking care of Dick. I would soon have time to myself, but I wouldn't have my backyard sanctuary anymore. I wouldn't have Dick to be with, play with, love, and discover new adventures together.

Why couldn't everything come together at the right time? Why couldn't Dick get to enjoy his retirement? Why couldn't God give us just one more year together? Maybe two?

I tried not to get lost in the "what ifs" and pulled myself back to refocus and look at the blessings in our lives. I had that one year before Dick got sick when circumstances had led me to leave my job and I had delayed taking another one. We had enjoyed spending more time with one another, building our own website, and planning and taking our anniversary trip. That year was a gift. Our time together now was a gift.

I spoke with Linda about her photography on our field trip. She said she treated it like a job. She got up early every day and had a plan in mind—photographing the seals at the Ellisville Harbor State Park in Plymouth or the birds at Jenny Pond. I loved photographing wildlife, birds, and of course, butterflies. I usually photographed in my own backyard because it provided such a rich environment and that's what my schedule allowed.

I was worried that I wouldn't have much to photograph in our new, meager courtyard. But I made a realization that day—when we moved to Plymouth, I could seek out places like Linda did. Rather than thinking about losing my backyard, I needed to look at Plymouth as my bigger backyard, with new adventures awaiting in the horizon.

CHAPTER 38

Preparations for Moving– A Setback

A friend advised me to pack one box a day in preparation for moving, and that's exactly what I did. We filled a lot of trash bins over the next seven months; made multiple trips to the book bin and put out regular pickups for Big Brother. The kids were finally forced to make those tough decisions about taking their own stuff or tossing it out.

It hurt to throw things out as each item held a special memory. I carefully packed our camping, hiking, and scuba gear, acutely aware that we would probably never use them again. As I packed our flippers, I doubted I would ever be brave enough to go scuba diving without my buddy—I couldn't imagine trusting my life to anyone but Dick. Would I ever get to use my hiking gear to walk the Appalachian Trail? No, I couldn't imagine doing it without Dick, and certainly not on my own.

It was so sad packing up those items and memories that sometimes I was paralyzed.

In January, there was a scheduled week to make design decisions on our new condo-choices of materials, color, style of carpets, countertops, tile, and more. My sister Jerri, who had a lot of interior design experience, was flying in to help us with the selections. We made preliminary visits to the design center, so we had some ideas of what we wanted. As it turned out, we had a medical procedure that week that prevented us from following through. Fortunately, Jerri acted on our behalf and I was able to return to Plymouth and rubber stamp her decisions by the end of the week.

Over the past several weeks, Dick's physician had been reducing his Keppra while increasing another seizure medication to take its place. During the two weeks he was off the Keppra, Dick had more energy and could think clearer. But because of increased seizure activity, which they determined were continuous, partial seizures, he ended up in the hospital and had to resume a high dose of Keppra to regulate the seizures. It was a frightening experience. For several days Dick had trouble initiating and making decisions and needed cueing for basic functions like getting dressed. By the end of the week, we were so grateful to see his personality come back; he became more animated, made jokes, and asked when he could get out of the hospital.

During the tense time Dick was in the hospital, we received a countless number of caring, encouraging notes, messages of prayers and strength, and offers of meals and help from our Helping Hands community. I always shared these with Dick, and they buoyed both our spirits. This was the first time Dick felt compelled to respond and asked me if I could help him write back on Helping Hands. I posted this announcement for him on the Lotsa Helping Hands site on February 1, 2013.

Dear Friends,

I have done my best to be the best doctor and loyal friend I could be over the last fifty years. I have been rewarded many times over by the dedication and kindness you have shown me even as I have been slowly losing bits and pieces of my memory, physical capacity, judgment and general knowledge.

As most of you know, the course of glioblastoma is often less than a year, but you have all contributed to making this last year profoundly satisfying. I have gotten to visit much of my dearest family and friends. Belatedly, I realize that much of my brusque, distant and irritable behavior may have been due to this tumor.

My deepest regret is that I have been unable to reciprocate all your kindnesses. I appreciate every kindness and act of respect you have shown me.

Sincerely,
Dick Gross

CHAPTER 39

Designing our New Home

When Dick was feeling better, I shared all the design choices with him, and he wanted to know every detail. I really knew he was feeling more like himself when he wanted to know how much it was going to cost him!

My sister hesitantly told me, "I hope you don't mind—I chose one upgrade for you. I wanted you to have something special to make you feel luxurious."

We had tried to stick to the standard options to keep costs down. Jerri showed me a photo of an elegant strip of mosaic tile trim in the master bathroom shower and I fell in love with it. I still think of my sister every time I take a shower.

Jerri studied and measured every inch of our condo plans. She helped us decide which furniture to keep for the new house and which to get rid of. We had bought our Telemark dining room set thirty-eight years ago when we were living in Cleveland. It opened up to serve twelve people. We had shared an untold number of casual meals, birthday parties, and elaborate holiday celebrations at that table with family and friends. We'd raised caterpillars and chrysalises on that hutch. We couldn't even give that dining room set away, but its size and early American style definitely would not fit in our new condo. Jerri made one more trip to Massachusetts to help us with some new purchases. By the time she left, we had a detailed printout on graph paper of where everything would go for move-in day.

While I was in Plymouth in January for the design selection week, I stopped to check on our new home site. Seeing the foundation made moving more of a reality for me. I got started on choosing a realtor, arranging to get our underground oil tank removed, improving the septic system to comply with Title 5 requirements, making house repairs, and hiring a landscaper.

The most exciting call I made was to a highly respected horticulturist with local ties. I spoke with him about helping us design and install our new courtyard garden. We set a date for the spring when he would come take a look at our Lakeville garden design and then go to our Plymouth site to see what we could create in that space. Although the idea of moving was bittersweet, Dick and I were excited to be planning together, and we looked at the move as our next grand adventure.

CHAPTER 40

Las Vegas

In February 2013, my sister Jerri and her husband, Alan, invited us, my siblings, their spouses, and my mom to a four-day vacation in Las Vegas, where my mom lived. Jerri arranged for us all to stay in a suite of hotel rooms on the Strip. My nieces Amy and Heather were able to join us as well as Heather's four-year-old twin boys.

Traveling was not as easy anymore, but we made it work.

"I think it might be a good idea if we reserve a wheelchair at the airport," I said.

"Absolutely not," Dick fired back. "I can still walk. I want to do as much as I can for as long as I can."

"I know you do. I just thought . . ."

"I don't need any help."

As it turned out, when we arrived at the airport, the check-in agent assessed the situation and asked Dick, "Can I order you a wheelchair? It's a long walk to the gate. I think you'll be more comfortable."

She gave me a knowing look and I realized I must have looked as overwhelmed and frazzled as I felt.

I was shocked when Dick gratefully accepted her offer. "Yes, thank you."

The airline representative apparently ordered a wheelchair transport to meet us at the other end as well, and I was so relieved to see them waiting for us. Dick made friends with the attendant on the long walk and he assisted us right into a taxi to head to the hotel.

I suggested Dick take a nap when we got settled into our room. I was looking forward to some quiet time myself. There was a knock on the door and my sister greeted us with a hug.

Then I heard Dick yell out, "I can't find my wallet. It's not in my pants pocket. I lost my wallet!"

"I'll help you look," I said. I tried not to panic. I looked all over to see if it had slipped out onto the bed or the floor. My sister helped by checking at the lobby.

Dick was impatiently ruffling through his belongings. Suddenly, I thought, *this was a terrible idea. We never should have left home.* I think Dick must have had the same thought.

We called the taxi service, who later returned the call saying the wallet was not left in the taxi. Then I remembered Dick had insisted on paying the airline attendant the tip himself. It was awkward for him to retrieve his wallet and put it back while sitting in the wheelchair. I had gotten into the habit of paying for most things, but Dick's pride would not let him leave his wallet at home. We contacted the airport, and they said they would get back to us.

Dick and I were both too upset to appreciate seeing all the family members who stopped in to say hello. Dick went to nap but had trouble falling asleep. He was trying to remember how much cash he had in his wallet. I envisioned the nuisance of trying to replace all the credit cards and health insurance cards. I gave myself a headache worrying that Dick might have a seizure. Again, the thought ran through my head, *we shouldn't have come; I'll never leave home again.*

While I was still exchanging phone calls with airport security, the front desk rang to say someone was in the lobby with Dick's wallet. I could barely ask questions before bursting into tears of relief. The kind gentleman who had helped us with the wheelchair had found Dick's wallet on the side of the wheelchair seat. He, himself, hand delivered the wallet to our hotel. Life just seemed to embrace us with honest, caring people everywhere we went. I silently thanked God.

We were emotionally exhausted. We slept for a few hours and woke up refreshed and relieved. Once we gathered with family, we were able to put the episode behind us and look forward to our plans for the next few days.

We limited the amount of walking we did and built in afternoon naps. We attended The Beatles Love: Cirque du Soleil and a Celine Dion concert. Having grown up in the Beatles era, we found the music to be both nostalgic and captivating. Dick was mesmerized by the beautiful Celine Dion, whose stage presence was as sweet as her stellar voice. We bought one of her CDs, which Dick enjoyed listening to over and over again.

Jerri arranged an Academy Awards night in our suite. We all got dressed up and watched the show together. Jerri printed up ballots and we voted for who we thought would win in each category. After announcing the grand prize winner, Jerri engineered a Yankee swap with prizes for all. We hadn't laughed so much in a long time. We also celebrated my Uncle Harold's eighty-first birthday at a champagne brunch in a fancy hotel on the Strip with my aunt, uncle, and cousins who lived in Vegas. It was great to see Dick enjoying himself and getting away from the daily routine of medical appointments.

The best part of the trip was spending time with family—reminiscing, sharing, laughing, and building new memories. I was so excited about a special side trip I had arranged as a surprise for Dick—a helicopter ride over the Grand Canyon. Dick had always wanted to visit all the national parks, but we had only made it to Acadia and Yosemite. However, Dick didn't seem comfortable and didn't show much expression. I'm not sure if he didn't feel well enough to appreciate it or if it just didn't measure up to how he would have preferred seeing the sights—hiking through the park and stopping along the way to photograph the beautiful scenery. I suspect the latter.

Our Vegas experience reminded me of our trip climbing Kilimanjaro. There were some serious moments on Kili when Dick had some regrets, but in the end, he loved the adventure. Over the next few weeks I heard Dick recount glowing stories of seeing Celine Dion and the Beatles Cirque du Soleil to his volunteers, doctors, and therapists. I knew our travel days weren't over yet.

CHAPTER 41

Therapy

Despite our hectic schedule, there were two crucial things that I never missed during Dick's illness: my appointment with my therapist, Barbara, and my appointment with my hairdresser, Carmen.

Dick may not have felt the need for a therapist (or a hairdresser) but I couldn't do without! Luckily I had an experienced, master therapist in place, as I had struggled with the changes and losses that occurred when I had my accident and when our daughter became seriously ill. Barbara's office was a twenty-five-minute drive away and right up until our move, I made the trip every other week without fail.

Those first few weeks after Dick's diagnosis, I exploded with shock, anger, and sadness. Barbara's office, upstairs in a quaint carriage house, was a safe haven to let loose. When I heard Barbara's familiar call, I climbed the stairs and opened the door. I entered another world on the other side of that door. I always felt like I was entering a child's fairy tale—one with a good ending. There were stuffed animals of all sorts, fairies, and puffy couches laden with soft, textured pillows. Every inch was covered with happy surprises. The color scheme was soft shades of pinks and greens.

I would take a deep breath, sink into the couch, and release an audible sigh of relief. I felt a peacefulness wash over me as I entered this wonderland. I didn't have to be strong. I didn't have to pretend. I didn't have to hide my tears. I didn't have to fill pill boxes, make doctors' appointments, pay bills, update friends or family. I could allow myself to just be. I could complain, wail, fall apart, and know that at the end of the hour, I would feel better. I would be prepared to walk out that door, that serene space, and enter the world of reality with a fresh outlook and a renewed will to keep going.

Barbara helped me recognize my feelings and acknowledge them. She helped me sort out thoughts, possibilities, and ideas so that I could make clearer decisions. She helped me to assess my physical symptoms and to seek help for medication for depression and sleep. When I occasionally let thoughts seep in about the future so that it became paralyzing, she reminded me to live in the present and take one day at a time.

I remember the very first time I saw Barbara, years ago. I had tried a few therapists prior to her who were clearly lacking, but I knew right away that Barbara was a skilled therapist who could help me. At the end of our first session, she had asked me, "Would you like a hug?"

I was a little taken aback.

"No, I'm not comfortable with that," I had responded.

In my own professional career I had always been taught that physical contact was not acceptable with clients and had abided by that rule.

This time when I returned with a hole in my heart too big to fill, Barbara asked again, as our session ended, "Would you like a hug?"

I fell into her arms and was enveloped in a much-needed hug. This became our new ritual. When I left that safe harbor, I always had the same lingering thought—maybe I could just stay right here, in this storybook land, where it was safe.

Barbara would send me off with the familiar refrain, "Be gentle with yourself." I came to know that phrase like it was my own.

She was my go-to person. There was nothing that was too intense or too sad to share. I was fortunate that I had many good friends, but I noticed over time that my friends never looked me in the eye and said, "How ARE you?" There was banter back and forth and concern over the latest seizure or insurance setback, but I didn't sense the invitation to open up and expose my deepest feelings. The exception was my friends who were psychotherapists, and luckily, I had a few. Barbara helped me to understand that those responses were normal. Our friends were also suffering. It was hard for everyone to accept the feelings associated with a loss. It was too deep, too painful. My therapist friends were better able to hear and take on the pain. Recognizing this, I leaned on them more.

Dick was totally comfortable with the casual, everyday talk with friends; in fact, he preferred it. He was not one to dwell on emotions. I noticed even when he spoke to the rabbi, Dick didn't talk about death or dying. He was more likely to ask, "What's new in the congregation?" "How is your family?" They both knew why the rabbi was visiting, but Dick was not ready to go deeper.

* * *

Carmen had been cutting my hair for almost thirty years. I had followed her to two salons and finally back to Lakeville when she opened Carmen's Hair Studio. She had given Seth his first haircut. Carmen had gotten married and had three children since I started with her. She had a calm, even temperament. She was able to read her clientele's needs to know whether they just wanted quiet time, needed a good listener, or wanted to gab about the latest town news. She was not only an expert at her craft, but she truly cared. After my accident in 2007, when I was not mobile, she came to our home to do my hair. She made home visits to do comb-outs for all three of my girls' bat mitzvahs. Our family took over her salon on Samantha's wedding day.

I kept up my schedule, seeing Carmen every five weeks right until we moved in July. True to her nature, she was a good listener. I fully expected to make the thirty-five-minute ride back to Carmen's after we moved. However, after making the trip once, I realized I couldn't afford to add on an extra hour for travel time. There was a salon right in The Pinehills Village and I realized I had to make the change. I felt like I was losing a good friend.

CHAPTER 42

Taking Care of Me

In the first six months of Dick's illness, there were two occasions where I completely lost control. One day I went for a walk in the neighborhood when Dick was out at an appointment. I stopped at my neighbor Cindy's house to ask if she would like to accompany me. I barely got the words out before I burst into tears.

The pent-up emotions of the last few months came pouring out. I don't know how long I sat on Cindy's couch with her warm hugs and heart encircling me. I instinctively knew Cindy was one of those people who could listen, who could take on the toughest emotions, and who could be there for me, and she was.

Another day, my friend Kathy gave me a ride to pick up my car, which had been in for servicing. I don't remember what the trigger was—it may have been as simple as time out of the house without Dick or an uncomplicated, "How are you?" but again, the floodgates opened, and my grief couldn't be contained.

I realized I needed to build in more time for myself. I wanted to be as strong as I could for Dick so that I would have the necessary resources to take care of him. I needed to take care of myself, as my therapist had been reminding me all along. I had always thought there would be time for that later, and I dismissed everyone's concerns that I take care of myself. My weight and cholesterol level had skyrocketed.

As Dick's needs became greater, I was no longer comfortable leaving him alone. He tired easily, so it became harder to take him with me on errands. He would sometimes misinterpret what I said and get frustrated with me. In turn, my frustration level increased when he didn't understand what I was saying.

There were not as many appointments at this stage of treatment, so I thought about using Lotsa Helping Hands to request friends to come by and visit with Dick so I could take a class at the Y or go out once in a while. Dick was not keen on the idea, so I brought it up during one of our sessions with Dr. V.

Dr. V thought it was a good idea for me to get out on my own and reinforced that with Dick. But no matter how many ways Dr. V or I talked to him about it, Dick repeated, "I want to go with Robin to the Y." I understood how he felt but I still needed some time off by myself. Finally, Dr. V advised that I should not prepare Dick. I should just arrange for a friend to come over and go out on my own. Somehow, it didn't feel right. I wasn't sure if I could do that.

I often referred back to Gena's letter when I got stuck, and this time I gave her a call and explained my dilemma.

Gena said, "When Steve was sick, there were days when we would just sit on the couch together and watch TV. Steve might drift in and out of sleep and we wouldn't communicate much. One day, I had a friend stay with him so I could go out. When I returned, I was surprised and delighted to hear they had so much fun together listening to music and hanging out."

Gena's story gave me the courage to try.

I wrote an update on Lotsa Helping Hands, entitled "Taking Care of Me." I shared some of my concerns and let everyone know I would be posting a weekly date on the calendar over the next month for social visits. I gave some suggestions for activities Dick might enjoy—going out for ice cream, working on his computer dictation, or doing some packing.

Charlie, a member of our camera club, was the first volunteer to sign up, and Dick really enjoyed spending time with him. Charlie helped him put fixative on our canvas prints. Those prints had been sitting there gathering dust since Dick got sick. I knew Charlie owned his own business and worked full-time, so I felt a little guilty that he came to hang out with Dick so I could go out.

I thanked him for coming and asked, "How did you get the day off?"

He responded, "What's the use of owning your own business if you can't take time off to be with a friend?"

The second time, an elderly female patient of Dick's signed up. Dick had always been delighted to spend time with friends and former patients when they accompanied him to appointments. But this time, he had a disgruntled look when I returned. Two hours seemed way too long for him. It was a disaster. I realized later Dick felt like he had to be a host. He was more of a doer than a guy who just hung out. He loved doing a project with Charlie, but he was not one to sit around and make small talk.

He told me that night, "I don't need a babysitter."

"I'm so sorry, I thought it would be good for me to get out of your hair once in a while and give you a chance to visit with some friends."

"I don't need to spend time with friends. I just want to be with you. I'm sorry I can't help you with everything. You can leave me alone if you have to go out. I don't mind."

"I'm so sorry. I love you so much. I want to be with you too," I said.

I quickly took down the rest of the social dates from the Helping Hands calendar.

Despite Dick's memory failings, there was one thing he always knew—how much he loved me, and that never changed.

I was discouraged but I tried to figure out how I could build in some time for myself without using volunteers. It occurred to me that a few physicians and good friends of Dick's like Dr. Friedman and Dr. Bornstein, had recently retired. I called them and our friends Sandy and Paul, and asked if they might like to hang out together with Dick once a week. They all thought it was an excellent idea and no one ever mentioned to Dick that I initiated it.

The following Wednesday, they picked Dick up and went to breakfast at the local book café, Somethin's Brewin'. Once word was out, they were joined by even more friends. They spent every Wednesday through July at the café, telling jokes, talking politics and local news, and reminiscing. I understand sometimes they could be a loud, raucous group, and Dick loved every minute of it! He had never really spent time alone socializing with his friends. I often wondered if that's what would have happened naturally when he retired.

It gave me an opportunity to do errands, go for a walk, or make appointments for myself during the day. If I ran overtime, one of the guys always volunteered to stay with Dick until I returned home. One day I headed out to do some errands. Often when I was by myself, l let my defenses down. On this particular day, before I had gotten too far, I was blinded by tears.

190

I impulsively pulled off the road into Robert and Emily Nisenbaum's driveway. Robert had died the previous year of cancer. Dick and I both knew Robert, as our kids had gone to nursery school together and he had been a patient of Dick's. I had never met his second wife, Emily, and I had never been to their home. An impelling inner force drove me to get out of the car and ring the bell. Emily answered the door. I didn't know what I was going to say, but somehow I felt like I needed to be there. I managed to mutter, "I'm Robin, Dr. Gross's wife. I'm sorry . . ." Before I could continue, I broke down in tears.

"I know who you are," Emily said, "Come in, I'm sorry . . ." She embraced me with a giant hug and my grief poured out in heaving sobs. I felt like I'd always known Emily. Her kitchen, with the copper pots hanging from the rafters, felt like a safe space. We talked for a long time. I think I just needed to be with someone who could understand the depth of my grief.

I felt a strong connection with this woman whom I had never met and would never see again. For a little while, the tension just drifted out of my body. As I pulled out of Emily's driveway, I saw Sandy's car parked across the street at Somethin's Brewin'. I thought how ironic it was that right across the street Dick and his buddies were schmoozing and laughing, but I was glad that was his reality and he would not have to witness my pain.

The guys continued to meet after our move. Bob organized the group and they carpooled to Plymouth once a week. They went out to breakfast at Olio's, the coffee shop in The Pinehills Village Green, and when Olio's closed in December of 2013, they frequented other Plymouth breakfast spots.

Sometimes they would hang around afterward and help me out with a chore or two, like bringing up the outdoor furniture from the basement. Dick looked forward to those mornings with enthusiasm

"Are my buddies coming today?" he would often ask when he awoke in the morning.

The group started out with the purpose of giving me some time for myself. But as I overheard them joking and laughing, I realized it had become much more than that. The group had become meaningful, not only to Dick, but to his buddies as well.

We enjoyed attending the annual St. Paddy's Day party in March hosted by our friends Rob and Kyle Sepersky, where we connected with friends and colleagues we hadn't seen since the last one.

Our friend Phoebe approached me at the party and said, "I would like to come over once a week after work and spend a few hours with Dick. You can use that time to do whatever you want."

Phoebe was a nurse who worked as director of a senior center. Except for these annual parties, we hadn't seen much of Phoebe and her husband since our children were little when we were both active in the Lakeville Mothers' Club.

I thanked Phoebe for offering but I told her I wasn't sure that would work. I explained what had happened a few months previously when I put some social dates up on Lotsa Helping Hands.

"I work in that field. You know me, Robin; I can have a conversation with anyone!"

"Dick likes to be productive. He's not that much of a talker."

"Does he have an iPad?"

"He does, but he only used it at work for writing scripts."

"I could show him how to use it."

"I think he would love that," I said.

Phoebe spoke to Dick about wanting to visit with him once a week in the evening after work and he agreed. She came the following week and I went on a shopping spree. Spring was approaching and I realized I had nothing that fit anymore. I had jumped a few sizes. I couldn't believe that shopping for "fat clothes" could be so much fun!

The best part was that when I returned home, Phoebe and Dick were engrossed in conversation and hardly noticed I had returned. Dick showed me what Phoebe taught him about the iPad. He had an email address through the Mass Medical Society, but it had become too overwhelming for him to check because it was filled with professional notices. Phoebe established a personal email address for Dick on gmail and showed him how he could use it on his iPad.

Phoebe and her husband, Ed, and Dick and I had children around the same ages. In the next three months until we moved, Phoebe and Dick had heart-to-heart talks about the physical and medical changes he was experiencing, the trials of raising kids, and his concerns about their future and mine.

My therapist often used to say that the universe had a way of taking care of us when we needed it. The right people seemed to come into our lives at the right time. This proved true, over and over again.

CHAPTER 43

A Tough Day

After Dick's office closed, work-related mail was delivered to our home address. He would receive test results from specialists, requests for records from insurance companies, letters from patients, and lots of other business-related mail. I sorted through the mail that required a response and wrote back to providers, insurance companies, and patients. As Dick became more confused, I tried to be vigilant in opening and responding to his mail when he wasn't home, to protect him from unnecessary worry. I lost the battle one day in March, when Dick got to the mail first. He became very distressed over a request for records regarding a former patient. He was convinced he was being sued by his patient, and I could not persuade him otherwise.

He read and reread the letter over and over again, misinterpreting its intention.

"I've done nothing wrong, but I will have to call my insurance company and let them know about this letter. This patient is going to sue me."

"What makes you think that? It doesn't say that anywhere. It only says they are requesting information," I said.

"You are wrong! You'll see. They're going to sue me, and you will be left penniless!"

"I don't believe that is correct. They only want information. I will direct them to the appropriate place to retrieve the patient's records. You don't have to worry about it. Nothing bad is going to happen to you or to me," I told him.

Dick was in a ferocious mood with a scowl on his face all day. I couldn't distract him. He kept bringing the conversation back to the fact that he was being sued. My attempts at easing his worries were futile.

Dick became so agitated that I finally called Michele, Dick's former office manager, to ask if she could speak to him. She kindly drove right over.

"Dr. Gross, it's so good to see you. Robin said you got a letter you are concerned about. Can I help you with it?" Michele offered.

"You won't be able to help me, Michele. I have to call my lawyer. I'm being sued."

Michele patiently read through the letter. "You can relax, Dr. Gross. This is just a routine request for records from the Visiting Nurse Association. Oh, you know what? You definitely don't have to worry—the date of service is January 2013. You were not even in practice then! You were not the physician who ordered this service," she explained.

"Then why would they send it to me? That's not right. They want the records so they can go to court," Dick said.

195

Despite our best efforts at convincing Dick he was not being sued, he would not listen to reason. Although I knew it was getting harder for Dick to stay focused and make connections, I somehow believed that if I just explained clearly and often enough, he would understand.

I had a raging headache the whole day. I realized how horrible it must be for Dick to experience fear and loss of control when he couldn't put together all the information correctly. I wanted so badly to take away his irrational worries, but I didn't know how. I needed to find better strategies to help him through the tough days.

We were both exhausted from this emotionally draining day. As I opened the rest of the mail later on, I recognized the familiar handwriting and North Carolina return address of Dick's former patients, Fran and Dave Silvia. They supported us, long distance, through the two-year period with their steadfast weekly greeting cards. Fran always wrote a personal note reminding Dick to enjoy the day. Their card turned out to be a godsend that day.

It read:

Just for today—Do the things you like best. Ignore the routine. Put your troubles to rest.

Just for today—Laugh out loud, sing a song. Be assertive, be silly, be happy, be strong.

Just for today—Do it all once, and then if you like it, tomorrow, do it all once again.

Sometimes it's easiest just to think one day at a time.

That card couldn't have arrived at a better time. I read it aloud to Dick and it sparked something in me. I decided to forget about the letter, forget the bad day, forget the routine, and just have fun together! We danced, we sang silly songs, and we laughed so hard when we couldn't remember the words to "It's Howdy Doody Time"!

CHAPTER 44

Birth Day and Birthdays

Our new grandson, Ronen Samuel, arrived on March 26, 2013, and we headed for New York for the brit milah (covenant of circumcision) ritual a week later. The bris ceremony included passing the baby to all the generations, and my heart swelled watching Dick hold and hug his sweet baby grandson. The middle name Samuel was chosen after Dick's brother, Samuel. Dick was so proud to hear Samantha share the wonderful characteristics his brother possessed, and we all envisioned Ronen carrying on Sam's legacy of being a bright, hardworking, and compassionate man.

I overheard five-year-old Aerin confide in Dick, as she sat in his lap on the couch, "Zayde, everyone dies sometime. I'm afraid to die."

She said it very matter of factly, in a clear, strong voice. "Don't be afraid, Aerin. Zayde's not afraid. I have lived such a wonderful life and I've been able to help others. Seeing you, Jacob, and now Ronen has given me great joy. You have a long life ahead of you, Aerin."

And Aerin changed the subject and popped off his lap just as abruptly as she had gotten on in the first place. It was interesting to me that Aerin was able to talk about death, while it was much harder for the adults. She was already processing and questioning it in her mind. She knew her Zayde was going to die and she looked to him for answers. Dick's simple response seemed to offer Aerin the reassurance she needed.

Samantha and Adam hosted a birthday party at their New York apartment that weekend for Dick's sixty-fifth birthday, which fell two days later. We invited family who had come from all over the U.S. for the bris and our friend Lou from our Monet's Garden gang and his girlfriend, Lindsey. The feeling of love and connection that night was palpable. Dick was just glowing, so pleased to be alive and to be celebrating life.

We had a wonderful dinner, but everyone knew Dick's favorite was desserts and I have never seen such an array of birthday goodies! There was a luscious double chocolate cake, a carrot cake with velvety white cream cheese icing decorated with frosted carrots and walnuts, homemade brownies covered in M&M's, all manner of delectable Italian pastries, and fancy cupcakes in all flavors. I don't know whose eyes popped more—the kids' or Dick's. His appetite was generally poor, but that night he rallied and tasted everything.

Aerin was wearing a two-piece outfit they got on a trip to India. It had a long, flowing skirt and a crop top that showed her belly. It was emerald green embellished with glittering jewels. Aerin did some Indian yoga stances and danced for us as five-year-olds do—with wild abandon. It was the best entertainment we could have possibly had.

Although we all knew this might be Dick's last birthday, there was no sadness that night. We reminisced, we laughed, we ate more than we could imagine; we played with the grandchildren and plastered that new baby with hugs and kisses.

We extended the celebrations by staying at a Hilton Hotel in Times Square. One night we saw the Broadway production of *Wicked* and another night we enjoyed an early birthday dinner with our dear cousins Iris and Harold.

Since I was not up to the challenge of driving to New York, we were grateful that our daughter Sandra did all the driving. The day after we returned home was Dick's actual birthday and we spent a quiet day at home recovering from four days of celebration.

There is no present that seems appropriate for a dying man, but Sarah figured one out and presented Dick with a heartfelt birthday letter.

Dear Dad,

I love you so much. You are an amazing role model and I am very impressed with what you are accomplishing in your lifetime. You helped so many people as a doctor and made a beautiful name for yourself in Lakeville/Middleboro. I was so proud of you when I worked at the Honey Dew Donuts coffee shop and everyone from the policemen to the dogcatcher knew that I was Doctor Gross's daughter and appreciated me because of it. Wherever I go in Lakeville, I hear stories of how much you mean to people. I know you got Sandra out of at least one parking ticket. You touch many lives.

Growing up, you always made sure that our family experienced the best of everything. I feel so blessed that I have already explored the world through our travels, and you always found a way to provide us with educational camps, programs and studies. I never had to struggle too much for opportunities or worry about failures because you were always there behind me to catch me if I fell. I hope you know that you have lots of people around you to catch you too.

You introduced me to the fun of science and invention with your ideas for the pool water heater and microwaved crystals. You encouraged my science projects on hydroelectricity, Viking ships, and Morse code, and Samantha's psychology word experiments, etc. Your love of knowledge and books and technology always pervaded the house and left me with a great appreciation for science projects—erector sets, growing crystals, and playing with the colors on TV with magnets affecting the electrons in the cathode ray tubes. There was never a subject you didn't know something about, and we were always taught to question and find the answers.

You always set an amazing example of hard work, resilience, and independence in your medical practice. I love how you created your world. You treated your patients like gold and even when I messed up and told people to come in during your lunch break, you saw them. You also never let us accept dishonesty or gray morality. You drove to my high school during your lunch break to sign a permission slip for me to join the National Honor Society even though the honor society advisor herself had recommended I forge a parent signature. You wouldn't have it! You took all of your extra time to do the right thing. Your example taught me more about honor than any group or club.

When I was ill during medical school and Mom was also sick, you were so strong to hold down the fort and keep the household running. Everyone leaned on you and somehow you were strong enough to bear it with grace and love. You wrote me a beautiful letter when you knew it was the hardest time for me, and with your strength and Mom's, I pulled through. You were always the backbone to keep everyone up as they faced their personal trials and never needed support or even appreciation yourself. You are such a beautiful soul and I don't tell you enough how much you mean to me. We have been through the hardest times together already, and we know that we can do it. You are the most amazing, sweet, genuine man, and I am so proud that you are my father. Thank you for everything. I love you.

    Love,

    Sarah

CHAPTER 45

Nourishment of Body & Soul

Dick and I both grew up in kosher households and maintained a kosher household ourselves. We did not eat pork products or shellfish inside or outside the home. We had separate meat and dairy dishes and silverware, and two Passover sets as well. After using kosher meat for twenty-five years, we gave it up; it just became too difficult to purchase. Dick was not a fussy eater. He enjoyed whatever I made and was easy to please (totally unlike the children!). Dick always had a sweet tooth—brownies were his favorite food.

During his initial six weeks of radiation, Dick felt nauseous and said food tasted "like cardboard." Breakfast was his best meal and by dinner he was mostly picking at his food. I did not request meals on Lotsa Helping Hands, as there was no reason I could not cook. However, my cousin Iris, an incredible cook as well as a gracious hostess, brought us meals once a week. She and my cousin Harold would bring a meal fit for a king and queen, best of all, with her famous fudge brownies in tow.

There was always enough for at least another meal. Because Iris kept in touch with my mother on a regular basis, she knew when we were expecting company and would prepare a dinner for ten or twelve if we were expecting the kids or out-of-town family. When we got home from the Dana at 7:30 p.m., tired and hungry, it was such a welcome gift to have a delicious home-cooked meal waiting for us. Iris filled our freezer before they left for Florida in October 2012.

Because Dick was consistently losing weight, his doctor recommended a consultation with a nutritionist. We met with one at Dana-Farber who advised that Dick should eat high calorie foods and have frequent, small meals throughout the day. The nutritionist suggested we continue to meet with her on a regular basis.

Dick responded, "It's really hard for us to get into Boston. We had to make a special trip today, because when we come for our usual appointments, we are booked solid the whole day. I have referred patients to an excellent nutritionist in Middleboro, Kristin Hatch. Could I follow up with her instead?"

"Kris Hatch?? I know Kris. She's an outstanding nutritionist! We went to school together. Of course, Kris is more than qualified."

Dick later exaggerated, telling his doctors and everyone he knew, "They all knew Kris Hatch at the Dana-Farber. She's famous."

We called Kris to set up an initial appointment. We were both acquainted with her as we had friends in common. Kris lived a short distance from us, so she offered to come to our home. After talking about some basic principles, introducing us to Boost Plus, and giving us some handouts, Kris said, "What I would like to do is cook for you. I'll bring you a meal once a week. You can tell me your favorites."

"It's so kind of you to offer but that's too much for you. It's complicated. We don't eat certain foods and we eat kosher style," Dick explained.

"It would be a privilege for me to cook for you. Dr. Gross, you are the reason my private practice got off the ground. Your referrals got me started. I can't thank you enough.

"I understand about kosher restrictions. I will always give you a couple of options so you can make a choice."

We went back and forth awhile but Kris was very persuasive.

"We would at least like to pay you for the groceries," I said.

"I will definitely not accept payment. This is my offering of friendship and love to you."

My eyes welled up as I went over and gave Kris a hug.

"Thank you, Kris," Dick finally said, "That is very generous of you."

When Kris left, we perused through the many dietary handouts she gave us, and Dick asked for my help to create a nutrition notebook. On the front cover, in his shaky handwriting, Dick labeled it:

Nutrition

Live Long and Prosper

Kris was an amazing cook. Each meal was presented like we were eating at the Ritz, complete with delivery of a vase of beautiful flowers. She researched kosher cooking and borrowed my cookbooks. She always paid attention to Dick's reactions and noted his favorites. She prepared a travel snack bag for the car for when we were stuck in traffic or out all day at appointments.

At Dick's request, Dr. Reardon prescribed an appetite stimulant pill, Marinol, twice a day. That combined with Kris's delicious food, suggestions, and tips, improved Dick's intake.

Kris instructed us, "You need to do the opposite of everything you have learned in the past. Dick needs to eat calorie-rich, nutrient-dense foods."

I started off buying calorie-rich foods for Dick and low-fat versions for myself but quickly decided it was easier just to buy one product. At the grocery store I chose whole milk, butter, eggnog, red meat, etc. I felt like I needed to apologize to the clerk in the checkout line! The abundance of all these yummy foods was too much temptation for me, so I decided to just give in and not worry about gaining weight. There would be time for that later. The good news was that Dick didn't lose weight that month. The bad news was that I gained five pounds!

When our daughter Sarah visited for a few weeks, Kris prepared special vegetarian selections for her. Sarah was so appreciative of Kris' kindness she asked if she could help her cook. Kris was pleased to mentor Sarah, so when Sarah was home, she would go over to Kris' house and they would cook together. They became close—preparing, sharing, cooking, and chatting, while providing love and sustenance well beyond the actual food.

Kris and I communicated by email on a regular basis. She would send a preview of her upcoming menu. "I will be making beef stew with many veggies, raspberry/pineapple salad, and honey cake. I'll also do butternut squash soup. It's a tasty soup, would be easily tolerated and good for lunch the next day. How does that sound?"

Dick admitted he felt bad that Kris was doing so much work, especially when he couldn't tolerate eating much. And I felt guilty about accepting help for a task, like cooking, that I could do myself. I often acknowledged Kris on my Lotsa Helping Hands updates, but I felt like I could never adequately thank her. Then we got a note from Kris reminding me that we didn't have to, and that allowed us both to accept her generosity.

You are welcome. It gives me such joy to be connected with you this way. It is definitely not necessary to thank us. I love cooking for you/look forward to doing so, and expect nothing in return—only for you to enjoy the food, to have you feel our care for you, and to have well-nourished bodies that will give you the best energy and outlook possible. You do excellently with the latter, regardless of the day, it seems.

Every few weeks we would have a more formal talk and look over weight management and other issues. On the first snowy, winter day, Kris had trouble walking from the car to our kitchen door as I hadn't gotten out to shovel the walk and the snow had frozen. I felt terrible when I realized how icy it was. Kris usually had so many casserole dishes, and, of course, fresh flowers, that it required two trips to the car, so I went out to help her for the second one.

"The snowplow we hire does the circle driveway and the drive to the garage but there are still a few places that we have to hand shovel. I'm so sorry I didn't get out here to shovel before you came," I apologized.

"Don't worry," Kris replied. "I'm going to send my husband, Jeff, over to shovel the walk for you. If there is ever anything you need, please call us. If it's something we can't do for you, we will find someone who can."

On Dick's birthday, April 8, 2013, Kris let us know ahead of time she was preparing a special birthday dinner for Dick. It was an incredible meal, complete with a chocolate birthday cake for Dick's sweet tooth.

"Kris," Dick said, "you outdid yourself! I'll have to take a picture of those gorgeous roses—the rainbow colors are dazzling! Thank you for making my birthday special. Please join us for dinner."

"I can't, but thank you for asking. Happy birthday," she said as they exchanged a birthday hug.

The next day I sent Kris an email thanking her for the elaborate birthday dinner:

Dear Kris,

The dinner was fabulous!! We really enjoyed it. The chicken piccata was delicious. We had never seen a "singing balloon." Dick got such a kick out of it. The flowers are amazing! Rainbow roses—wow!! Your note was lovely and very meaningful to Dick. You are just such a beautiful person, Kris, and we are blessed to have you in our lives!

Love,

Robin

She replied:

Robin,

Thank you. I was very delighted to be able to make Dick's birthday dinner and am so glad you enjoyed it. I remember, months ago, you mentioned that Dick's birthday would be coming up in April/thinking about how to celebrate it. What a wonderful week of celebration you had with your family, around such an important event! I so admire your courage to forge ahead with more daily activity than most people would contemplate with just usual life. Most definitely, REST seemed most in order for his birthday this year.

I know that Dick is the first to say, on his birthday, and all days, that his greatest asset in life has been you—a wife who is consistently supportive, full of energy, insightful, always planning ahead, caring for the small and large details of all things, with humor— and then he never fails to mention your beauty.

Jeff will be glad to take care of the walk/he will be in touch with you. Also glad to do anything else that you may need.

Will look forward next to making a fish dinner for you.

Love,

Kris

Kris continued to play a major role in our lives until we moved in July. She and her husband, Jeff, both helped out when needed, including airport runs to pick up family.

I believe God often puts people in our lives for a reason, and Kris was one of those angels.

CHAPTER 46

Spring 2013

I think of spring as a time of rebirth, but the spring of 2013 felt like the tide was turning for the worse. Dick was having frequent seizures and lost ground after each one. He had increasing difficulty with orientation, memory, balance, and mobility. It was becoming a struggle for him to make the stairs to our second-floor bedroom. Despite my repeated suggestion that we move down to one of the children's old bedrooms, Dick steadfastly refused.

I knew it was out of his love for me that Dick wanted to assist me with tasks like packing and lifting boxes, but for safety reasons I had to be stern with him. He started complaining that I was too "bossy." Dick accompanied me to my medical appointment one day where our friend Kyle was working in her husband's office. Dick greatly respected and admired Kyle both as a nurse and a friend. When Dick confided his frustration to Kyle, she assured him he could be the "boss" that day. Dick thought that was just grand and reminded me about it all day long!

Despite my fear and ambivalence about moving, I felt like life would be easier once we moved. We would have our bedroom on the first floor. We would be done with packing and all the maintenance our large home required. Although I tried to savor each day, part of me couldn't wait till July rolled around.

Dr. Reardon referred us to Dr. Ellen Bubrick, an epilepsy specialist, because of the difficulty in controlling seizures. She took a thorough history and made some recommendations and changes in medications that, thankfully, helped in the control of Dick's seizures over the next few months. As we got to know Dr. Bubrick and filled her in on Dick's experiences as a doctor, she used to say he was one of her favorite patients, and she was one of our favorite docs. Seeing a specialist involved more doctors' appointments, more trips to Boston, and trials and changes in medications, but it was worth it when we finally reached a more stable period.

Although Dick had printed some pictures on canvas when we returned from Monet's Garden, this spring was the first opportunity he had to gallery wrap them since he became sick. He wanted to show me the process so I could do it on my own. Dick had experimented and come up with his own special technique for folding the corners of the canvas so they lay perfectly flat. He had it down to a science; it frustrated him now as he folded and refolded, but couldn't remember how to do it.

I felt terrible that I had never paid attention as Dick had steadfastly wrapped the prints. He would occasionally bring them up from his workstation in the basement and fold and staple them as we watched TV together in the evening. I reminded Dick that our camera club friend, Scott, owned a similar printer and did canvas gallery wraps. I suggested we invite him over to help out and Dick agreed.

Scott came and demonstrated how to fold the corners so they were smooth, and we made a demo so I could try it myself. I was surprised how much strength it took in your hands to staple the canvas to the wood frame. I was motivated to work hard at it when I saw how pleased Dick was with the final result. Making photos was important to him, and he was so proud of me for carrying on his passion.

He told me later that evening, "People will forget about me being a good doctor. But the photographs will live on for a long time. They are something tangible that my great-grandchildren can look at and remember me."

I put my hands on his shoulders and looked right into his eyes, "People will never forget you or what an exceptional doctor you are. We have all those beautiful handwritten letters that your patients sent you, lauding your medical wizardry. You will be remembered for all of your virtues and talents. You will always be remembered by your family as being the best dad, grandfather, and husband. You will be missed more than anything in the world."

In April, Dick became eligible for Medicare, which once again meant a change in health insurance. We chose the most comprehensive supplemental plan available. Just like last time, despite my best planning efforts, there were some glitches in the transition. Getting the medications, deliveries, and the specialty pharmacy orders correct was time consuming and challenging. We asked Dr. Reardon to send in a prescription for erlotinib under Dick's new insurance. The good news was that it was approved! So despite the hassle of changing insurance twice within one year, we no longer had the expense and challenge of getting the erlotinib from India.

We were invited to spend a spring weekend at Dick's cousins' new summer home in Gloucester, Massachusetts. It was a lovely spot by the beach, and we took the half block walk down to the shore with our camera packs. We hadn't taken Dick's camera case out since December when we went to photograph the snowy owls. His gait was shaky, and the extra weight of the backpack made it difficult to balance. Just as we were admiring the jagged rocks at the ocean's edge, Dick went down with a thud. There was a little blood and embarrassment, but the hardest thing for both of us was the realization that he was losing his physical abilities. That was the last time Dick ever wore his camera backpack.

Although the local Mass Medical Society had feted Dick early in the fall, the state level event was in April 2013 at the Seaport Hotel in Boston. I was excited for Dick and looked forward to a memorable evening. As we were getting ready, I noticed he was having trouble with his tie. I offered to help but he couldn't show me what to do. Dick didn't remember how to tie his tie!

I felt a terrible sense of fear and alarm. It had always looked easy when Dick had done it, but now I was flustered, and I couldn't figure out how to tie it. I was all dressed up, sweating, scared, and trying to hide my panic from Dick. We couldn't just show up to a formal affair with Dick half dressed. It was getting late and we needed to get on the road. I looked on YouTube and there it was—how to tie a tie. I tried to stay calm and followed step-by-step directions until I had a presentable finished product.

There was another foreboding occurrence that night. On the way to Boston, Sarah called to inquire about the lumbar drain procedure Dick would undergo later that week at the Brigham. I heard Dick's end of the conversation and realized by his responses that he couldn't describe the procedure and wasn't sure what was being done. He and Bharani had thought of the shunt and suggested it to the neuro-oncologist months ago! I was shocked to hear that he couldn't explain it to Sarah.

After fighting terrible traffic, we arrived late and somehow the excitement of the night had dissipated. We were seated with the contingent from the Plymouth District, including Dr. Rick Pieters, the incoming MMS president-elect, and his wife, Edie. I started to feel sick almost right away. By the time dinner was served I was so nauseated that I couldn't eat the filet mignon or anything else on the plate. It was so unlike me. Dick didn't take one bite of his dinner either. He never had an appetite at that hour, so I wasn't surprised.

After we heard the congratulations given to all the individual district recipients of the Community Clinician of the Year awards, including Dick, I bolted out of my seat and escaped to the bathroom. Edie followed.

"Are you all right?" she asked.

"I'm feeling so nauseous. I don't know what's wrong."

I tried to hold back the tears, but I was unsuccessful. I explained about the tie and the call from Sarah. "I just don't know how we can keep going like this. Changes are happening so fast. I don't know how I will be able to drive home tonight. I feel so terrible."

"Don't worry about that," Edie said. "We'll give you a ride home. We're just worried about you. You turned white. I knew something was wrong. It sounds like it has been a very difficult evening. You've had a lot to deal within a short time."

Dick was very subdued that night. He was mostly concerned about me and didn't mind leaving early. Our doctor friends drove to our home in Lakeville, one driving my car and the other driving their car. I knew it was way out of their way to drive from Boston to Lakeville, as they lived north of Plymouth, but I felt too sick to argue.

Rick was an admirer of Dick's photography. Months later, after we moved to Plymouth, we invited Rick and Edie to visit and presented them with a canvas photo as a thank you for accompanying us safely home.

Bharani suggested to me the next day that I may have experienced a migraine without the headache symptoms. That had never happened to me before or after, but I believe that's exactly what occurred that night. I tried hard not to show my stress, but my body couldn't hide it. Fortunately, my symptoms resolved without further incident, but the experience left me with a new understanding of the road ahead.

CHAPTER 47

Attempted Lumbar Drain

In May 2013 Dick's tumor had been stable for one year. However, he was still experiencing confusion and walked with an unsteady gait, which made Bharani and Dick question whether a lumbar drain procedure might be helpful. A lumbar drain is used to treat normal pressure hydrocephalus (NPH). The condition's hallmark symptoms are dementia and a wide stance-shuffling gait, and the symptoms can be reversed. The process involves draining excess fluid from the brain. Dr. Reardon felt there was a slim chance that Dick's increased confusion was a result of NPH. However, if it was, Dick's cognition would improve from draining the excess fluid surrounding the tumor. The procedure would require a three- to four-day hospitalization at the Brigham. We consulted with Dick's surgeon, Dr. Johnson, and decided to go forward with the procedure.

He would eventually have the procedure done in October, but before then, we had two false starts.

It took a lot of planning and energy to get to Boston. I canceled all of our upcoming appointments and volunteer drivers. I postponed signing our mortgage paperwork. I made arrangements for our cat and the mail. I got the house in order in case there was another showing. I packed for the hospital and printed a current list of meds. I remembered to take the one med they always had trouble getting through the hospital pharmacy. I warned Dick's cousins who had given me the key to their Chestnut Hill home to use anytime, that I might stay overnight on the second or third night of Dick's admission. I called the service station to let them know it was our car that got towed into their station on Sunday. I played phone tag with the Green Company who finally reached me at the hospital to let me know there was a color choice for a new option at our condo. The preparations alone left me drained.

I went for a massage that morning so I could make it through the drive to Boston. The stress was taking its toll on my body. A few days earlier, after driving to the hospital in stop and go traffic, I could barely walk when I got out of the car.

On the afternoon of May 13, 2013, Dick was admitted to the Brigham for the lumbar drain. Bharani met us as usual and we were grateful for his company. After waiting several hours, the hospital personnel came in to tell us that it wasn't safe to perform the procedure as Dick was taking a daily baby aspirin, which causes increased risk of bleeding.

I was angry as the procedure had come at a difficult time while we were preparing for our move. How had they missed the fact that he was on aspirin? Didn't they know how hard it was for patients like Dick to wait long hours and accommodate to change? I couldn't imagine going through all this again.

I was especially upset about everything Dick had to endure. He had a long wait for admission to a bed, had to respond to multiple mini-mental tests, had an IV inserted, blood work done, PT assessment, and didn't get to rest all day, although naps had become a necessary part of his routine. After they explained they weren't going to do the procedure, they expected him to wait another hour until the doctor was finished with surgery, as the surgeon wanted to explain to him person-ally why he couldn't proceed. Dick became increasingly impatient but waited it out to speak to Dr. Johnson, whom he respected very much.

At that point, we both just wanted to go home. Dick asked the staff to take out his IV. They kept stalling as they said it was hospital policy to leave it in right until discharge. Dick knew it wasn't neces-sary at that point and he wanted it out. As he became more agitated, I kept going to the nurse's station pleading with them to take it out. Dick finally resorted to taking things into his own hands.

"I'm going to pull it out myself," he said.

"Please don't," I said as I covered my eyes, "The nurse promised she would be right here."

I ran to tell the nurse, with an accusatory tone, that he was taking it out himself and she finally sent someone to remove it.

After speaking to Dr. Johnson, we started walking out around nine p.m. when the nurse stopped us and said, "I'm sorry, you have to wait. I haven't printed out your paperwork yet."

We waited until the frustration became unbearable.

Suddenly Dick yelled out, "I'm not waiting any longer! You don't need the paperwork. I don't even think the insurance will pay for this hospitalization because there was no medical service performed."

"Everything should be covered by insurance," the nurse tried to reassure him. "Let me call a wheelchair transport for you. Your wife can bring the car around while you sign the paperwork and we'll meet her down there."

"I refuse to pay for parking!" Dick said in agitation. His face was beet red and I could see the veins in his temples pulsing.

"Where did you park?" she asked.

"We're parked in the Dana-Farber lot."

"Well, you will have to take that up with them," the nurse said.

I was fuming inside but I told Dick, "Don't worry, I promise you: we will not have to pay for parking. I will take care of it."

I was relieved to go to the garage and escape the tense situation. I couldn't have lasted another minute trying to get Dick to wait for the paperwork. I burst into tears the moment I turned my back to leave the floor. It was such an exasperating day. I hated it when Dick got agitated and the situation was out of our control. I hated watching him become upset and irrational. I hated the life of pills, doctors, and hospitals. I hated glioblastoma.

I tried to control my sobbing to explain to the parking attendant why I didn't want to pay the fee. I managed to get out bits and pieces of what happened, but he didn't even need to hear my story. He just whisked me through with no charge.

As disheartened and depleted as we both felt, when Sandra called on the way home, Dick, in his incredible way of viewing the world and talking to people, told her, "We were treated like we were in a spa for the day. It was such a good thing that they canceled the procedure and saved me from hemorrhaging to death!"

I was completely shocked by his response, but his positive interpretation helped relieve my tension headache. Those moments when the real Dick shone through the disease were priceless.

We arrived back in Lakeville close to eleven o'clock that night, frustrated and exhausted. I usually wrote updates on Lotsa Helping Hands twice a month, but that night I needed to vent my frustration. I banged out a blog, entitled "A Rough Day," detailing all the things that had gone wrong that day. I felt much better afterward. I made mention of looking forward to hanging in the garden with the birds and the butterflies for a few days with no appointments and no stress.

The next day I had forty-six messages of comfort: "You are surrounded by love and admiration," "It's perfectly ok to cry and cry some more," "You are a model of courage and perseverance." Dick's cousin Jean wrote, "What troupers you both are. Dick's positive spin on the story is topped only by your ability to find joy in the butterflies and the birds, even in the midst of what you are going through."

Our Helping Hands support network was always invaluable in keeping our spirits up.

We were so busy packing and selling the house that we decided to put off the lumbar drain until after our move to Plymouth.

CHAPTER 48

Faith/Religion

I've felt God's presence as long as I can remember. As a child, it was not cool to admit that you actually enjoyed attending Saturday services. Although most kids' attendance at Shabbat services was spotty, it was a given that I would respond yes to roll-call attendance taken the following day at Sunday School. I was one of the few Jewish children in Fall River, Massachusetts, who lived within walking distance of the temple, so I could trudge through even in a snowstorm, and I did. The enormous sanctuary, with its mosaic dome ceiling and brilliant stained glass windows, was mesmerizing and the service, uplifting.

After high school I participated in a one-year program in Israel—the Young Judaea Year Course. During our five months studying in Jerusalem and one month on a moshav settlement, I felt the absence of a religious and spiritual presence. When it was time to choose a kibbutz for our three-month stay, I was in the minority who chose to go to a Kibbutz Dati (religious). Although I disliked the separation of the females in the back of the synagogue, I loved the familiar prayers and cadence of the service, the holiness of saying blessings before and after meals and the sanctity of keeping Shabbat.

In college I chose the kosher meal plan offered at the Hillel building. I was a regular at Friday night services. Dick and I met at Hillel and continued to attend services there through our early years of marriage. The CWRU Hillel rabbi officiated at our wedding in Tiverton, Rhode Island.

When I was a child, my family's life revolved around the temple. Dick had a similar upbringing in Winthrop, MA. When Dick and I bought our first home, we joined the conservative synagogue in New Bedford, MA, twenty-five miles south of Lakeville. Although our four children attended Hebrew school there, we never felt like we truly belonged. It was a tight-knit, closed group, and we were the outsiders commuting from a strange place called Lakeville. When the rabbi of forty years retired, there was a significant change, as a new young rabbi, Rabbi Raphael Kanter, took over the leadership.

As my kids got older, I started attending Shabbat services on a regular basis, a year before Rabbi Kanter arrived. Services were held in the oversized sanctuary, and I had to leave before they were over to pick up my children from Saturday School dismissal. Rabbi Kanter moved services to the more intimate chapel and coordinated them to end at the same time as Saturday School. Then everyone was invited to a kiddush luncheon afterward. Rabbi Kanter instituted many changes such as these, which built a stronger sense of community.

With his positive influence, the synagogue quickly became more welcoming to interfaith families and those who had not lived there for generations. The congregation began to attract members from outlying towns. Rabbi Kanter developed a Keruv (interfaith) Committee and Dick and I were active in it. There were a few new interfaith families from the Lakeville area who joined our synagogue and we sat together at Shabbat services and the kiddush luncheon afterward. It was the beginning of enduring friendships. Dick and I finally felt like we belonged.

Attending services centered me for the week. I was able to transport myself to a place where I could forget the stresses of the week. The chapel's southern wall is enhanced by beautiful stained glass windows. As the sun's rays strike the glass, light streams into the chapel infused with soft, glowing reflections. I always felt like God's light was shining down upon us.

I heard a friend chant the haftorah in memory of her father on his yahrzeit one Shabbat and decided I would love to honor my father in this way. It is a complex process as you need to learn the *tropes*, the symbols that tell you the melody. At the same time, you also need to read the Hebrew letters and vowels. My friend Carol tutored me. I practiced at night when I got into bed, playing the tape Carol made for me and then singing the prayer aloud. It was very meditative. Dick loved to hear me sing.

He would often tell me, "You put me to sleep with your beautiful voice."

I chanted my first haftorah in 1994 for my dad's yahrzeit and did it on the anniversary of his death for many years. I felt a strong connection to God when I was chanting. Dick took on the role of chairman of the Search Committee for a new cantor at our synagogue and with the committee's recommendation, the synagogue hired Cantor Nathaniel Schudrich the following year. Dick and I signed up for the cantor's class on chanting haftorot and we enjoyed learning together. Later we took the cantor's class on chanting Torah tropes. Dick was smarter than me in just about everything, but reading Hebrew and learning the Torah tropes was one of the few things where I was more proficient. Although Dick's knowledge base was far greater than mine, he never made me feel like I wasn't just as smart as he was.

I usually went to services when Dick was working on Saturdays. After participating in services for two hours, I always enjoyed socializing afterward and eating lunch with fellow congregants. When Dick's schedule allowed, we took pleasure in attending services together, and for a few years we participated in the mentoring program, acting as mentors for pre bar and bat mitzvah students.

Dick regarded religion more as an intellectual pursuit. Where I liked to feel enveloped by the power of God and the spirit of tranquility, Dick liked to use his time during services to read the Torah portion and commentaries.

Dick believed in the traditions of the Jewish religion and felt it was important for the survival of the Jewish people to keep up religious and cultural practices. He did not feel like he had a personal relationship with God. He came from a science background and was more of an objective thinker who observed facts. He believed keeping the commandments was a code for how you should live a just and honorable life.

We never entertained the idea of life after death. We never even talked about that as a possibility. Neither of us had a simplistic view of God as rewarding good and punishing evil, yet I often thought life would be a lot simpler if it worked that way. Through the two years of Dick's illness, we witnessed the hand of God in the people who helped us. I was constantly amazed at the outpouring of love and assistance from family, friends, patients, and acquaintances. I began to form a new understanding of God as residing in people. The power of goodness was so strong, it felt tangible.

I often asked myself, *Would I be such a good person? Would I give up a vacation day to drive a friend to Boston for treatment or help someone pack up for a move? Would I cook elaborate meals for someone I did not know very well? Would I call every week for two years to check on a cousin or mail a weekly get-well card to a former doctor over a two-year period?* I promised I would try to dedicate myself to being a better person and to pay forward all the kindnesses we had received. I tried to convey in my Helping Hands updates the gratitude that we both felt and hopefully I succeeded.

I did not generally ask for things from God because I knew that's not how it worked. I prayed to God for strength and guidance. But yes, I must admit, I prayed to God for a miracle that first night when it was clear we were dealing with terminal brain cancer. *Just this once,* I thought, *I need a miracle. Please God, spare Dick.*

I remembered reading the Book of Job and Rabbi Kushner's book *When Bad Things Happen to Good People,* years earlier. I knew there were no good answers. Innocent people suffer terrible misfortunes in life.

What I took from Rabbi Kushner's book is that belief in God can't be tied to seeing God as all-powerful. Bad stuff happens. Bad stuff happens even to good people. God doesn't make it happen. But we can still look to God to provide strength and comfort. I see God in people. I see God in the kindness of people who help each other, in the courage of those who are facing death, in the dedication of those who work to make the world a better place.

Dick did not become angry or bitter or dwell on "why me" when he got sick. He focused on what he could do to make things better. He researched treatments for glioblastoma, he made sure that he provided the best resources to his patients when he could no longer care for them himself, and he provided for me and his family for the future.

God surrounded us with angels who brought help, encouragement, and hope on a regular basis. We were reminded daily of being part of a community who cared. Our Lotsa Helping Hands community not only provided practical help, but also renewed our spirit with their love and support. I did not get the miracle I prayed to God for in those first nights of diagnosis. But I got miracles of a different sort: a miraculous husband who accepted his prognosis with courage and grace and focused his energy on making life the best it could be, and a miraculous community of people who carried us through our journey.

CHAPTER 49

My Mom

There was a flurry of calls between my three siblings and me in February 2013 when my mom became ill. After living most of her life in Fall River, Massachusetts, my mom had retired to Las Vegas in her eighties. She spent the summers with us in Lakeville. She had so much energy and pizazz for life, Dick used to tell everyone, "My mother-in-law moved to Vegas to become a showgirl!"

My sisters, who lived in California, flew to Vegas at the first alert that something was wrong. Mom was diagnosed with a large hiatal hernia and had a surgical consult, but we determined it would be best to get a second opinion in Boston. My sister Priscilla accompanied Mom to Boston and Mom stayed with us while she was evaluated. We were very distraught to see she had lost a drastic amount of weight and was in significant pain.

The Boston physician did not want to schedule surgery until Mom had a consult with a GI specialist, which we expedited. Mom developed a bad cold, so because of Dick's compromised health, she went to stay with my brother, Neal, and his wife, Karen, in Providence, Rhode Island. When she developed pneumonia and her condition declined, my sisters flew in to help. They had just hired some professional help to start the following day when my mother took a turn for the worse. She was crying out in pain. She became confused; she started speaking in Yiddish, talking to my father who had died thirty-five years earlier and calling for her mama. She was giving up and talking about dying.

That was not like my mother. Although widowed at the age of fifty-three, she was strong and resilient. She ran my father's factory after he died. She was a spirited, positive person, always helping others. My mom was a people person. When I was growing up, she seemed to know everyone in town. I remember her talking on the phone a lot, which she still does to this day, keeping in touch with relatives and friends all over the country on a regular basis.

After the kids left home, she took people into her home. She volunteered with the Greater Fall River United Jewish Appeal in resettling Russian immigrants: she housed them before they got settled, helped furnish their first apartments, and got them started in their new lives. She sponsored my father's family, who immigrated to Fall River from Russia in the early 1980s. She housed a Community College student from Sweden. Her door was always open, and she made enduring friendships.

While working full time as an adult, Mom became a part-time student and got an associate's degree from Bristol Community College. She then became a substitute teacher in the Fall River public school system until she moved to Las Vegas. She was always positive and supportive in anything we did. The highest compliment

I have ever received in my life was when people told me I was like my mom.

My brother, Neal, called me around 8 p.m. that night to say they were taking Mom to the Miriam Hospital emergency room. There was fear in his voice. We were all scared she was dying: our mom, Lorraine, who was the strongest person we knew. She just couldn't die. *Please God make it not true.*

I wanted to go to my mom immediately. I had always felt bad that I had not been able to get home to see my dad before he died. I called Ruth to stay with Dick so I could go to the hospital, but she insisted on driving me, so I called my friend Kathy, one of Dick's favorite volunteers.

The ride to Providence was agonizing. I kept fearing my phone was going to ring, but thank God it did not. It was difficult to see my mother in such a terrible state. They did an abdominal CAT scan and found pervasive lymphoma. The ER physician showed us the scan and we saw that several areas of her body were covered with disease. We were all devastated to hear the news although the physician explained to us that lymphoma was treatable and curable.

How did they miss the lymphoma diagnosis in Boston just two weeks earlier, we all wondered? We later found out that although they had done a scan, they had given her a previous test with dye so that they could not read the scan clearly. That seemed like a poor excuse to me. I knew if Dick was healthy, he would have diagnosed her sooner.

I cried all the way home, not just ordinary tears but shuddering sobs that left my body feeling hollow. I cried for Dick, I cried for my mother, I cried for my father, and I cried for me. I felt ripped apart and thought I would never feel whole again.

When I got home, I slid into bed next to Dick. I could barely tell him the news. He held me and stroked my head. I cried softer tears now as he held me close.

My mom remained in the hospital for one week, recovering from the pneumonia and being seen by oncology. Surgery for the hiatal hernia was put on the back burner while the primary problem was addressed.

My brother, Neal, had organized a spectacular, first-ever family reunion at his place on Martha's Vineyard and more than fifty relatives from all over the U.S. attended. We missed my mother, the family matriarch, but various family and friends took turns staying with her at the hospital while we were on the Vineyard.

We knew my mother was stabilized and on the right track when, by the end of the week, she was asking for her cell phone, wanting to know every detail of the reunion and where and when next year's reunion would be held.

CHAPTER 50

June 2013

Suddenly, July loomed closer and I was getting anxious about the move. *How will I ever be ready in time? What will we do with all the extra furniture? How will I get to see my mom once I move? Will volunteers come all the way to Plymouth?*

There were so many questions and details to take care of. We still had to sell the house and take care of finishing touches on our new home. Dick and I had always worked on projects together, but lately I felt like I needed to take responsibility for everything. It was overwhelming. Dick desperately wanted to help, but his capacity was diminished both physically and mentally. We opened the pool that summer so we could show the house at its best. Dick had always taken care of the pool maintenance and I had difficulty keeping it operational. I was indebted to our good friend Bob Smith, who nursed that pool along and kept it going all summer.

We had a lot of chores that needed attention in order to get the house ready for sale. We hired our friend and Dick's patient, Ron Dunham, who had helped us through the years with home repairs and additions. He not only refused payment in the end, but he made return visits to take down pictures from the cathedral ceiling living room and other tasks that Dick could no longer do.

There were days when I felt like I was drowning in a list of things to do. *What had I been thinking? Why did I ever agree to a move?*

My college roommate Marcia called to say she had a two-week vacation and wanted to offer her services for whatever we needed. She came down from Somerville on two separate occasions to help us pack. Our friends Peter and Robyn came several times from an hour away to assist in packing, and Dick's sister-in-law and niece flew in from Florida to help.

We were constantly amazed at and grateful for everyone's generous support. We never would have gotten the house ready for sale and moved out without the help of so many friends and family. They were our saviors.

"What do you think we should do about Aristophanes?" I asked Dick one evening as he cuddled our cat and stroked its soft black-and-white fur.

Aristophanes was used to being out of doors for the fifteen years we owned him. He loved hunting and roaming in the backyard and the neighborhood. He stayed out all night in the summer months and was in and out of the house all day long. He loved to curl up on Dick's lap in the evenings. I could hear his contented purr from the next room. We both loved Aristophanes, but I didn't think he would fit into our new lives.

"Can't we take him with us?" Dick asked.

"Well, I suppose we could, but," I said hesitantly, "pets are not allowed to roam free in The Pinehills."

"Couldn't we let him stay out in the courtyard?"

"Our courtyard is not contained. It's open at either end."

"I would hate to leave Aristophanes behind," Dick said, as he hugged him closer.

"Me too, but I'm not sure it's fair to Aristophanes to make him an indoor cat after he's had his freedom for so long. There's not a good space for a litter box in the new house."

I felt terrible as soon as I said those words.

A heavy silence hung in the air. Then Dick said, "You're right. Do you remember when our cat Sophocles died? He was old and could barely get around, but I was glad he died fishing in the pond, doing something he loved rather than being sick indoors. I wouldn't want Aristophanes to give up what he loves. Maybe one of the kids could take him."

"Maybe," I responded although we both knew that was an even less likely scenario than the kids taking the furniture.

The next day I told my friend Ruth how guilty I felt suggesting to Dick that we shouldn't take the cat with us. Selfishly, I was thinking how much extra work it would be for me. Dick loved Aristophanes and the cat was soothing to him.

Ruth solved our dilemma when she called the following night and asked if she could adopt Aristophanes. She had cared for him before when we went away, and she loved Aristophanes. Thank God for Ruth! Dick agreed that letting Ruth and Marty adopt Aristophanes was the best solution, and I felt a tremendous sense of relief.

We researched physicians in the Plymouth area so Dick would have a local PCP. I reached out to Dick's many contacts at the Mass

Medical Society and received a strong recommendation for Dr. Thomas Browning. We decided to set up the first appointment before we moved so there would be a smooth transition. When I got directions to his office, we realized it was located right in The Pinehills Village Green. Dr. Browning also worked as the medical director of a local hospice two days a week. He knew of Dick's reputation; they had a good rapport and Dick appreciated Dr. Browning's keen sense of humor.

At the end of June my mom went to the Fall River Jewish Home for rehab and I was very grateful to volunteers who stayed with Dick so I could visit, attend her care plan meetings, and take her for infusions. As soon as I got there, she would start pushing me out the door, telling me, "You need to get back home to your husband."

As she progressed, she moved into an assisted living facility in Providence near my brother. God was looking over her and she eventually beat the lymphoma and got a clean bill of health.

We had gotten to know Sandra's boyfriend over the last few months and we were glad to see her so happy. We were relieved she was doing well and headed in the right direction. Dick told me, "Sandra will make an excellent nurse someday. She is a hard worker and I am very proud of her."

"It's a good feeling when your kids finally grow up and 'find themselves,' isn't it?" I said. "You helped Sandra a lot by letting her work in your office and mentoring her. You should be proud too."

For the first time in their adult lives, all four children seemed to be on the right track. Not only had Sandra found her calling but Seth had found his place in the army. Sarah and Vivek seemed happy, and Samantha, Adam, and their children were thriving.

There was a pre-closing walk-through scheduled by the Green Company in June to go through the new house and identify any problems. It was a forty-minute drive each way, Dick's stamina was poor, and there was nowhere to sit in the empty house. After fifteen minutes, Dick declared, much to the surprise of the customer representative, Lois, "It looks fine to me. Let's go."

Lois asked, "Don't you want to look in the bathrooms and check upstairs?"

"No," Dick replied, "I'm sure it's fine. I'm tired."

I ran upstairs to have a quick look around. Luckily, Lois was advocating for us and noted and marked down some minor flaws that needed to be addressed. I think we were the first customers to ever breeze through the process without any complaints!

Dick's tumor continued to be stable, and Dr. Reardon suggested Dick stop one of his oral chemotherapies in June. It was the one that caused the most side effects, so Dick was looking forward to feeling better and having more energy.

I had never used the Helping Hands calendar to request assistance with cooking, but the week we moved, I requested dinners. I was surprised at the huge response. A number of people told me they were so glad they had an opportunity to help, because, due to their work schedules, they couldn't assist with driving during the day. It was an intensely hot week and volunteers were creative in making meals that were cool, refreshing, and delicious.

Dick saw everyone working hard around him. He wanted so much to do his share. He started going around the house spraying WD-40 lubricant on all the doors and windows. He became obsessed with it. He sprayed so much on the glass sliders in the living room that I was worried he would stain the carpets.

"Thanks for your help," I told him. "That's enough now. The doors are fine."

"No one will buy this house because the doors squeak," he replied in an irritated voice.

I was afraid no one would buy this house because there was gooey lubricant all over the doors and windows!

Despite Dick's rampant spraying, in June, we ended up with two offers on the house. We were thrilled that it went to a young couple who had obviously fallen in love with the house and garden. My voice cracked and my eyes filled with tears as I assured them it was an amazing house and yard in which to raise a family.

We celebrated our forty-first anniversary by having lunch at Somethin's Brewin' and watching the new *Star Wars* movie. Nights out were a thing of the past. We looked through the photos on the computer from our fortieth anniversary trip to Keukenhof and Monet's Garden.

"That was the best trip we ever took," Dick said. "It was so romantic to see you in Monet's Garden amidst the lush flowers and against the backdrop of the green bridges over the pond. I should have taken more pictures of you."

"I'm so glad we met Gena and Charles and all the rest of the gang."

"Gena has been such a support to you and to me. She went through a lot, losing her husband so young, but she enjoys life. I want you to be like that too. Will you promise me that, Robin?"

Tears erupted and wouldn't stop as the photos in front of me turned into a blur. My body shook and he steadied me.

"I wish you could always be with me," I said. "I love you so much. I need you. I don't want to let you go—ever."

"I love you more than the day I married you, if that is possible," Dick said.

"Me too, I was the luckiest girl in the world to have found you."

"You are going to be all right," Dick said. "You can take care of yourself. So, remember I want you to be happy and enjoy life like Gena, okay?"

"I promise, I will," I told him. But my heart was breaking, and I didn't think I could ever feel whole without him.

It was our tradition to look through our wedding album on our anniversary, and this year it held even more meaning. I got out our thick, navy blue leather album with gold lettering and we started meandering through the pages.

"Look how skinny you were then. My handsome groom," I said, as I gave him a kiss.

"You were so beautiful, and you still are."

"I've definitely gained a few pounds since then."

"No, you look exactly the same," Dick insisted, and, in his eyes, I did.

As we looked at the tables of guests, we usually commented on how many people had died. This time neither one of us said anything. I thought about it as I looked at the picture of Dick and his brother, Sam, his best man. *They were two young, handsome men with bright futures. Who could have predicted that their lives would be cut short from glioblastoma? It just wasn't fair. Life was not fair. Glioblastoma sucked.*

Our favorite picture was the one where we were walking down the aisle holding hands after the ceremony. We looked more relaxed and we were grinning from ear to ear.

"Happy anniversary," I told Dick as I gave him a kiss.

"Happy anniversary," Dick said. "Let me take you to bed, my bride."

CHAPTER 51

Garden Memories

As much as I loved our house, it was my garden that I would miss the most. When the children were little, I would steal a little time for myself out in the garden—a time to breathe, to re-energize. I loved gathering herbs and cutting flowers, listening to the call of the birds and the throaty croaking of the frogs and getting down in the dirt to pull weeds. Most of all, I loved photographing the flowers and the butterflies.

When I was working full-time, I would rush home to enjoy some time in the garden on long summer days. I always had my camera in hand and loved capturing the beauty and adventure that awaited. I had started writing a nature blog and had loads of stories dancing in my head that I was excited about sharing through words and photographs. Nowadays, when Dick took a nap, the garden again served as my oasis. I would photograph the birds nesting in the birdhouse or check the pipevine plant for butterfly eggs and allow myself to forget. Just forget about brain tumors, treatments, and the future.

We had beautiful memories in that garden, and I longed to carry them with me, so I conceived a plan to do just that. I asked a photographer friend, Greg Lessard, if he would come video Dick and me in the garden. Although he didn't have much video experience, he readily agreed to do it with his iPad and wouldn't accept any payment. It was unscripted, but we mapped out a plan to start at one end of the garden and make stops at key places to tell stories of our garden adventures.

We started at the far end of the garden where Dick had put up a baby swing between two tall trees and later built two wooden swings as our family grew. We told stories of all the swinging adventures—how the kids would slide off and jump into a big pile of leaves in the fall, how Samantha toppled off the swing and skinned her knee and how Dick dug out the big rock that was the culprit. That rock later became part of the stone wall Dick built to border our raised vegetable garden.

We reminisced about our pet peacocks, whose pen eventually replaced the swings: about the racket they made and how they sometimes escaped into the neighbors' yard or the golf course. We would send the children on a grand adventure to corral them back and Seth was usually the one who was successful in returning them to the yard.

Then we moved over to the pond that we put in for our twenty-fifth anniversary. We shared the story of being surprised one morning to discover mallard ducks swimming in our small pond! Our resident garter snakes had entertained us one afternoon crawling up the waterfall and sliding down, as though they were enjoying a slide at the water park.

As we walked over the large expanse of lawn on the north side of the yard, we talked about all the parties we had hosted there—my mom's seventy-fifth birthday party, petting zoo birthdays, Samantha's wedding shower, a Hawaiian luau with our gourmet group, Sarah's engagement party, and a Four or More Party, to which we invited everyone we knew with four or more children.

The videotaping project was tiring for Dick, so in order to include the other end of the yard, Greg came on a second occasion. It worked out well, as the grandchildren were visiting, so he caught them on camera as well. Our daughter Sarah, home that week to help us move, also got to participate.

I was surprised when Sarah interrupted Greg and said, "I would like to say something."

Sarah is a very private person and shy in front of an audience. She brought over chairs for Dick and me.

"Sit down. I have something important to tell you."

Dick and I were both cautious but suspected it was good news from the broad smile she wore.

"I'm married!" Sarah said, "Vivek and I eloped and got married over July 4th."

"Congratulations," we said in unison as we jumped up to hug her.

Tears came to my eyes, but they were happy ones. I immediately began to process the information with mixed emotions.

"You got married? You didn't want a big wedding? We would have given you one."

"No, we didn't. You had that beautiful engagement party right here in the yard for us. That was like a wedding."

Sarah, always accommodating, knew this wasn't a good time for a wedding. The thought also flashed through my head that now Dick wouldn't have to worry about her. He would know that she was taken care of. I imagine Sarah was thinking the same thing.

Our expressions of surprise and joy over Sarah's marriage were captured on video. That same day, Seth called from Afghanistan. This rare occasion was also captured on our backyard video.

Just as the garden had reflected thirty-three years of our family life events, so too did the video mirror the cycle of life.

CHAPTER 52

The Big Move

Moving day on July 19 turned out to be a record breaker, reaching over 100 sweltering degrees. The heat was so pervasive, it felt like we were stuck in a cloud of sticky marshmallows. Our Lakeville home was not air-conditioned, and our merry band of helpers was hot, sweaty, and not so merry. Two of our daughters came home to help. Our friends Barbara and Bob, Peter and Robyn, and Bharani spent the day alternately cleaning, packing, organizing, and spending time with Dick. Sandra's friend Mark and his girlfriend, Kim, came over mid-day and gave us an infusion of new energy. I generally keep good humor in tense situations, but that day I was just plain mean and grouchy.

I screamed at Kim as she started packing the vacuum, "No, don't pack that! Get it out of that box! I need the vacuum out till the end. We'll have to take it in the car."

I didn't recognize myself—ordering people around, swearing under my breath, yelling at those who were volunteering their time in that miserable heat to help us through this ordeal. Everyone was doing the best they could. I was trying to organize and direct, but I fear I came across as a madwoman without an ounce of gratefulness. My clothes felt like they were an armored suit, glued to my hot, sticky body. There was usually a cool refuge in the family room, which had a room air conditioner, but that day, with the doors swung wide open, there was no relief to be had, inside or out.

The movers worked very hard, but their pace was slow because of the sweltering heat. As one o'clock approached, I anxiously asked the foreman what time they would finish loading. He approximated about 2 p.m., so I suggested Sarah and Sandra take Dick out to lunch and meet us at the Plymouth home. When the movers were finally ready, they decided it was too late to pick up the boxes at our storage unit but instead headed right to Plymouth to start unloading.

Barbara, Bob, and Bharani accompanied us to Plymouth to help unload the cars and organize the medications and other essentials. Around 5 p.m. I realized that our bed would not be set up in time for Dick to go to sleep at his usual hour of 8 p.m. He had already had a very tiring day with minimal naptime.

My sister's friends Tina and Mark who lived in The Pinehills, had graciously invited us for dinner that night so I called Tina to update her on our timeline. She said they were willing to do whatever we needed and that we were welcome to spend the night if necessary. I ended up sending Sarah over with Dick so they could have dinner, escape the chaos, and have a clean, safe environment to spend the night. Sandra and I stayed behind to supervise the move.

The Big Move

We followed the movers back to Lakeville around 8 p.m. to get the last few remaining items. We were hot, tired, and hungry. I remember telling Sandra a few days later, "Someday we will look back and laugh at all the crazy things that happened that night!"

On our way back from Lakeville, my fuel gauge said empty and the closest gas station was closed. The local Back Nine Pub closed just as we got there, so we went to Burger King and had to wait twenty minutes in line. Who knew Burger King was so popular? We reached another gas station, Sandra opened her food, and it was the wrong meal order! I couldn't find the key to the storage locker anywhere, so it was just as well the movers never got there that day. It took them until 12:30 a.m. to finish unloading in Plymouth and they somehow forgot the TV, which we had to pick up as Verizon was scheduled to come the next day.

I felt guilty that I had not been able to give Dick much attention and had to leave him in a strange place on the first night of our move. I missed him terribly as I slept by myself in our new bedroom, but I knew I made the best decision possible and he was in good hands with Sarah and Tina.

Although we had nicknamed our Dana-Farber days as "marathon days," this was indeed a "marathon day" to top them all.

CHAPTER 53

Rebecca's Landing Neighborhood

The next day our friend Josh set up our computer, printer, and telephones and got everything operational. Over the next days and weeks, I unpacked and put away what we needed and relegated the rest of the boxes to the basement, as obstacles were a hazard for Dick's uneven mobility. Our son-in-law, Adam, came down for a weekend and set up the stereo equipment and TVs and put storage units in the basement.

In August Jerri and Alan came for a visit and helped us put up pictures and rearrange some furniture. Jerri was able to see how our place had transitioned from her graph paper design to reality. Dick loved seeing our own canvas prints up on the walls. It was a hot summer and I loved having an air-conditioned house for the first time in my life. Dick, who was always cold now, put up with it.

Although I continued writing updates on Lotsa Helping Hands, I didn't put dates up on the help calendar very often. Many volunteers drove a good distance to Lakeville to transport Dick from there and asking people to drive to Plymouth felt like too much. Instead, we transitioned to in-house services. I contacted the Visiting Nurse Association located in The Pinehills and initiated referrals for occupational and physical therapy to assist Dick in getting used to his new environment.

The Green Company was very attentive to detail and customer service. They presented us with a personalized photo book of The Pinehills, our Rebecca's Landing neighborhood, and documentation of our house as it was being built. Dick loved showing all our guests the book, which included a photo of us with glowing smiles, taken the day we bought the condo. One day I noticed the house was swarming with guys washing the exterior windows, from the garage to the second story. I woke Dick from his nap as I knew he would want to see our condo fees at work!

Just weeks after we moved in, a spectacular rainbow caught my eye out the back deck. I grabbed our camera gear and helped Dick out to the deck. We got some great shots and spent the last moments of the lingering rainbow just hugging and holding hands. We both knew we had witnessed something special.

"I think God has given us a sign that we picked the right place," I told Dick, and he heartily agreed.

Dr. Reardon advised a break from infusions, as there had been no new tumor growth for some time. It was the first time since Dick was diagnosed that our days were not structured with radiation treatments, rehab, or medical appointments, and we no longer had the task of moving hanging over our heads.

Now that we were settled in, I started thinking about Gena's letter and their bucket list trip up Route 66. I asked Dick, "Is there anything special you would like to do over the next few months? Would you like to take a trip somewhere? Maybe to the national parks or to Italy?"

We had always talked about going to Italy someday. That would have been our next big trip.

"No, I'm more interested in seeing people than places. Traveling will be getting harder, so I only want to visit with family and friends."

Dick was much more realistic than me with my romantic notion of taking him to Italy. Shortly after, we heard that Seth would be returning from Afghanistan in November. He had to remain on base in Seattle, Washington, for at least one month after his return, so we decided to plan a trip to meet him there. We would get to see our Monet's Garden buddies, Gena and Charles, who both lived in Seattle. I called Gena, who immediately took over as travel planner.

She sent us links and descriptions about museums, concerts, restaurants, and other photographic opportunities in Seattle. Based on our interests, she came up with a travel itinerary, building in lots of flexibility and time for naps for Dick. It turned out Charles was having a fiftieth birthday celebration in November. Going to see Seth, visiting Gena, and attending Charles's party gave us something special to look forward to. It was not the trip to Italy I had dreamed of, but I realized in the end, that Dick was right—being with people you love is much more important than seeing the Colosseum.

In those early weeks we experienced the kindness of our new neighbors with warm welcomes, visits, and invitations. Rebecca's Landing held a get-together by the pool every Friday evening where we got acquainted with everyone and made some special friends.

I met a lovely woman, Annie, a retired physician's assistant, who looked at me sincerely with her memorable blue eyes as she tucked her business card in my hand, and said, "Call me anytime." Annie became an important part of our circle of care in the last few weeks of Dick's life.

The neighborhood social committee held a monthly coffee for the women, and there were a group of guys who went out to breakfast together on Fridays. Dick was quickly welcomed into the breakfast gang. Rebecca's Landing definitely felt like the pot of gold at the end of the rainbow.

Dick looked forward with great enthusiasm to his morning out with the neighborhood guys. On Thursday nights Francois, Roger, and Dave called about picking him up the following morning. Dick had so many invitations—there was competition to drive him! The guys always looked out for him. They reported to me if he ate and how much. Dave told me one day that Dick insisted on treating the gang to breakfast. They let him the first time because it gave Dick so much pleasure. The second time, Dave let Dick think he was paying but didn't take his money.

As the months progressed, Dick had more and more difficulty managing money. The guys helped him when he needed to make change, left an exorbitant amount of tip money, or misplaced his wallet. Even when he couldn't make change anymore, Dick still had a great fund of knowledge. He didn't need to know what day of the week it was to have an intelligent conversation. He still had a sense of humor and showed genuine interest in others.

We also enjoyed some time to ourselves to explore our new surroundings. We visited Plimoth Plantation, attended a play at The Pinehills, and visited a butterfly house just twenty minutes from our home. We bought Gena a house gift there, and Dick bought me an early birthday present—a butterfly necklace and earrings. He couldn't have picked a more perfect gift!

Dr. V was correct when she warned us that the move would prove to be a difficult transition for Dick with all the physical changes. When we headed out to the car, Dick started toward the basement door as in our old house the garage was at the basement level. The location of the bathroom by the study often eluded him. He had great difficulty with the light switches, which also took me a while to master! I labeled them all at the suggestion of his occupational therapist (OT).

She was excellent at focusing on his functional abilities in the new house. She made adaptations including a velcro pad on the main switch in the bathroom to help identify it from the other two that were lined up next to one another and a velcro sticker on the number two on the microwave so Dick could heat something up for himself with the quick start button. She put open/close arrows on the lock to our glass sliding door to the courtyard. Our new place became replete with "signage."

The OT came at variable times, but Jason, the physical therapist (PT), came regularly at 8 a.m. on Tuesdays. I read in The Pinehills newsletter that there was a Body Blast exercise class on Tuesdays at 8 a.m. at the Stonebridge Club. I approached Jason and asked if it would be all right if I went out to take the class while he worked with Dick. He said it was a great idea and he would even try to get there early if possible.

I started attending the class and looked forward to this "me" time every week. It felt good to focus on the moment and leave behind the world of brain tumors. I didn't want to take advantage of Jason's good will, so I always left class early in order to be back home before he left. Jason and Dick usually went for a walk outside as part of their session and would often run into our neighbor Keith, walking his dog, Mazie. Keith was a gregarious guy, always quick to shake hands, saying, "How are ya, good to see ya," followed by, "How are things goin'?" before you had a chance to answer the first question.

Keith noticed I was rushing home at nine a.m. to arrive before Jason finished. He offered to come visit with Dick when Jason left and stay with him until I got back. Keith had a heart of gold and Dick loved spending time with him. Keith worked at Fenway Park, home of the Red Sox, and could talk sports, which is something I was never good at.

Keith always encouraged me, "Take your time. Stop and run an errand if you need to. We're having so much fun here—Dick won't miss you."

I noticed Dick was sporting a new Red Sox baseball cap. Keith got tickets for the game at Fenway Park for Seth when he came to visit that summer and both Seth and Dick received new Red Sox shirts.

At the end of the eight-week PT sessions, Keith generously volunteered to stay with Dick so I could keep attending exercise class. Yes, we had definitely landed in the right place.

Right after our move, I looked into starting a Jewish group at The Pinehills, since we were an hour's drive from our synagogue community. The Pinehills staff assisted me in putting a notice in the newsletter in the hope of getting together a planning committee. I had the first meeting of eight women at our home in July 2013, and we held our inaugural event in September of that year for the High Holidays. We became an official Pinehills Club and decided on the name Shalom Pinehills.

Another member, Nancy, had also moved into The Pinehills in July, and her husband, Steve, became one of Dick's favorite volunteers. Dick and Steve had both graduated from RPI and shared a love of photography. As Dick's needs became greater, Nancy stepped up to become the committee chair of Shalom Pinehills. Another original member, Alex, had lost her dad to glioblastoma and her husband to cancer. She was a recently retired RN and also became a valued volunteer.

We had our "thirty-day walk-through" with a Green Company representative, who assessed any problems and marked all the paint nicks created when we moved in. They followed up with a repairman who painted over all the trouble spots, fixed stuck windows and drawers, and made sure everything was in perfect working order. Dick was so pleased and relieved to know that the Green Company had followed through on all their promises and that I was part of a condo association that would handle the major upkeep of our home.

A few blocks from our home is a beautiful wooded trail that leads to Clam Pudding Pond. When we bought the house in December, it had been too cold and slippery for Dick to walk to the pond, but it was important to me that he saw it. So as soon as we were able, I took him, and he delighted in the enchanting walk through the woods to our very own neighborhood pond. We saw a blue heron taking off, fish jumping out of the water, and turkeys jumping up into the trees.

By summer's end, I was anxious about taking Dick to the pond by myself because of his declining balance and stamina. With his PT taking one arm, and me the other, we successfully made the walk to the pond, but I feared it would be our last.

As we sat down on the dock bench to take a break and enjoy the vista, we were surprised by a splash as one of our neighbors emerged from the water, shook himself off, and exclaimed for all to hear, "Another glorious day in Rebecca's Landing!"

And it was.

CHAPTER 54

The Pinehills

A break from rehab allowed us more time together and we enjoyed getting to know our new neighborhood. My intention was to hold a housewarming party after we settled in, but it turned out that wasn't necessary. We had a steady stream of visitors right from the beginning. They always called first and hospitality was not expected. We often took our company to the local coffee shop, Oleo's, in the Village Green.

It was hard for Dick to get used to the idea that we no longer had a mailbox in front of our house. He liked being able to go outside and pick up the mail. But we developed an even better tradition—in the late afternoon, we went to pick up our mail at the post office and stopped next door at Oleo's. We relaxed at one of the outdoor umbrella tables to read our mail and have a snack, feeling like we were at a European café. Dick usually ordered an éclair and a coffee or hot chocolate.

The owner's dad, who helped manage the restaurant, could see Dick was struggling to keep weight on and knew his fondness for sweets. He would come by our table to say hello and never failed to slip Dick some extra Italian cookies. We'd only been in The Pinehills about a month when a familiar face came by Oleo's, greeting us by name. The second time that happened, we felt as if we truly belonged.

The Pinehills offered many clubs and activities; it felt like one big summer camp adventure and we both loved summer camp! I requested a friendly visitor from the Neighbor to Neighbor program before we had met many of our own neighbors. An elderly gentleman who lived in a different part of The Pinehills came to visit with Dick so I could do some errands. I was concerned when I returned one day; they told me about their misadventures getting lost when they took a walk in the neighborhood and couldn't remember their way back.

Dick was bemused as he told the story to Dr. V.

"My wife got a volunteer who had Alzheimer's to help a man who has a brain tumor!" he exclaimed.

Every few months, The Pinehills held an orientation for new residents, where the staff gave presentations about the general community. Residents went around and introduced themselves, stating where they came from, which neighborhood they had moved into, and how they happened to come to The Pinehills. We were so enamored with our own neighborhood of Rebecca's Landing that I felt certain we had chosen the best neighborhood of all. As we listened to the stories everyone shared about how they were welcomed into their respective neighborhoods, it struck me that every person in that room thought the exact same thing.

That's when I realized that Dick had been right in having the foresight to make the move. My fears started to melt away. We were going to be okay. *I* was going to be okay. We had come to live in a very special place that was feeling more and more like home.

I didn't feel comfortable leaving Dick alone because he was not yet familiar with the layout of our new home and was at risk for falls. I managed to run to The Market in the village or to the drug store when he napped. I started having my counseling sessions with Barbara by phone unless family from out of town was staying with us.

The Pinehills has an extensive array of walking trails. The Rebecca's Landing neighborhood women walked twice a week and called themselves the "Street Walkers." When I read the introductory email about the walking group, I longed to join them. I wished I had the freedom to walk the trails, bike, and swim. The neighborhood pool was just beyond the back of our home. Sometimes when I was on the deck, I could hear the faint chatter of voices or gleeful squeals from visiting grandchildren. The weather was beautiful that summer and I desperately wanted to go for a swim.

I often asked Dick if he wanted to go down to the pool with me, but he was never interested. He wasn't up to swimming and he was not the kind of guy who would just sit around the pool. On one particularly gorgeous summer day, Dick was getting ready for a nap and I said I was going to take a quick swim. He told me to go ahead and enjoy myself.

As soon as Dick fell asleep, I raced down to the pool and luxuriated in the strong summer heat and the cool, refreshing water. I loved the feel of the water as it flowed over my body. I swam laps and felt so invigorated. I laid down on a lounge chair, closed my eyes, and forgot for a few minutes. Just forgot. Forgot everything. I enjoyed the moment—the cool breeze, the birds chirping, the glorious sun.

I thought I ought to get back, but I knew from experience that Dick would be asleep for at least an hour. I still had more time. *I'll just take another quick dip*, I thought. A few neighbors were in the pool and we just lazed around and talked as we half-heartedly swam. I finally dragged myself away from utopia.

As I headed toward my house, I had a feeling in the pit of my stomach that something was wrong. My steps quickened as I turned the corner. There was a figure way down the street that looked like Dick, walking away from me with a woman I didn't recognize. A feeling of dread overcame me. My head pounded as I ran.

"Dick, Dick," I called out.

"Mrs. Gross, we were looking for you."

It was Juliana, who came to clean our house once a week. Oh my god! I had forgotten Juliana was expected that day! She told me how Dick woke up upon her arrival and went to sit in the driver's seat of the car. When she asked if she could help, he said he wanted to go find me at the pool. I felt sick, like I had a giant weight on my chest.

I grabbed and clung to him with force. He and Juliana were heading in the opposite direction of the pool, but of course, Juliana wouldn't have known where it was, and Dick was disoriented in our new neighborhood. I was upset that I had let my desires take over, but at the same time, I was angry that my reverie had been broken and in reality, I could not do a simple thing for myself, like go for a swim.

That was the day I realized I could no longer leave Dick alone.

I did a lot of research to find someone I could use on occasion when I needed to go out. The next time I had an appointment I hired a caregiver to stay with Dick. After the second time, Dick informed me, once again, "I do *not* need a babysitter."

He was quite adamant, so I went back to what I knew worked. He enjoyed spending time with friends. So occasionally, I asked our new friends and neighbors to spend time with Dick or posted dates on the Lotsa Helping Hands site. I had always felt comfortable requesting help for people to drive Dick to appointments, but it felt like entering new territory when it came to requesting help so that I could go out.

It seemed acceptable to ask for help so I could keep a dental appointment. But was it okay to ask for help so I could get my hair done or go to the nursery? No, I didn't think so. That was entering muddy waters. It felt selfish. There were things I wanted to do and places I wanted to go. But I reminded myself, I would have plenty of time later. I could join the Street Walkers, swim in the pool, and take photos like Linda Fuller, whenever I wanted to someday.

* * *

That week, I had an appointment at the dental office in Middle-boro where we had been going for over thirty years. Our dental hygienist, Ann, had taken care of our whole family and we always caught up on news at our visits.

I told Ann that I was anxious to get right back that day as I'd left Dick with a friend and she assured me they would get me out on time. I told her that a friend had generously given me a gift certificate to a spa in Lakeville before we moved but I never had time to use it. Now I was afraid to leave Dick alone and had to factor in driving time.

"I have Fridays off," Ann said. "I'd love to come see your new place and spend some time with Dr. Gross one day while you go to the spa."

She was quite sincere in her request, so we set a date. Dick and Ann had lunch at Oleo's while I enjoyed a much-needed massage.

My back had been bothering me from the physical labor and stress of moving.

Dick later joked with a smile, "When friends saw me at the coffee shop with Ann, they all wanted to know, who was the beautiful, young lady I was with?"

CHAPTER 55

Settling In

There was a woman who lived in The Pinehills, named Mercia, whose husband had recently died of glioblastoma. She heard through a friend that we would be moving to The Pinehills and even before our move, she was anxious to share information with me about an online support group for caregivers of glioblastoma patients. However, I felt too overwhelmed to call Mercia or join the support group until well after our move. When I finally gave in and called her, I was so glad I did. My hesitancy had been that I wasn't sure how much I really wanted to know about what lay ahead. But Mercia was a wonderful support—she stopped by often, brought home-cooked meals, and invited us to her home. Although I felt like I didn't have time for anything else in my life, with her encouragement, I took the plunge and joined the private Facebook support group called the "GBM & Brain Tumor Women Warriors." Dick liked to call them the "Women Worriers."

I introduced myself to the group with a brief description of our situation and received a flood of warm and genuine welcomes. I was reassured the forum was a place where I could swear, scream, or bitch and didn't have to hold back on anything. I could also look to the members for guidance in the maze of treatment and care-giving options. They hosted an online get-together called "Wine and Whine" on Thursday nights, and although I didn't drink, I occasionally joined them. I was amazed at how these women could keep their sense of humor and find gaiety in the little things in life. Many of them were still employed while caring for their spouses and not as fortunate as I was in having family and friends to help.

There were two reasons why I never really took to the support group like Mercia did. One of the very first times I went on the site, there was a huge discussion of when to take off your wedding ring. I was shocked by this candid exchange. At the time, I couldn't relate at all. I just wasn't ready to hear that conversation and it put me off.

Over time, the women's names became more familiar to me. I recognized those who had lost their spouses and were now the ones giving words of encouragement and support. I recognized the newbies like myself whose husbands were fairly stable but were still struggling with day-to-day changes. I tried to reach out to the women who were at the stage of initial diagnosis, seeking advice about where to get treatment and what medications people had tried. And then there were the heart-wrenching stories of those who were actively dying. Most often I couldn't respond to these. It felt too raw. I watched as Mercia and many others showed such empathy and strength to guide these women through the worst of times. Nobody understood like they did. They always seemed to have just the right words. I had great admiration for them.

The second thing I found upsetting was the fact that some of the women were caring for children who had glioblastoma. I was having such a hard time accepting our own fate; I could not even begin to think about the trauma of losing a child. So I just checked on the site once or twice a week or if I had a specific question. I was not on there all the time like many of the women . . . until the last two weeks, when I really needed them.

* * *

We hired our friend Ron to make modifications to the extra room in our new house, which we converted into a study. Although we set it up as we had in our old house with two chairs and two computers, Dick rarely used the study. It became my favorite room.

Again, Dick wanted to feel like he was contributing, so he took his favorite can of WD-40 and started spraying the doors and windows. It became out of control. I was worried he was doing damage to our attractive new home. I felt terrible but I finally hid the can. He asked for it once and I pretended I couldn't find it. Thank God he did not remember to ask for it again!

Gena, who continued to be our guiding angel, sent us two gifts when we moved into our new home. The first was a gift certificate to Morrison's, a local nursery. I decided to wait until spring to use the certificate so I could see where I needed to fill in the landscaping. One of our petite buddleia bushes did not make it through the rough winter, so I purchased a buddleia labeled "tutti frutti petite" in a striking fuchsia color. Instead of replacing the plant by the path to the courtyard, I planted it center stage in a sunny spot next to the pond where we could see it from indoors. I don't know if the plant was mislabeled or whether it was a gift from God, but eventually it grew to eight feet tall and became a mecca for butterflies.

Gena also sent us a mezuzah, a parchment scroll inscribed with Hebrew verses from the Torah, contained in a decorative case. It is a Jewish custom to put a mezuzah on the doorposts of your home. It was the most exquisite mezuzah I had ever seen, sparkling with an array of vibrant, iridescent colors against a royal blue background. Dick remarked how thoughtful Gena was. She was not Jewish, but she knew how important our religion was to us.

We knew the local rabbi in Plymouth, Rabbi Lawrence Silverman, as he had an association with our New Bedford synagogue. When he had called to say he would like to come by and welcome us to Plymouth, I asked if he could help us to dedicate our new home. He suggested we put up the mezzuzot, cover them, and he would say the blessings for our new home when he arrived.

A job that would have otherwise been a pleasure for Dick became a task as he struggled with the hammer and nails. I helped him, and between the two of us, we got them up. Rabbi Silverman sang the traditional blessings and we unveiled the mezzuzot. It was bittersweet, as we were happy to be in our lovely new home and neighborhood, yet we knew Dick wouldn't be there to share it with me for very long. I was reminded of the beautiful "Blessing of Our Home" photograph that Dick had made, and which hung in our hallway. He printed a photo of a delicate white iris from our backyard and embossed over the photograph the following prayer:

Blessing of the Home

Please allow light and gladness, peace and contentment, to dwell in this home, and bestow abundant blessings and holiness to those who visit and to those who live here. May the illumination of the holy Torah and commandments shine here always.

If only those words could protect us from the inevitable. I wished it were that simple.

Although we already had the doorposts of our home well covered, Dick came up with the perfect solution for where to place Gena's gift. Our courtyard was the real entrance to our home, and it was framed with an arbor.

"Let's put the mezuzah on the post of the arbor," he suggested. "The Torah says to inscribe the words upon the doorposts of your house and upon your gates," he quoted.

"Brilliant idea," I responded.

"I still have a few good marbles," Dick joked.

I gave him a kiss. "You will always be the smartest man I know."

We affixed the mezuzah to the post of the white painted arbor. It shone brilliantly and created a warm, welcome feeling, infused with holiness.

About one month later, our daughter Sarah gave us a mezuzah as a gift, decorated with a blue and gold ornate design inlaid with enamel. The Hebrew letter Shin (Almighty), which is also an acronym for "Guardian of Israel's Doors," was embellished on the front.

On one of Rabbi Kanter's visits, he suggested we place it on the door entering our bedroom. When Dick tried to put it up, I was surprised how his skills had deteriorated in just four weeks. He labored with that hammer and nails but was determined to do it himself. What would have been a two-minute job took him ten minutes of concentrated work. Even now, whenever I pass through the bedroom door and see the four or five holes in the wall that marked Dick's initial attempts, I remember the frustration he felt.

In December I asked Dick if he would like to give a holiday gift to the guys in the neighborhood breakfast gang. I suggested we could print and mat photos of the rainbow over Rebecca's Landing. I knew Dick loved to share his photos, and it would be a way of sharing a part of himself with his new friends. He agreed that would be a perfect gift.

I once told Dave, one of the breakfast gang, "I'm sorry you didn't get to know Dick when he was himself."

He looked at me with surprise and said, "Oh, but we did. We knew he was a kind and generous person. And really smart."

CHAPTER 56

The Courtyard

Our new house faced the courtyard on three sides, so we had a good view from our kitchen/dining room area, bedroom, and study. The outdoors, however, was a far cry from the model home and our vision of our future garden—it was literally a sandpit with a temporary, tarred pathway leading to the porch.

At our Lakeville home, a chorus of frogs and creatures had serenaded us after dark. Here, with no vegetation to offer shelter to wildlife, it was so quiet at night that we had trouble falling asleep. I was seriously considering getting a CD of rain forest sounds when, a few weeks after we moved in, a lone cricket took up residence in our courtyard. We were never so happy to hear that familiar raucous, chirping.

I had diligently been calling our landscaper to let him know we had moved in and were ready to begin our project. But when he didn't respond by mid-August we decided to move ahead and hire someone else. I got names of local landscapers and we went to visit gardens they had designed in The Pinehills. It was getting much harder for Dick to walk around, and I think he would have settled for the first one, but he persevered because he knew it was important to me to be thorough and make the best choice. For the most part, the gardens we saw were conservative and designed to be maintenance free.

I was not looking for maintenance free. I was planning on spending hours working and photographing in the garden. Our Lakeville garden had a cottage garden look, with orphan plants springing up all over; there was nothing formal about it. There were plenty of natural hiding places for the birds and the butterflies. I didn't want a few hydrangea bushes in a row. I didn't want a courtyard ninety percent filled with pavers.

I found a local landscaper whose garden designs had some character, and he met with us to go over our ideas. In the end, the landscaper said he had no experience with water features and there was not enough space to vent a fireplace. Although I hated facing that sand-filled patio every morning, I was not going to give in. My garden was too important to me. Of course I had to weigh all that against the clock.

Finally, we discovered Susannah Davis, of Davis Land Design in Marion, MA. Her email address began with "ohsusannah." I liked her already.

Susannah was very accommodating and scheduled an appointment at our place right away. She understood my desire to have a garden that would attract wildlife. Susannah was a cancer survivor and appreciated our need to move forward quickly. She found a fireplace kit that could be built so it vented from the front and she had an experienced resource for building ponds. Susannah had a spiritual and artistic sense and seemed to know exactly what I wanted before I said it. I knew at our initial visit that she was the one.

Dick and I were very excited about the project. We fell in love with the drawings and design concept that Susannah presented. Her selection of trees, bushes, and flowers incorporated most of my desires, and I added a few of my own favorites. Dick had been gradually trusting me to take care of all business matters. I knew I was at the helm when he never even asked to see the estimate. He was so smart; I'm sure he recognized it would be an expensive proposition but probably didn't ask because he knew how important it was to me, and he wanted me to be happy. I signed a contract the third week in September. Susannah and her team were committed to getting the garden in that fall and they worked hard to make it work. Dick's buddy Dave was on the condo board and with his help, the board approved the courtyard design we submitted in record time.

There were a lot of tasks to take care of including bringing in soil material and a gas line, hiring an electrician, choosing pavers, lighting, and plant material, building the fireplace and pond, and putting in an irrigation system. Susannah and her team were easy to work with, and despite weather delays, our courtyard was gradually transformed. It was beginning to feel more like home. But could they possibly get all the work done in time? Most important, would Dick hang on to see the transformation?

We brought a few special items with us from our Lakeville garden which Susannah incorporated into the design—a bird house, peacock sculpture, a plaque with the words "Butterfly Crossing" and a sundial Dick had bought me which was manufactured at the Colonial Brass

Company right in Middleboro. By the second week in November, Susannah's crew were putting the finishing touches on the fireplace and placing mulch on the beds.

A few years back we had given our friends Tricia and Larry some fish from our Lakeville pond when they built their own. Tricia said she had a large population of fish now and would be happy to deliver some. We had a new generation of our own fish!

Our enchanted courtyard was complete just in time to show it off to our Thanksgiving company. Now we had the familiar music of the fountain's rushing water to fall asleep by, and we hoped the frogs would soon follow. At night the dramatic lighting and lit fireplace danced with fervor. Susannah and her crew had created a natural, sacred space and I had no doubt the birds and butterflies would find us in the spring.

Susannah told me, "I gave you a gift of some native-looking bulbs by the pond and I threw in a few surprises for you in the spring."

We forgot about Susannah's surprise until a lovely mix of pink, purple, and blue bulbs greeted us in the spring, when the whole garden looked even more glorious. We were mesmerized by the luscious pink tulips with beautiful double blossoms, which looked more like roses than tulips. There were fragile blue forget-me-nots— Dick's favorite! I wrote a note to Susannah to thank her for the spring treasures and she wrote back thanking us!

Every time I read your blog I feel so utterly blessed to have been a part of your courtyard and to have met your family. Thank you again and again. My heart goes out to you both. You are both very courageous people. You are a rock—Dick is so fortunate to have such a steady, kind, and wise partner in this difficult part of his journey.

We really rallied a great team to get that courtyard done in record time. There was an abundance of positive energy and a great effort by all. We wanted so very much to know that you both would be able to enjoy it.

I felt toward Susannah the way Dick's patients had described their relationship with him. Not only had we picked the most talented, professional landscape designer ever, but we had made a lifelong friend. Susannah signed up to become a member of Lotsa Helping Hands and became an important part of our support system.

CHAPTER 57

Seth Returns Home

In November 2013, we were eagerly awaiting news of Seth's return from Afghanistan. As soon as we heard he was returning to base for re-entry orientation, we booked a flight to Seattle. We were so relieved that Seth was returning home safely and that Dick was strong enough to make the trip. This time, when I preordered a wheelchair to help us through the airport, Dick didn't complain.

Dick had always done the driving when we rented a car, and I missed being able to rely on him. I negotiated the trip out to the Joint Base Fort Lewis-McChord with the help of a GPS. We went through rigorous security at the visitor center before we finally got to see Seth. It felt like we waited an eternity and I had a migraine brewing.

Although we had had sporadic phone calls with Seth during his ten-month deployment, we had lived with the fear that he might be hurt or killed. When I saw for myself that he was alive and whole,

268

and none of our fears had come to pass, my tears flowed freely. We held each other in a giant family bear hug. Seth is not an emotional type of kid, but it was certainly an emotional reunion.

Seth had recommended I make reservations at the Lakeside Recreational cabins in a lovely, secluded area of the base, as he knew we would enjoy that setting over the base hotel. He gave us a tour of the base and his barracks. Dick was too exhausted to do anything else, but it was comforting just to spend time together.

The next morning, we accompanied Seth to the commissary for breakfast. Suddenly, Dick slumped over in his chair and seized. Seth called out, "Man down." Dick couldn't have picked a better place to have a seizure as there were army medics and personnel right there who knew exactly what to do. Dick chose not to go to the hospital. We settled into the cabin while Seth headed back to work. As I got Dick into bed, I began to doubt whether being in that isolated cabin was a good idea after all. I was scared he might have another seizure because of the stress of travel and the time difference. I made a note to tell Gena we might have to modify our schedule of sightseeing.

Fortunately, Dick woke up refreshed and we spent time sitting on the back porch overlooking the lake and watching the birds. I was thinking about Gena's letter. We didn't often talk about the future, but I asked Dick if there was anything he wanted me to do when he was gone.

He replied, "I want you to go on a photo trip and smile like Gena."

I clasped his hand, leaned my head on his shoulder, and imagined myself being strong and independent like Gena, perhaps being a model for someone else someday like Gena had been for me.

"I will," I assured him, as I squeezed his hand and we sat in silence a while as I fought to hold back the tears.

Seth had shared with us the previous day that his unit had been responsible for shrinking and dismantling bases. We were grateful to hear that he had not seen combat in Afghanistan.

We reminisced about Seth as a little boy with so much fury and energy, and how much he had grown and matured during his enlistment.

Although based near Seattle for a few years, Seth had never been into the city. He was able to get two days off to accompany us into Seattle. We got Seth his own room at the Hilton, a real luxury for him after having roughed it in Afghanistan. He was very grateful to have a king size bed with crisp, clean sheets, TV with cable, and a huge private bathroom with all the hot water he could ever use.

Gena picked us up every morning for sightseeing, returned us to the hotel to rest, and picked us up again when we had evening plans. Having gone through a similar journey with her husband, Gena knew better than I the challenges Dick was facing and was sensitive to our need to explore mainly by car. She took a wheelchair out of her trunk when we arrived at the Kubota Japanese Gardens. Dick never said a word, but calmly climbed in so we could all relax and enjoy the outing and even take some photos. The Chihuly Garden and Glass Museum was our favorite attraction, although the Hot Cakes Dessert Shoppe, which featured molten chocolate cake with ice cream, was a close second for Dick!

Seth had to head back to base the evening before his twenty-fifth birthday, but we had celebrated all week long. Seth told us that the government was cutting thirty thousand soldiers, but he hoped to reenlist in the army and apply for a position as a diver. We were so proud of him and his career plans. Although there was always uncertainty in our lives now, it was not the sad farewell we had when

Seth was deployed. We told Seth how proud we were of h
much we loved him.

He told Dick, "I'm proud of you too, Dad,
you," and promised to come home to visit as soon a
We enjoyed a few more days with Gena as our private gui
honored to attend an elegant dinner party for Charles's fifti

On the way home, I was thinking about the rou
the trip—arriving with a migraine, Dick's seizure, and
rains. By day three, I was having another one of thos
I thinking?" days. But by day seven, after dry, sunny d
wined and dined, reuniting with Seth, Gena's sunny dis
generosity of spirit, I was ready to do it again!

I said to Dick, "I know this trip wasn't easy and the s
lot out of you. Maybe we should have waited until Seth
to visit?"

"Absolutely not. I loved being with Seth and wou
wanted to wait a day longer to see him. It was great to s
Charles again. Our trip to Monet's Garden was like a f
seeing them brought back so many wonderful memorie

"And," Dick said with a smile, as he gazed into my
love going on adventures with you."

CHAPTER 58

Losing Patience

"The insurance is willing to give you another round of physical and occupational therapy," I told Dick. "I've really enjoyed ⎯e lighter schedule, which has given us more time to spend with ⎯ch other and getting to know our new neighborhood. What do you ⎯ink? Do you want to start rehab therapy again?"

"I want to try to stay as active as possible. But I think I can do ⎯at just hanging out with you. You keep me pretty busy! What about ⎯ing to the Y together? I'd rather be out in the community and ⎯ercising with friends than having therapy at home."

"You just gave me a great idea!" I responded. "I read in The ⎯nehills newsletter that they have a yoga class. How would you like ⎯ take yoga together?"

"Sure, let's try it."

Dr. Reardon gave us the go ahead. The yoga instructor was ⎯onderful and made Dick feel quite at ease using a chair as an

accommodation. I couldn't relax for a minute as I was constantly glancing back and forth to make sure Dick was all right. But it was his neighbor, on his other side, who noticed Dick leaning to one side with his head on his shoulder, still, with his eyes fixed. It was in the midst of our second session when Dick had a partial seizure. I reached for my pocketbook, but my hands shook so much that I had trouble getting the Ativan pill out. Someone called 911. Luckily, there were many helping hands nearby, including a nurse. As we anxiously waited for the ambulance, I couldn't help but think this was my fault. I never should have brought him to yoga class.

We had our first experience at the Jordan Hospital emergency room in Plymouth, a place we later got to know well. All the physicians agreed that yoga was not the cause of the seizure. My own theory is that it was caused by abruptly stopping the medication modafinil (wakefulness drug) a few days earlier because of a delivery problem from the mail order pharmacy. The physicians said there was no correlation, but I was still furious with the prescription company. The doctors increased Dick's seizure medication. We knew the routine—his gait worsened, he was more confused, and he slept a lot. No more yoga for us.

We still laughed and had fun together. But creeping in, more often now, were times when Dick misinterpreted information, didn't remember correctly what happened, and got agitated. Often those conversations would end in Dick's telling me, "*You* need cognitive therapy." I tried to be patient but sometimes I got short with him and would then feel terrible afterward.

Although I rarely used my camera anymore, I took it out one night there was supposed to be a full moon and set it up on the tripod by the door to the back deck. Of all nights, Dick had a fall as he was

273

getting up from the couch, tripped over the tripod and camera, and they both crashed to the floor. Dick was pretty sore from the fall, but more upset about the camera. The camera body seemed to be intact but my favorite go-to lens broke.

Because Dick's short-term memory was unreliable, I was hopeful he would forget about the incident the next morning. No such luck! Instead, he had a false memory of the event that included me pushing him. Because the event was so distressing and emotional to him, I think it altered his perception of what happened. He was also angry that I hadn't put away my equipment when I was finished with it. This was one lesson I'd heard him repeat multiple times through the years to me and the kids—put away your tools when you are done with them.

It was our first time at the Hunt's Camera store in nearby Hanover, so no one knew us there. Of course, Dick didn't hesitate to tell everyone that the camera fell, and the lens broke because I pushed him. I was so embarrassed. Dick looked pretty normal except for his almost bald head with a prominent scar. Would people believe him?

The salesman declared the lens irreparable, which I had suspected, but thankfully the camera was operational. This was the first time I ever purchased camera equipment on my own. Dick had always spent hours researching lenses and getting the best prices. I relied on help from the salesperson and ended up getting a new 18 to 200 mm Tamron lens that had just come out and was on special that weekend.

I whispered to the salesman when Dick was out of earshot, "My husband has a terminal brain tumor. His cognition is poor and he has false memories. His balance is poor. I didn't push him."

The salesman gave an imperceptible nod, glanced up and over at Dick, but didn't look too concerned. I was never entirely sure what he really believed.

One day Dick expressed interest in working on a photo. He hadn't worked on the computer or on developing photos for a long time, but this had always been his area of expertise. I manned the computer while he sat on a chair next to me, directing. I tried hard to get the colors the way he wanted them. But no matter what I did, he was not satisfied. He got quite agitated. I tried to tell him that I was doing what he suggested. I made suggestions of my own which I thought looked much better, but he didn't like those either.

When I couldn't get the outcome he wanted, he exclaimed, "You're doing it all wrong!"

"I'm sorry. I wish I could get the photo the way you envision it. I am trying my best. I know you were always the expert at developing photos."

He left the room in a huff.

There were incidents where we both tried each other's patience. But luckily, there were lots more of the good times.

Two years later, I attended a "Psychic Halloween" party in my neighborhood. Each person met with a medium privately for twenty minutes. She had an uncanny ability to read me. She felt Dick's presence in the room and communicated some things he wanted to share with me.

She said, "I have no idea what this means, but he says, '*You got the colors right.*'"

I knew exactly what he meant.

CHAPTER 59

Third Time's the Charm

We had delayed the lumbar drain several months because of our move but we were motivated to reschedule it after reading an article in the *Boston Globe* which cited dramatic results with the lumbar drain for normal pressure hydrocephalus (NPH). The article stated NPH could develop with brain tumor patients. The procedure was set for September 30. We had a repeat performance—admitted to the Brigham, IV placed, and after several hours wait, the doctor came in and told us they could not perform the procedure. Dick would be at risk because he was still receiving the chemotherapy drug Avastin. They recommended holding his next infusion and doing the lumbar drain a month later. It was another frustrating experience, but we had cleared the week and the weather prediction was for unseasonably warm weather, so we tried to look at it as a bonus week for ourselves.

It was rescheduled to October 21. We were disappointed that we would miss the baby naming for Dick's great niece in Atlanta, but we didn't want to delay any longer. Like the previous times, there were so many last-minute details to take care of before we left, but we managed to get to the Brigham on time for our noon appointment. We then proceeded to wait for a bed in admitting for six and a half hours! I was so grateful to Bharani for being with us. I don't think I ever could have gotten Dick to wait it out without his help.

More than once Dick implored, "Let's go home."

It was heartrending to listen to him. I desperately wanted to give in and take him home, but I tried to keep our goal in mind and put up a good front. The staff apologized and gave us lunch vouchers, but Dick was not impressed. At one point I accompanied Dick to customer relations because he wanted to file a complaint. I figured that at least going through the motions would distract him so he wouldn't dwell on leaving. I didn't often use Facebook, but that day I posted about our long wait at the Brigham. Then I read everyone's supportive comments to Dick and that really helped to pass the time.

Once situated in a room, we waited another few hours for the doctor to place the lumbar drain. Dick refused oxycodone and a local anesthetic, but he did fine. The seizure specialist had ordered an EEG to check seizure activity, so they completed that as well while Dick was an inpatient. Our Boston family and friends and our rabbi from New Bedford came, which helped make the days go by quicker.

By day four, we hadn't noticed any cognitive changes. Sometimes it can take longer, so we were still hopeful. I was anxious to return home to see how our courtyard was proceeding but Dr. Johnson convinced us to give it one more day. I think he just did not want to give up.

It was difficult to judge the efficacy of the procedure, as Dick was more confused than usual because of the change of environment in the hospital setting, coupled with his lack of sleep. The physical therapist noted no changes at discharge.

When we got home, Dick returned to baseline. I was grateful for that but deeply disappointed that I did not notice any improvement in cognitive ability. Life was getting harder for him all the time, as his short-term memory and his grasp on interpreting the world around him were failing. We did notice some physical improvements: he was no longer shuffling his feet at night or when he was tired.

We left for our Seattle trip to see Seth shortly after the procedure, on November 6. I started noticing changes in Dick's abilities during that week. He astonished me by remembering the number of our hotel room. He was introduced to Gena's cat, Merlin, and when he awoke from a nap two hours later, he recalled the cat's name. When we returned home, Dick was looking at everything with new interest and more discerning eyes. He questioned things that he hadn't noticed before.

"We need to move the pictures on the living room wall so they are centered. Why don't we have everything in the basement up on planks?"

He wanted to fix his bicycle. He wanted to know what all his pills looked like and what they were for. I couldn't believe it! It was remarkable to see his mind turning gears again and his inquisitive self coming back to life. When Bharani visited, Dick was so excited to show off that he could not only walk with no difficulty, but he could dance! He danced me around the kitchen and Bharani has the video on his phone to prove it.

For the past four months, at our appointments with Dr. V, Dick's performance on the mini-mental status exam had declined dramatically. Dick could not recall any of the four words he was asked to remember. He could not identify them with cues or when given three choices. On our appointment the week we returned from Seattle, Dick remembered two out of the four words and recalled the others right away when given choices. In the past months he had difficulty counting backwards from 100 by sevens; that week he was not only able to do it perfectly, but quickly as well! His drawings were excellent in form and content. This was the first time in that office when the tears rolling down my cheeks were those of joy. Dick's medical exam that day showed his balance, gait, and strength all improved.

Dr. V and Dr. Reardon were astounded by the gains Dick had made. Dick was thrilled to be able to think more clearly and contribute more in decision-making. We were so glad we persisted in going through with the procedure despite two failed attempts. The third time was the charm.

The downside of Dick's recovery of some skills was that he became overconfident. He tried to ride his bike but still didn't have enough balance and coordination and fell in the process. He thought maybe he was well enough to drive, and I feared he might try to take the car.

I returned home with a migraine one night and could barely lay out his pill box and water and open the right slot for Thursday night's pills before I crawled into bed. I asked him if he could take the pills on his own and he assured me he could. In the morning I realized he had taken my pills instead. He loved his newfound independence and I loved seeing him be more himself, but although his abilities were much improved, he still needed direction and supervision.

CHAPTER 60

November/December 2013

Around the end of November, Dick began to lose the gains he had made from the lumbar trial, and shortly after, he was back to his previous baseline. It was so hard for me to see him slide back. His rational, observant self was getting sucked up into the mire of the brain tumor. He was aware enough to be upset about losing the abilities he had enjoyed so briefly. One Saturday morning, he insisted I bring him to the local ER as he was concerned about his decline in functioning.

We had an appointment with Dr. Johnson the following week to determine whether Dick needed a permanent shunt or whether they could repeat the lumbar drain periodically, so I suggested we wait till then.

"No, something's wrong. We need to go to the emergency room right away," he said. I agreed to go as I did not want to start an argument.

He was assessed at the local ER and they recommended we go to the Brigham ER. Because it was not an emergency, I would have to drive him myself. We were sent home after ten frustrating hours and were informed that Dick would have to wait until his scheduled appointment with Dr. Johnson on Thursday. I was aggravated that Dick hadn't listened to me when I suggested that in the first place. But I bit my tongue and managed not to say, I told you so.

A few days later, we saw Dr. Johnson, who agreed that Dick needed a permanent shunt. He described the process, which would require a two-day hospitalization. They would put a hole in Dick's skull and insert a catheter, which would drain the excess cerebrospinal fluid internally to the abdomen. We would hopefully see positive changes within a week or two after the shunt was placed. There was a risk of infection, but we felt the potential gains outweighed the risks, so we set the date for the preop appointment in late December.

We attended a few neighborhood gatherings that fall, and Dick surprised me by staying awake for four-hour stretches. He really enjoyed the stimulation of being with other people. He looked forward to his weekly outings with his Lakeville friends and to breakfasts with the neighborhood guys.

He would often wake up in the morning and say, "What time are my friends picking me up today?" and if they weren't scheduled to come that day, I tried my best to distract him.

"You are a very popular guy," I told him, "but I want a little time with you too, you know. It's my day today and I'm looking forward to spending it with you."

He laughed and told me, "You are always my favorite companion."

Since we had decided to take a break from rehab, it was nice to have a more relaxed schedule, which gave Dick more energy for company and outings. He loved seeing his colleagues from all over the region at a Mass Medical Society event at Plimoth Plantation and enjoyed a visit from his sister-in-law and niece from Florida.

Dick had a dental cleaning appointment at Dr. Messier's office in Middleboro.

When the hygienist went home sick before they could contact us, Dr. Messier himself cleaned Dick's teeth. Dick was very honored and repeated that story to whomever he saw over the following weeks. Dick was thrilled to see two of his patients while we were in town. He enjoyed the perks of running into his old patients—greetings of "Hi, Doc," catching up on news on both sides, and hugs from all the women.

We had a wonderful Thanksgiving at our new home, surrounded by all the children except Seth. My mother had recently moved into an assisted living facility near my brother and sister-in-law in Providence, and they were all able to come for the holiday. Bharani, who had become part of our family, also joined us. When we went around the table and shared what we were thankful for, almost everyone focused on being grateful for being together.

Dick said simply, "Being alive."

We enjoyed an extended visit with Sarah, Samantha, and the grandchildren. It made us so happy to hear the delight in six-year-old Aerin's voice when she arrived:

"Guess what Nana and Zayde? We are going to stay for a *whole* week!"

Chanukah fell close to Thanksgiving that year, so we had the bonus of celebrating the holiday with the grandchildren. Eight-month-old Ronen had a special relationship with his zayde and smiled continuously when he was with him. Dick loved to sit on the couch, holding the baby against his chest, while I cushioned him on the other side. Ronen had crystal clear blue eyes just like his zayde. Watching them together brought tears to my eyes.

I was so grateful that Dick had lived to see the birth of his third grandchild. At the same time, I longed to see Dick watch Ronen become a bar mitzvah and marry someday. Oh, how I wished Dick could see Sarah, Sandra, and Seth's children someday. Raising our children had not always been an easy road, and I wished Dick could enjoy the benefits of their adulthood, maturity, and successes.

I took lots of photos so that Ronen would have memories of his zayde holding and hugging him with so much love. And of course, Bharani took photos every time he was with us, whether it was a Thanksgiving feast or a surgical consult. I had recently looked at some of the photos Bharani routinely sent us online. I almost didn't recognize myself! I glared at the pictures. Who was that fat, washed-out woman with frizzy hair? Could it be me? Yes, it was, and I was mortified. *How had that happened? How did I get so huge? How did I get so old?*

Maybe I should skip our nightly bowl of ice cream and start walking up and down the stairs in the house, as Dr. Edelman had suggested. But in reality, I knew that I wouldn't do any of those things. Not now. I needed to focus on Dick and enjoy our time together. I *needed* my ice cream right now.

On the last night of Chanukah, we attended the Shalom Pinehills' Chanukah party at the Stonebridge Club, with over fifty Pinehills residents in attendance. Dick had encouraged me to start the group when we moved in, so I was pleased that he got to see the fruits of our labor.

I got a call from a neighbor, Esteban, whose wife passed away in December. He had been dedicated to her care the last few years as she suffered from cancer. He asked if he could help out by visiting Dick. Esteban was a physicist and Dick had majored in physics as an undergrad. They talked about books, scientists, and astronomy. Despite his brain cancer, Dick was able to engage in conversations with Esteban that were beyond me. Esteban became a regular volunteer and often came over, bearing home-baked banana bread, which he confided was the only thing he knew how to bake. It was delicious.

Seth got a two-week military leave in December. We were so proud to show him our new home and neighborhood, and he got to visit with my mom at her new apartment at the assisted living facility. Seth joined us at our neighborhood holiday party and accompanied Dick to his weekly breakfast with the neighborhood guys. I couldn't help but wonder as Seth left—would this be the last time he and his dad spent time together?

Christmas week, our son-in-law Adam came to help us with a few things. He brought a long, sturdy, worktable that he no longer needed in their New York apartment and set it up in the basement so we would have a place to work on gallery wrapping photos. Dick still hoped to have a production line. I wasn't so sure.

We got a ride back to New York with Adam to attend a fiftieth wedding anniversary party for Dick's cousins. Even with door-to-door service, travel was exhausting for Dick. Once we arrived in the city, Dick never left the hotel room. He didn't feel up to attending the anniversary party the next day, so Samantha and I took turns staying with him. I felt so bad that although we made the effort to come all that way, he missed the event. But Dick's cousins and extended family came to visit him the following day. Seeing them, one on one, in a private, quieter setting worked much better for Dick anyway.

Although the traveling was stressful, he was still thrilled to have made the trip and visit with everyone, especially the grandchildren.

Samantha and Adam had recently bought their own place in the East Village, which was undergoing renovations before they moved in. I knew Dick would love to see their first house so I asked Samantha if we could get a tour, but she said it was in a state of disarray from being torn apart and rebuilt. Besides, it was on the second and third floors of the building and the stairs were long and treacherous. She also commented that if her dad saw how small it was and how much they paid for it, she thought he would be upset. I snuck a preview and knew she was right!

For the past twenty-five years, we had sent out a holiday letter, complete with a photo collage. I read my draft of the 2013 letter to Dick and he wanted to add to it. He dictated the following addition:

I regret that I am unable to write legibly and focus my attention to complete tasks for myself. Robin has been a real saint and she's been a great nurse. Her social work skills have been successful in getting us through the maze of insurance and medical forms.

Robin and fabulous friends, family, colleagues, and volunteers have gotten me through this cancer that's typically fatal. I've improved and that miracle is due in part to our wonderful community of friends.

Love,

Dick

I looked at Dick in amazement as I put my arms on his shoulders. "Do you really think it is a miracle? Do you think you will get better?"

"I will eventually die from this disease, but I have lived a whole year and a half with it. Not just survived—lived! I am so lucky I have you. I never could have gotten through this without you. You dedicate all your time and energy to me and make every day joyful. I am lucky not to be in any physical pain. Thank you for organizing the Lotsa Helping Hands site—I still don't understand how it works exactly but I'm grateful for all the people who are so giving of their time. I appreciate life. I appreciate every day. I appreciate you. I'm sorry sometimes I'm so grouchy."

"You are forgiven. I can't imagine what a pain I would be if it was me who was in your place!" I said as I planted a kiss on his cheek. "I love you so much."

"I feel blessed to have been given the past year and a half and hopefully more," Dick said.

"I still pray maybe there will be a miraculous cure," I whispered in his ear.

"I'm afraid it will be too late for me, my darling, but I hope there will be a cure someday."

I cried silent tears.

CHAPTER 61

Shadows of Night

A nother shunt was placed on December 30 and although we
saw some improvements, they were not consistent. Dick's
gait and balance were better for a while but then he began to have
more frequent falls and started using a cane. Although we still had
many good days, gaps in Dick's functioning became more obvious.
He was approved for cognitive therapy again and assigned a new
speech therapist. This was our first negative experience with in-home
providers. The speech therapist came late in the evening, was totally
disorganized, and gave Dick third grade worksheets. It was insulting.
At the second session, I told her not to return. I could do better
myself.

I often napped alongside Dick during the day and then I was too
tired to fall asleep at night. I had rarely shopped online before, but I
became addicted, looking through sites like Wayfair, Overstock, and

One Kings Lane. I was able to divorce myself from the everyday challenges and lose myself in mazes of lamps, coffee tables, and outdoor furniture. I had carefully chosen a small, teak table and chairs for the courtyard, one of the last finishing pieces we needed.

Often, around midnight, I would hear Dick's voice calling out from the bedroom, "Robin, where are you? Come to bed. It's too late for you to be up."

I would be bounced back to reality from my safe space in the study.

"I missed you," he would say. "I can't fall asleep without you."

Through the years, this was a frequent refrain. Dick was often exhausted from work and would go to bed earlier than I would, but at 11 p.m. he would call out to me, "Come to bed, my darling. It's late. I can't fall asleep without you. You'll never be able to get up for bootcamp at 4:45 a.m.!"

I left my fantasy world of online shopping in the study, crawled into bed, and snuggled up next to Dick.

"I love you," he said. And we gave each other a kiss goodnight.

As I tried to fall asleep, I wondered, *when Dick was gone, who would call me to bed when I stayed up too late?*

I woke up abruptly one night with a terrible cramp in my foot.

"Dick, wake up. I need help."

We had lived this scenario many times before. Dick expertly pulled my toes forward until the cramp disappeared.

"You should be okay now. Walk around the room a few times."

"Thank you for working your magic," I said.

Then with a sickening feeling, I remembered: Dick would not always be there for me. There would be no one to wake up in the middle of the night when I got a cramp in my foot. No one to pull my toes forward to stretch the muscles. No one to hold my head with just the right pressure when I had a migraine.

The incident triggered a memory of the day that Dick saved Sandra's life. I had accompanied her to the hospital for a routine colonoscopy. In recovery, her O2 sats went down to 90 and they had to give her oxygen. I called Dick, as I was concerned. He said it sounded like it might be either an aspiration pneumonia or a pulmonary embolism (blood clot). They eventually took Sandra off the oxygen and sent her home, attributing her difficulty breathing to anxiety.

It was the first night of Passover and I still had a lot to prepare. Sandra's bedroom was upstairs. I would have put her to bed and gone down to the kitchen to finish cooking. It might have been hours before I checked on her.

I called Dick on the way home from the hospital to let him know Sandra was discharged. He dropped everything in his office and met us at the door of our house with a pulse oximeter. Sandra's oxygen level was so low we had to rush back to the hospital, where she was admitted to the ICU for three days for aspiration pneumonia. *What did people do who didn't have a doctor in the house? What would I do?*

I was drawn back to the present. "I won't be able to fix the cramp alone when you're not here." I cried and I couldn't stop.

Dick calmly said, "Yes, you can, and I'm going to show you how. You see how our sleigh bed is shaped at the footboard? All you have to do is place your foot up against the board and press your toes into it."

He demonstrated and then had me try it.

"You can do it," he said.

"I know I can, but I wish you could always be here to help me," I whimpered.

He held me tenderly and said, "I'll be with you. You'll hear my words and you'll know what to do. I love you so much."

"I love you too."

I lay awake for hours that night. I had rarely let myself think about the future, about the possibility of being alone someday—it hurt too much. But I tried to reassure myself with Dick's thoughts—he would always be with me, in my mind, and in my heart.

CHAPTER 62
Winter 2014: Highs and Low

Over the next few months, I felt like we were on a roller coaster, and I hate roller coasters. We were in and out of the hospital. Dick was convinced that the shunt was malfunctioning, but the medical professionals determined it was working fine. He was diagnosed with anemia and diverticulitis. He was bothered by severe itching, a side effect from one of the chemo drugs, which never subsided. With the help of iron pills and supplementing his diet, Dick became more alert and energetic. One of our inpatient stays in Boston was particularly grueling. I was so glad that Bharani, Sandra, and my cousin Melinda were there with us through it all. They made a ten-hour wait in the ER feel like a social convention.

Just one day after discharge, Dick had a seizure and a fall. The EMTs were quite insistent this time that Dick should be taken by ambulance to the hospital, but Dick refused.

"I just want to sleep in my own bed, with my wife by my side," he told them.

We had many interactions with the EMTs from The Pinehills Fire Department, who were always professional, kind, and respected Dick's decisions, but this time I sensed the urgency in their voices.

After they left, I asked Dick, "Are you sure you're safe staying home?"

"I'm not sure," he said. "But I am sure I don't want to go to the hospital right now. We just came back. I am exhausted. I don't want to wait for hours and then have to provide another long history for a medical student and resident. You know I am DNR code status. If I have a seizure where I am unable to process information, that's the end for me. I don't want to live like that. It's important you know this information. You are my health care proxy."

Of course I knew. We'd had this conversation multiple times and it was always an emotional one.

"I know. I understand. I just want you to be the best you can be for as long as possible. I love you so much. I can't imagine life without you."

We held onto each other like we were on a sinking lifeboat. My eyes welled up although I tried to contain my tears because I knew Dick couldn't bear to see me cry. Dick's arms, wrapped around me, helped calm the storm in my heart.

"You'll be okay," he said, as he gently wiped the tears from my eyes. "You are strong and capable. I love you so much, honey," Dick said.

"I wish I could be as strong as you," I replied, finally breaking down as the tears burst forth.

"You are," Dick consoled me. "I am so proud of you. You have done the best possible job taking care of me. I couldn't ask for anything more. You are the best wife in the world. I am such a lucky man to have found you."

And, as he often did when we had these tough conversations, he ended with, "I have lived a happy and fulfilling life."

We lay down together, emotionally exhausted, but content that we were in our own bed, we had each other, and had somehow dodged another bullet.

I shared some of our ups and downs on Lotsa Helping Hands in my January update and received this insightful note from our camera club friend Scott.

Dick has such a humble, genuine way about him, I felt it the second I met him. While I'm sure the "hard talks" are not something you enjoy, I have to believe that Dick could not be more honest when he says how much he loves you and speaks of his fulfilling life. He seems to have found peace and acceptance with what he's going through, and I am sure he wants nothing more than for you to find that peace as well.

Perhaps what matters most to him is that the time you both spend together be as high quality and magical as possible. . . .

Enjoy that special love you both have for one another, just as you have in all your yesterdays. . . . Be reminded to enjoy it today, tomorrow and forevermore. . . .

Dick was so appreciative of the responses we got on Helping Hands that in February, he asked me to help him write a letter on the site. He had two pieces of paper with the start of two letters he had been working on. It took a lot of patient studying to decipher them but I did the best I could to combine them into one letter. I posted it, at his request, on Lotsa Helping Hands on February 18, 2014.

Dear Friends & Family,

I am delighted to be pain free. I delight in having so many old friends. I regret that neither my memory nor penmanship permit me to write you individually. We're delighted to have company. Please call anytime you want to come over. I'd love to see you all. I regret my declining cognition, and I'm profoundly saddened by my inability to judge space and time. I'm delighted to have all of you in my life. Please forgive me if I've become more repetitive. I love you all. Please keep me posted on how you are doing. I rely on Robin to explain and remember everything for me.

Thank you all for rising to my aid. It seems odd, but your kindness and consideration have made this a wonderful year. I appreciate your giving me so much fellowship and compassion. I wish you prosperity, long life, and happiness. Please enjoy the spring and all the goodness about.

Love,

Dick

Folks responded to Dick's letter on Lotsa Helping Hands, and we had visitors, or were invited out, several times a week, which helped make the long winter more lively. We enjoyed a visit from our nephew Ben on his winter break from Dartmouth College. The kids came in from New York and we celebrated our grandson Jacob's fourth birthday. Dick's friend and colleague Dr. McNamee came to visit him with greetings from the rest of the medical staff. Our new Shalom Pinehills Club sponsored a wine tasting for the Jewish holiday of Purim, which we attended with many of our new friends at The Pinehills. Dick loved seeing his old friends at the six-month reunion of his LIVESTRONG class in East Bridgewater. Dick's sister visited from Minnesota, and my sister and brother-in-law came from California.

My cousin Melinda came many times that winter laden with delicious meals and Dick's favorite: batches of the world's best fudge brownies.

Dick's patients Lisa and Ron Grace had a talented young daughter, Brianna, who was a professional musician. They called to ask if their daughter, also one of Dick's patients, could come to sing for "Dr. Gross." She performed an amazing personal concert for us right in our own living room! We were so fortunate that Brianna was able to come before she moved out to Nashville. Keeping active socially was a gift for Dick. He inevitably rose to the occasion when he was with friends and family. He was still able to contribute to the conversation and make jokes, and he loved being surrounded by family and friends, both old and new.

Although it was a tough few months, we also shared beautiful moments and magical memories. Dick had taught me how to print canvas photos, gallery wrap them on stretcher bars, and affix wire on the back. Those winter months were the first time I had to try my hand at it independently. My first few attempts proved difficult. I didn't have the strength in my hands to staple the canvas to the stretcher bars and the staples wouldn't stay or came out crooked. I looked online to see if I could pick up any tips and discovered that many photographers used a pneumatic stapler. I researched and ordered one online.

Our friend Bob helped me set up the air compressor and pneumatic stapler in the basement next to the worktable Adam had brought us. I was intimidated by the power of the machine and the din it created, but it worked. We got a production line going for printing canvas photos! Dick was so excited to make an excursion to Winberg's Hardware in Lakeville where his friend Paul Winberg helped him pick out supplies. First thing on Dick's list—he insisted on buying safety glasses for me.

I asked Dick one day how I was doing.

He responded, "The mark of being a good student is when the pupil's work surpasses the teacher, and that's what you have achieved."

"Only because I had the best teacher in the world!"

We had an opportunity to display some of our photos in The Pinehills Cabana in February, and Dick was enthusiastic about our upcoming exhibit at The Stonebridge Club's Great Room in July. They had a rotating display of Pinehills resident guest artists each month.

I read that the Plymouth Arts Center was having a call for submissions for a juried photography exhibit. I knew it was a very competitive show but decided to submit a photo from each of us. A few weeks later I received notice that Dick's photo was accepted.

"Guess what?" I said to Dick, "I submitted two photos to the Plymouth Arts Center photography show and yours was accepted. Congratulations! I'm so proud of you. I have to bring the photo in by Saturday."

Dick was excited but worried that we wouldn't have time to print it.

"We can just take down the one from our wall. Don't worry, you have to price the photo very high because they take a thirty percent commission, so nobody will be able to afford to buy it!"

I invited some family and friends to the opening reception at the end of March. We situated Dick in a lone chair in the exhibit room where his canvas hung, and he delighted in greeting everyone and hearing comments from passersby. Friends from both our New Bedford and Plymouth photo communities came to congratulate Dick.

By the time the exhibit ended on May 3, Dick's condition had advanced. I was not able to leave the house to pick up the photo, so I asked a neighbor.

She came back empty-handed, saying, "It sold!"

We just stood there open-mouthed, repeating, "It sold? It sold?"

We had sold a few photos before but never to a complete stranger. Dick was shocked and elated. Now he could add selling a photograph to his list of accomplishments, but more than that, it gave him confirmation that his work was really professional. We danced around the room in joy.

We also finished up the last details on our house that winter. Dick decided he wanted a rocking chair and I helped him pick one out. Our neighbor Larry helped us assemble it. Larry had previously helped us put together our new end tables and assorted other purchases. He was retired and let us know that we could call on him anytime, and I did. He always answered the phone, "Larry Lynch, at your service." Larry joked around a lot and had a special way of doing all the work but making Dick feel like he had contributed.

One day the light on the refrigerator water filter went on alerting us it was time to replace it. That was something Dick could have done intuitively in the past. He and I read the instructions over and over again, trying to follow them to a T, but between the two of us, we just could not get the filter in right. I finally resorted to calling Larry, who twisted it into place in seconds. I think it made Dick feel good to know that I had a Larry Lynch in my life.

We made choices about various types of window coverings. Dick had definite ideas about designs and colors. He wanted the roman shade in the bedroom to be a blackout shade so he could sleep during the day. He also thought it would be a good idea to choose the option of the cordless lift shade in the bedroom so he could do it himself. I didn't think we needed that luxury since I was perfectly capable of doing it manually.

"I'll always be here with you. I can pull the shade for you," I said.

"You know what, it doesn't matter," Dick said. "This is going to be *your* house. You are the one who is going to live here, so you should get what you want. I want you to be happy. If you like the orange tone better on the cornice over the living room windows, you should get it. If you want to get the cord on the bedroom shade, you should get it. Go ahead, *do what you want.*"

I was shocked for a moment. Dick rarely talked about my being alone, and the reality just knocked me for a loop. We had both made every decision about the house and its furnishings, living the fantasy that we would always be there together. My lips trembled as I spoke, but I hoped they didn't betray my sadness.

"We've always made choices together. I respect your opinion. I think we are a great design team. We've been a great team in life, haven't we?"

"Yes, we have, the best," Dick replied.

"I love that we created this place together. I'm glad you are here to help me. You are right—we should get the blackout, cordless shade in the bedroom."

I fell into his arms with the knowledge that what he said was true.

The roller coaster continued, but we had a firm grip on each other. We relished the slow parts of the ride and looked out and enjoyed life along the way.

CHAPTER 63

Valentine's Day

We had back-to-back appointments at Dana-Farber and the Brigham on February 12 and 13, so we decided to take advantage of the Boston hotel discount program offered to Dana-Farber patients and stay overnight at the Marriott in Coolidge Corner rather than fight the traffic. We had signed up for a Valentine's luncheon at The Pinehills Stonebridge Club, but as it turned out, Dick needed some follow-up testing which made an additional night's stay in Boston necessary.

Instead, we had lunch at a nearby restaurant, but our own private celebration of Valentine's Day came later that day. The last major item we needed for our home was a dining room chandelier. We had looked online and at local lighting showrooms with no success.

It was getting much more difficult for Dick to go shopping. I noticed as we drove up to our hotel that Neena's Design Lighting was situated a block and a half away. Although Dick's balance and stamina were becoming more challenged, he was willing to attempt the walk. We took it slowly and held on to each other. One more block and we would never have made it.

The store's showroom greeted us with an array of glittering lights of every size and style, but one stood out to both of us. It was a round, gold chandelier with crystals hanging in eight tiered levels of circles. The crystals were shaped like inverted triangles and the overall look was a feast for one's eyes.

"That's the one," Dick said.

He was right. It was a perfect fit for our dining room.

"Let me check how much it is," I said, before we got too excited.

I was disappointed when I saw the price tag. Definitely more than we intended to spend.

Dick was usually the one who was mindful of our budget, but he said, "Let's get it. It will look gorgeous. Happy Valentine's Day!"

I gave him a kiss right in the middle of the store. "Happy Valentine's Day!"

We both envisioned the crystals with the sunlight hitting them, throwing rainbows on the dining room ceiling.

The chandelier was not in stock and it would be a six-week wait, as it was coming from overseas. Although we had gotten a good report at Dick's medical visit that day, I still felt some anxiety when I marked my calendar with the delivery date. Four weeks approached and I called to check on the delivery details.

"Sorry, there has been a delay," the clerk reported. "It will be four weeks from today."

"No," I responded strongly, "That's not acceptable. You don't understand. My husband's dying. I don't know if he'll be here in a few weeks. You need to get it delivered now. You promised it would be here in six weeks. We can't wait any longer."

"Let me get more information about the delay. We'll do the best we can to get it to you as soon as possible."

"That chandelier was our Valentine's present to one another. He needs to see it up." My voice cracked as I started to cry. I was shaky and sweating. "You really need to help me out here. This needs to happen now. I can't wait."

"I'll have the owner call you back," the clerk said.

The owner told me we were eligible for a discount due to the delay but the best they could do was April 15. If it came in sooner, he would call me. I knew he was trying to placate us with the discount but that wasn't important to me. I knew it wasn't his fault, but I was furious. I kept my angst from Dick. He didn't have a good sense of time and I didn't want to upset him. I marked the calendar once again and I counted the days.

When the package finally arrived, I called the electrician to put it up. He didn't come when he was scheduled and then he canceled due to illness. I called a few other electricians but there was going to be a long wait. I needed it done right away! That bare wire hanging out of the wide expanse of the dining room ceiling was shouting out at me. I was so frustrated. I could see Dick slipping every day. I sensed time was closing in on us.

Debbie, the aide who was assisting that day, heard and saw my distress.

"My husband's friend Rick is an electrician. Do you want me to call him? He's a great guy. He coaches my kid's hockey team. I'm sure he can help you." Debbie said.

"Yes, please call him."

Rick came the next day to assess the project. It was a Sunday, and his wife and five children came on their way home from church. His family stayed in the car while Rick came in to look at the chandelier. I went out and thanked them later. Rick said he would return the following morning to put up the chandelier.

He placed each crystal with care and their brilliance sparkled. This was the last item of furnishing to complete the inside decor of our new house. We were elated. We kept flipping the light switch on and off like kids, delighting in the sparkle of the crystals.

"I knew that was the one when I saw it," Dick said.

"Yes, you did. You have fabulous taste. It looks elegant," I proclaimed as we hugged and kissed. "You've made me a beautiful new home."

I breathed a huge sigh of relief that everything was done, but I had a nagging thought. *Did this mean Dick might die soon? Had he been hanging on to finish the last detail in preparing this magnificent new house for me?*

No, I concluded, crowding out those thoughts. He had to see Sandra graduate from nursing school. He had to hang on until summer to enjoy our courtyard filled with flowers and butterflies. He had just received an invitation to his fortieth medical school reunion in the fall and he wanted to attend.

Enjoy each and every day, I told myself. Today was the day that mattered, and it was a glorious day with rainbow reflections flitting across the room and Dick beaming in the new light.

CHAPTER 64

The Cancer Returns

When PT and OT reevaluated Dick in February, they determined he did not require services, but recommended instead that the LIVESTRONG Program would be an excellent way for him to keep active and maintain his skills. The next session was starting at the Middleboro Y in March, so I called to make sure Dick would have a spot as they had promised. After several tries, I finally reached the LIVESTRONG coordinator, who said it was the national LIVESTRONG policy that you could not take the class twice. Although I knew he was a young kid, just following the rules, I reminded him that the Middleboro staff had invited Dick to take the class again at their facility. I knew it was a free program and offered to pay for the class if that was the issue. He said there was a possibility he could arrange for someone to work out with Dick individually and he would get back to me.

I was furious. Working out individually would defeat the purpose of LIVESTRONG—being with people who shared a common bond and the camaraderie and support that developed between them. If I had been told at the outset that Dick could not take the class again, I would have accepted it, but I felt like I was strung along with promises of "if it doesn't fill up" and "he can take the next session." I never mentioned to Dick the tension I was having communicating with the Y. He had an idealized view of the Y and I did not want to change his perception. If I had trouble understanding their response, how could someone with a brain tumor comprehend it? But this time, I decided I would not take no for an answer.

I instinctively knew this would be Dick's last opportunity to participate. I wrote a passionate plea to the Interim Executive Director of the Middleboro Y. The answer was still no. I was horrified by his cold response. My husband was dying, and I didn't care about the rules. I knew how much it would mean to Dick to attend LIVESTRONG at his own Y and I was not going to let it go.

I looked up the regional CEO of the Old Colony YMCA Association and noticed his social work credentials. It was my hope that with his social work training in human relations and social responsibility, he would recognize that the Y had strayed from its mission. I wrote him a two-page letter requesting that Dick be allowed to take the LIVESTRONG program at the Middleboro Y.

I ended with the following:

The mission of the Y is to enrich the quality of life for everyone in our communities and to assist all people to develop to their fullest potential. This is exactly what I am asking for my husband. The average life span for a patient with glioblastoma is 14 months. We are fortunate he has exceeded that timeline. My goal is to continue to bring vitality and enjoyment into his life.

The staff and participants at the E. Bridgewater LIVESTRONG *program were a tremendous support for him. We have always enjoyed exercise as part of our life and I do not want to deny him that opportunity now. There is no question that participation in the* LIVESTRONG *Program would allow my husband to enjoy a better quality of life. The Y literature states that their business practices must be consistent with their mission, and I believe that not allowing Dick to take the program at the Middleboro Y is in conflict with their mission statement.*

The CEO was quick to respond, and I was very relieved that he honored my request. We attended the first LIVESTRONG session at the Middleboro Y on March 17. Two participants approached Dick after initial introductions and gave him a big hug. They were so happy to see him that their reaction brought me to tears. I knew at that moment I had made the right decision to fight for Dick's participation.

One of the participants was a former patient and another was a nurse who had worked with Dick many years ago at the old St. Luke's Hospital in Middleboro. I heard her tell Dick she had witnessed him saving many patients' lives in the early days when they had no specialists and Dick was on call 24/7.

After the aggravating battle to get into the class, we had to miss the second session due to an emergency medical appointment, and by the third class, we sadly recognized Dick would not be able to return because his functioning had deteriorated so quickly. I was disappointed that he had not been allowed to take the class back in the fall, but since there was nothing I could do about it now, I focused my attention on the present.

March was the first time in the past year and a half that I missed writing my biweekly update on Lotsa Helping Hands. With all the ER visits and hospitalizations, I didn't have the time or energy. I couldn't drag myself to the computer. I didn't know what to write. I couldn't make sense of the changes I was seeing. As I helplessly watched Dick losing skills, it became harder for me to share those struggles with our Helping Hands community. I needed to take a break. I would curl up next to Dick on the bed and nap alongside him.

At our monthly appointment on March 20, the MRI showed diffuse tumor growth. I shouldn't have been surprised. I knew Dick's behavior and abilities had become erratic. Although he had a good period after the shunt, his walking had worsened again. He was bent over now and walked deliberately with small steps. He got confused more often and did things like leaving the water running in the sink after he washed up. When he spoke, it took him longer to form the words he wanted to say. Dick thought it was the shunt that wasn't working, but I suspected it was more than that. It was still a hard blow to hear the reality. I had become so used to hearing "the tumor is stable" at our monthly trips to Dana-Farber that I had been lulled into believing that would go on forever.

Dr. Reardon asked Dick whether he wanted to continue treatment, and there was not the slightest hesitation in his reply.

"Yes, I do," he said bravely, as he looked over at me and then at Bharani. "I've had better than average results until now. I've been able to enjoy every day and I hope to keep doing so."

Part of me was surprised at his determined response. As I sat and waited while he got his infusion later that day, I wondered whether we could keep going. How long could we keep this up? Another part of me was relieved at his response. Maybe he could hold out a little

306

longer. Maybe there would be a cure. A part of me never gave up hope. Even if we had one more day; just one more day waking up with his kiss on my lips, watching Dick rock his baby grandson in his arms, hearing his laughter with his friends, drinking in his scent as we held on to each other in bed at night—it would be worth the fight. Dick made his own decision that day; there was no discussion—he was not ready to die.

When I finally forced myself to sit down and write an update on Lotsa Helping Hands, I thought about everything that had happened over the last several weeks. I thought back on how much Dick enjoyed seeing his medical colleagues at the Sepersky's annual St. Paddy's Day party, his weekly breakfasts with the "boys," and seeing our synagogue community at "Shabbat Across America." I thought about what Dick had been saying all along—that these past two years had been the best years of his life. I looked at the last month through his positive lens and recognized that the love he felt was what had kept him going this long and what pushed him to try to keep going a little longer.

CHAPTER 65

Decline

I wrote to Jenn, our nurse practitioner at the Dana-Farber, regarding the dramatic changes I was seeing in Dick. I told her Seth was coming home for three weeks in July and asked her if she thought he should come sooner.

"Yes, even if it's for a short visit. It might be better for him to come while Dick still has some good days," Jenn responded. "Do you think you and Dick might be interested in hospice?"

"Dick doesn't like hospice," I told her. "He had some bad experiences when he's referred patients to them. He told me hospice tends to prescribe too much pain medication."

Jenn suggested I might discuss hospice further with Dr. Browning, Dick's new internist. When I later spoke with Dr. Browning, he explained that Dick could not be on hospice if he was still receiving treatment. I wanted to respect Dick's determination to continue treatment, but I wasn't sure it was the right decision. After much thought and discussion back and forth with Dick's physicians, Jenn's suggestion seemed to make the most sense—give the Avastin infusion one more cycle and, if there was no benefit, think about moving to hospice.

Dick's abilities varied a lot and we tried to take advantage of the good days. Before getting the news about the reoccurrence, we had planned on attending my nephew-in-law Kenny's fortieth birthday party in New Jersey. Dick felt he was up to it and many of my extended family would be there, so we decided to stick with our plan to go the following week. My brother, Neal, drove us in my minivan with my sister-in-law Karen, Sandra, and my mom. On arrival, Dick said he felt sick and nauseous the entire ride, although he had not expressed a word of complaint the whole way.

"I want to go home right now," he said emphatically.

"It's a five-hour drive. We can't go home right now. You'll feel better after you rest awhile and then we can go to the party tonight."

"I don't want to go to any party. I want to go home *right now.*"

After going back and forth awhile, I realized it didn't make any sense to try to reason with Dick, so I just laid down next to him and tried to comfort him. He felt too sick to go out that night, so we took turns staying with him. The following morning, Dick felt better and he attended the brunch at my niece's home.

Sarah drove to New Jersey for the birthday party and was coming back to spend her spring vacation week with us. Since she was driving to Massachusetts, she offered to take Sandra and her dad. They thought it would give me a break and give them more time to spend with their dad. I arrived home before they did and called to see how they were doing. They had gotten lost and were somewhere in Rhode Island. Sandra complained that Sarah drove too slowly, and Sarah complained that Sandra was not a good navigator. Dick was getting agitated.

When Sandra gave her dad the phone to speak to me, Dick shouted in an angry tone, "I'm going to die soon, and I want to die in my own home!"

I was shocked by his outburst. I tried to stay calm on the phone, but inside I was feeling sick to my stomach. When I hung up, I sobbed uncontrollably.

What had I done? I never should have left him. I shouldn't have taken him to New Jersey in the first place. I was furious with myself. The next hour felt like an eternity.

When they finally arrived back home safely, I hugged Dick like it might be the last time and told him a hundred times how sorry I was and how much I loved him. He just wanted to go to bed. When he recovered after a long nap, we vowed to each other: no more traveling!

Looking back on the incident a day later, I realized it was a poor decision to go to New Jersey, and I should have made that judgment call myself. We had always made decisions together, but I knew that going forward, I needed to make the best decisions for both of us, no matter how hard they might be.

Dick's functional abilities were continuing to decline. The reality was the tumor was spreading and I could see evidence of its poison every day. I was so glad both Sandra and Sarah were spending time with us during their spring breaks.

Sarah, assessing Dick's declining skill level, suggested we should order a walker.

Dick overheard and responded, "I don't need a walker."

Sarah replied, "Dad, it will be safer. What would you recommend if it was one of your patients?"

He had a look that said she was right but replied, "I'm fine with the cane. I'll be better about using it all the time."

Sarah later told me privately, "Mom, I went ahead and ordered a walker which should arrive in a few days. Dad's going to need it."

My sister Priscilla also spent time with us that week, as she had flown in to be with my mom for her upcoming cataract surgery. It was a running joke that every time Priscilla came to visit, either my mom or Dick ended up in the hospital—and this time was no exception. I believe God sent her at that particular time because I needed her.

Dick fell one evening and had a grand mal seizure. He hadn't had one since the day he was diagnosed. He was hospitalized at the newly named Beth Israel Deaconess Hospital-Plymouth. The seizure dramatically impacted Dick's mobility. Although the hospital team recommended a rehab facility upon discharge, I insisted on taking him home. They agreed only under the condition that I get in-home services, so I hired help from a private agency for three hours a day. Dick also became eligible for an hour of assistance in the morning through his Medicare benefits.

At the doctor's recommendation, I contacted the children when Dick had the seizure. Samantha drove in with the baby and arrived in time to help us with the transition home from the hospital and then stayed for a week. Adam arrived with the other grandchildren to spend the weekend. Dr. Reardon and Jenn advocated with the Red Cross, so Seth was granted an emergency leave from the military to come home for five days. I never could have managed without all the help, as Dick was having difficulty with basic activities of daily living. Thank God

Sarah had the foresight to order the walker, which awaited us upon our return from the hospital and was now a necessity.

Dick loved having all the children home. Our neighbors kindly opened up their homes when we needed extra space for everybody. We had so much fun watching old family videos together. We laughed at the kids' complaints—how could I have ever dressed them in frilly matching dresses or let them get that ridiculous haircut? Dick loved holding baby Ronen while I took unending pictures of the two of them. Aerin and Jacob seemed to understand that their zayde was dying and that their loving presence was a comfort to him. They would nap right alongside him. Seth and Adam helped out with spring chores, like bringing up the outdoor furniture from the basement. How lucky we were to have this time together.

CHAPTER 66

Deterioration of Mind and Body

I remember the exact moment when Dick forgot how to eat. In late March, we were invited to our friends Tina and Mark's home for dinner. Dick didn't seem to know what to do with the food set in front of him. I offered him some food on his fork, and he ate it. I ended up feeding him the entire meal. I was devastated that Dick had reached this stage in his decline. I was also embarrassed. Fortunately, Tina and Mark took it all in stride. Going forward, Dick would usually need prompts or assistance in eating.

On April 3, Dick had his second infusion since the cancer had returned. By the end of that week, I realized the hospital's recommendation of 24/7 care was more realistic than four hours a day. My family encouraged me to seek more help. Our house cleaner, Juliana, recommended her friend, Poliana, who was a licensed practical nurse

(LPN). I interviewed Poliana and hired her. She would act as the case manager and arrange coverage with friends and family members of hers who were trained Certified Nursing Assistants (CNA). The caregivers were all Brazilian. Although they spoke English, Dick enjoyed learning Portuguese words from them and tried to speak to them in their native language. I was amazed by his adaptability and desire to learn new things. I was so grateful for the team's help, as Dick's mobility was poor, and he was sometimes incontinent. I recognized how fortunate I was that we could afford to hire help as I knew many women in my Women Warriors Facebook group had to do it all on their own.

Dick's mental abilities were variable. Some days he was like his old self, and other days he had a glazed look and was less communicative, as though he were occasionally having mini-seizures. There were more frequent bouts of moodiness and agitation. At other times, particularly when we had guests, he seemed alert, oriented, and engaged.

Our friend Greg came by with his wife and new baby and brought us the video he had made of our Lakeville backyard. Dick was thrilled to meet Greg's new daughter and to watch the treasured memories of our garden. We had another visitor in early April, Natalie Ward, the manager of the Mirbeau, a French-style inn and spa being built in The Pinehills. The Mirbeau, scheduled to open in July, would have a Monet-inspired theme and gardens. I had contacted Natalie a few weeks earlier to inquire whether they were interested in purchasing any of the photos we had taken at Monet's Garden in Giverny.

Natalie admired our canvas prints but shared that the Mirbeau had already purchased the artwork for the inn. She suggested we could possibly create postcards or some small items for the gift shop once they got established, and Dick was excited to hear this.

It was frightening to see changes happening so quickly. I had to hire the caregiving team to start covering nights as I had trouble getting Dick up to the bathroom. I hated giving up our privacy.

Some days Dick's thinking was not clear. One day that vividly stands out in my mind, he became agitated and began yelling at me. I felt like he was possessed of an evil spirit.

"You never washed a dish in your life! You don't know what you are doing!" Dick cried out at me.

My eyes started to smart, and my stomach churned. I was stunned. This was not my husband speaking. He would never have said such a thing. He thought the world of me and always told me so.

Leandro, the aide that day, saw me struggling to keep control. He pulled me aside in the kitchen and said, "You know it's the brain cancer talking, not him."

I knew that, but it didn't make it any easier.

"I need to go out for a walk," I told Leandro, as I was overcome with the feeling I must escape. "I'll have my phone in case there's an emergency."

I started down the street, crying hysterically. Feelings of shock, anger, and despair overtook me. Dick's words gnawed at my insides. Although I knew his insults were not true, hearing them come out of his mouth was devastating.

I called my friend Susan, whom I had known since elementary school, and whose kind, reflective manner always had a calming effect on me. Between my broken words and sobs, she somehow pieced together what was happening. Susan reaffirmed what Leandro had told me.

"It's the brain cancer speaking. Dick loves you more than anything in the world. When he was first diagnosed and I worked with him

315

on meditation/hypnosis techniques, Dick confided in me. He mostly talked about how much he admired you and loved you. He was more worried about you than about himself."

I had been racing down the streets without realizing it, and I had to catch my breath before responding. I slowed my pace and looked at the unfamiliar surroundings. I wasn't even sure where I was or the best route back.

I took a deep breath, stood in place for a few minutes, trying to gain control of my emotions as I spoke to Susan, "I didn't recognize him, Susan. I don't think he recognized me. I wish I could will him back. I don't want the end to be so terrible for him—for both of us. I don't want to lose him, Susan!"

"You've done a great job," Susan said. "You are still doing a great job and you will continue to be there for Dick. I know it's not easy. You are in my thoughts every day."

"Each day is getting harder. I feel so depleted. I hate glioblastoma—it's such a wretched disease."

"You are doing the best you can, Robin. You are a strong woman. Remember, I am your friend through good times and bad. You can call me anytime, even if it's the middle of the night. You know that, don't you?"

"Yes, I do, thank you. I need to get back now. Thanks for being there for me, Susan. I love you."

"I love you too."

I rushed back to the house through the maze of streets to find that Dick was napping. I was so emotionally exhausted, I laid down next to him and fell asleep. When we woke up, Dick was his old self and didn't seem to have any recollection of what had occurred. "I love you," he said, with his signature grin.

Unfortunately, Dick's brain cancer mind also became obsessed with frightening delusions, usually occurring late in the evening. One night he believed that his grandchildren had been kidnapped and became agitated and frightened. I called Samantha so she could reassure him the grandchildren were safe, but he couldn't accept the truth and made up involved scenarios why this was not so.

Another night Dick was convinced his sister, Cindy, and her husband were suspected of international espionage. It was so frightening when I couldn't calm him down or redirect his thoughts. I tried to show him the reality and convince him everything was all right, but it made absolutely no difference. I had almost always been able to soothe him and make him feel better. But this was totally new territory. I felt alone and terrified. I had always had Dick to talk to, to run things by, to help me make decisions. Now I was on my own.

Then, less than two weeks after Poliana and her crew started, she told me she could not continue to provide services, because Dick was now a "two-person assist." His physical abilities had declined so quickly that he couldn't control his body. He had more incidents of incontinence. Transfers to the chair and bed were getting very difficult. The aides were physically not able to do it alone. I offered to be the second person, but Poliana insisted that they couldn't use me, as the second person needed to be a trained CNA. I was terrified.

If Dick was not safe with a one-person assist, how would I manage? I could not afford to hire two people, twenty-four hours a day. I would not put him in a facility. I desperately wanted him to stay home and would do everything in my power to keep him there. I begged Poliana to stay until I could find some help and she agreed to provide coverage for a few more days. I knew we couldn't wait until our next appointment at the Dana-Farber. *I needed help now.*

It was evident the tumor was growing. Dick was also having trouble swallowing his pills and now I had to crush them and mix them in pudding or ice cream. I didn't think further treatment made sense. I knew Dick didn't want to live like this. We had discussed it many times. I was up all night agonizing over it, but I knew in my heart what I had to do. I called Jenn at Dana-Farber the next morning and requested that we cancel the next infusion and move up Dick's appointment to discuss next steps. Dr. Reardon would be able to see us on Monday, April 14, just two days after Dick's upcoming birthday party.

I asked for Jenn and Dr. Reardon's help in talking to Dick about stopping treatment and initiating hospice. They also offered to set up a meeting on the fourteenth with an end of life specialist at Dana-Farber who could introduce the idea of hospice and arrange a local referral. Although I wasn't sure it made sense, I asked if they could talk about the concept without using the word *hospice*, because of Dick's negative feelings about it. We all agreed this would be the best course of action for Dick at the time.

CHAPTER 67

Celebrating Dick's 66th Birthday

Samantha had approached me a few weeks earlier about planning a birthday party for Dick, whose sixty-sixth birthday was coming up on April 8. I told her I thought it would be a wonderful idea, but I had too much on my mind to plan a birthday party. I needed to focus on the day-to-day demands.

I quickly reconsidered, however, when I remembered how much Dick had enjoyed his retirement party. Being around family and friends always boosted his spirits. Samantha agreed to organize the party. We set a date for April 12, when all the children except Seth, who could not get additional leave, would be there.

On Dick's actual birthday on the eighth, my cousins Bonny and Melinda came down from Boston and brought a delicious lunch.

Samantha and the baby, Sandra, Bharani, and our friends Peter and Robyn joined us as well. We all gorged on a delectable chocolate birthday cake. Dick was fully oriented and in good spirits for the occasion.

Dick's mobility continued to decline and Poliana recommended we get him a wheelchair. I got the physician's order and insurance approval, and Dick was fitted for a chair. There was no opposition this time, as Dick himself recognized his decline. By April 11, the day before Dick's party, the wheelchair had become a necessity.

Samantha arranged a fabulous birthday party. She rented the Pinehills' Stonebridge Club, hired a caterer, and invited the entire Helping Hands community and some of our new Rebecca's Landing friends as well. Suddenly, it occurred to me—the Stonebridge Club was handicapped accessible, but our house was not—how would we get Dick down the stairs into the garage with the wheelchair? I was panic-stricken. It was all happening way too fast. One day Dick was walking and feeding himself, and days later, he couldn't do either.

I called our good friend Ron Dunham. Through the years, Ron had made renovations to our Lakeville home, helped us get it ready to sell, and made accommodations to our new home. I'm sure Dick would have thought it was an imposition for me to call Ron, but I didn't hesitate. I knew Ron was also a dedicated long-time patient of Dick's and by now, I had also learned that it was okay to reach out for help. Ron came over that day, took measurements, bought supplies, and installed a wooden ramp from the laundry room to the garage the following morning, just in time for us to make it to the party that day. Later, he installed a ramp from the front hallway to the courtyard, so Dick could enjoy the beckoning spring days outside.

It had been a severe winter, colored in white and gray, with long periods of time spent in the house. By the day of the birthday party, spring had blossomed. Two varieties of tulips bloomed in our courtyard: pink angelique tulips, which looked exactly like a sea of roses, and soft lilac tulips, which stood tall and proud beside the delicate pink ones. The "surprises" that Susannah had hinted at were poking up all over the courtyard in waves of pink and purple spires. Clumps of blue forget-me-nots were interspersed among the bulbs. How could Susannah have known these had always been Dick's favorite? Of course she couldn't, but she did know that they symbolized remembrance and undying love.

We had just started the pond fountain for the season; you could hear the rush of water in the background and see the fish that had survived the frigid winter. On the way to the Stonebridge Club, we passed an artfully landscaped area. On both sides of the road were stone walls filled with a harmonious arrangement of pale yellow daffodils, brilliant red tulips, and a punch of blue crocuses. It was a welcome, colorful, and peaceful scene after such a bleak winter. I wished I could come back with my camera.

Dick was greeted at his party by about fifty relatives and friends. He hadn't seen many of them in a long time, and it was a warm reunion. We positioned Dick's wheelchair at the head of the room, with a chair on either side, so friends could take turns to come sit beside him and share a birthday hug, a story, or a memory. After a while, I observed that Dick was only attentive to the person sitting on his right side. Every day there were major changes, and I finally figured out that on this day his left side seemed paralyzed and he could not direct his attention to the left. I slid the chair to his left away and everything flowed much better.

It was a wonderful sight to see Dick's face light up as he greeted everyone, from old patients to new neighbors. There is a poignant photograph from that day of my best friend Ruth leaning her head on Dick's shoulder and holding hands with him with such love and affection. There were a few moments when I had to step away to collect myself. I was overwhelmed with the fear and knowledge that Dick was saying good-bye. As the afternoon progressed and Dick got tired, he became quieter and didn't show a lot of expression, but I believe he was still listening and taking everything in.

We had ordered an impressive birthday cake decorated with chocolate ganache and fresh strawberries. The grandchildren delighted in helping their zayde blow out the candles. They brought another joyful dimension to the day as they ran around playing with exuberance.

We specified "no presents," but some people brought thoughtful gifts, and many gave Dick cards with heartfelt messages. I had a memory book for guests to sign and one of our new neighbors wrote, "We did not know you as a physician, but as a teacher you are teaching us how to live every day to the fullest." The patient who had written Dick a poem for his retirement party, gave him a poem for his birthday, this time in honor of me. I was very touched to receive such a magnanimous poem from someone I did not even know before she became part of our Helping Hands support system.

Over the next few days, as I read the heartfelt birthday cards and notes to Dick, it sparked an idea that I should reread the stash of cards and letters he had received a year ago. It was like hearing from old friends, and Dick appreciated, all over again, the kind, meaningful notes his patients and friends had written to him.

The day of the birthday party was unseasonably warm. With our courtyard bulbs sprouting in glory, the gorgeous view of the elegant

Pinehills landscaping and the luscious bowls of flowers decorating the tables at the party, Dick must have thought he was in a tropical paradise. When we returned home from the party, he said to me, "I can't believe *all* those people came *all* that way to travel to Bermuda to celebrate *my* birthday party!"

This time his delusion was a pleasant one and I didn't correct him.

CHAPTER 68

Last Visit to Dana-Farber

I was looking forward to the appointment at Dana-Farber on Monday, April 14 as I could see Dick was finally succumbing to the glioblastoma. The evening before, there was a substitute aide for the night shift. Nights had become more restless for Dick and this was a rough one. The aide fell asleep and Dick wet himself and the entire bed. I helped her clean up and make the bed with new linens and couldn't get back to sleep. I was already exhausted before we started the day at 6 a.m.

The early morning traffic was brutal. Every time the traffic came to a standstill, I tried to shake off the feeling that I needed to close my eyes—just for a second. I relaxed a little when we made it off the highway. Suddenly, I awoke with a start to blaring horns and realized I had fallen asleep and drifted into the intersection at a red light on Melnea Cass Boulevard. Immediately, I was fully awake and thanked God I hadn't gotten into an accident. I backed up out of the oncoming traffic. If I had any doubts about my mission to discontinue treatment that day, they quickly vanished when I realized I could have killed us both.

Bharani met us there as usual. The conversation between Dr. Reardon and Dick was a difficult one. Dr. Reardon explained that it didn't make sense to continue treatment since it wasn't working. He asked Dick's opinion, but Dick's thought process was not really clear that day. He was rambling on about unrelated matters. Dr. Reardon was very patient and repeated the same thing over in different ways as Dick didn't seem to be taking it in. I was never really sure he totally understood. I repeated to Dick that I thought Dr. Reardon was right, that the treatment was no longer helping, and it was time to stop. We had done the best we could, and his doctors had done the best they could. He didn't disagree.

Jenn had another appointment that day but stopped by to speak to Dick. We wished her well on her run for the upcoming Boston Marathon as we gave her a hug and said good-bye. It was sad to be leaving our treatment team, who had been with us right from the beginning. Both Jenn and Dr. Reardon encouraged us to stay in touch and assured us we could call on them at any time.

We then went to meet with a hospice specialist who talked about end of life alternatives and was careful not to use the word *hospice*, as I had requested. Again, I wasn't at all sure Dick was following the conversation. He was quiet and didn't seem to react with any emotion. They set up an intake with a local hospice at our home for the following day.

Before we left the Dana, Dick needed to use the bathroom. Even with the aid of the wheelchair, Bharani and I together had an extremely difficult time transferring Dick. He felt like dead weight. I got hot and sweaty in that small space trying to maneuver Dick's body, which was no longer pliable. There was a moment of panic when I thought we couldn't do it and Dick would end up on the floor. That, together with falling asleep at the wheel, confirmed for me that I had made the right decision to stop treatment. There was no way we could do this trip to Boston again.

That night was the first night of Passover. We had always made preparations for Passover far in advance: changing our dishes, getting rid of unleavened food, buying Passover foods, and hosting a seder, led by Dick, for fifteen to twenty people. I hadn't even realized Passover was approaching until it was almost upon us. I didn't feel the least bit guilty about not doing it all because I knew it was more important to take care of Dick.

I had bought some matzah and we had a simple seder with just the two of us that night. I started reading from the Haggadah; my first experience leading the seder and I lost my audience of one within the first five minutes! I looked over and Dick was fast asleep. It had been a long, hard day for both of us.

I wondered that night what the future would bring. *Would I ever hold a big seder again?* Although sometimes I complained that Dick should have included this English paragraph or that Hebrew song, I couldn't imagine having the seder without his leading it. I couldn't imagine hosting Thanksgiving dinner without him. I couldn't imagine life without him.

CHAPTER 69

Hospice

I was anxious before I even met with the hospice intake team. I was afraid they would mention the word *hospice* and Dick would get angry at them and even worse, at me. The nurse examined Dick while I met with the social worker and completed the reams of required paperwork. She explained the hospice program and what they offered. My immediate concern was that I needed twenty-four-hour help at home, and I quickly learned that they did not provide this service.

"What do you mean? If you don't provide caregivers, then what do you do?" I asked impatiently.

"We can provide a caregiver for one hour, five days a week. We will have a nurse come by to see your husband three or four times a week. They can check on him and answer any questions you might have. We have twenty-four-hour coverage available for medical emergencies.

"Three or four times a week? Changes are occurring so rapidly. That doesn't seem like enough."

"Well, we can make daily visits if necessary."

"I want daily nursing visits. But what I'm really worried about is the day-to-day care. I can't transfer Dick on my own. He is losing abilities quickly now. One hour, five days a week isn't enough."

"We have an association with a private group called Prescribed Care. They provide around-the-clock services. You would have to hire them independently, but I could give you their information and you could contact them directly."

"I'm not sure how helpful hospice is going to be for us if I have to hire help myself anyway," I said in an exasperated voice. My voice started to quiver, and I could feel the tears welling up. Maybe Dick was right, maybe we didn't need hospice.

"We will also provide you with an emergency medical kit, containing morphine and Haldol."

"But we don't need morphine. Dick is not in any pain. That's not really what I need right now."

"We can get you all the equipment you need at no charge—a walker, wheelchair, hospital bed . . ."

"I just bought everything we needed! I bought a shower chair and a commode. We drove all the way up to Weymouth to get a wheelchair and a very expensive cushion. No one told me hospice would cover the cost. It's too late now! I need help with day-to-day care.

"We also cover all the medications your husband will need."

"We have an excellent insurance policy and all his medications are covered."

I was antagonistic at every turn. I was angry that we had to be there. I was angry at glioblastoma, angry at the world. I was angry at myself for having to give in and call hospice. I was angry at Dick for leaving me. There was nothing this social worker could have said that would have made me feel better.

The nurse was finished examining Dick and they joined us at the dining room table.

"What about a hospital bed?" the social worker asked.

"We don't want a hospital bed. We want to sleep in the same bed," I responded.

The nurse explained all the reasons why the hospital bed would be best for Dick, including transfers and making it easier on the caregivers. She also explained the option many clients chose of placing the hospital bed in a different room so the patient would have privacy and it wouldn't be disruptive to a spouse's sleep.

"Can you put the bed right up against our bed so we can still sleep next to each other?" I asked, trying to hold back the tears. We had slept in the same bed for forty-one years. I couldn't imagine sleeping apart, certainly not in separate rooms.

"Of course, we can. There is a rail around the bed but we can put that side down so you can be next to one another."

Dick seemed to know exactly what was going on and said to me, "I'm going to need the hospital bed."

I should have given him more credit. A week later, he casually mentioned the "hospice nurse" in conversation. It was so silly of me to think he wouldn't recognize hospice in his midst! And to think, I was so furious on the day of the intake when the social worker said the "hospice" word too loudly, I almost kicked her out! Somehow, I needed to believe I was protecting Dick, but he knew all along. Just as he knew he had glioblastoma before the surgeon actually told him, he knew that the end was near.

I hadn't signed the final paperwork yet because I was so angry, and I wasn't sure hospice was the right decision. The social worker was still trying to appease me.

"We also provide social work services and we have a chaplain."

"I don't think we'll need that. We have our own support systems."

"Well, it is available for your children also."

When I reviewed out loud all the benefits she had described, that I felt we *didn't* need, the social worker became defensive.

"You don't need to sign with hospice services if you don't want to," she said. "Maybe you want to talk it over and think about it."

I was so stuck on the idea that they didn't provide twenty-four-hour care that I was having a hard time controlling my emotions and thinking clearly. I felt panicked.

I can't do this alone, I thought. *We can't go back to Dana-Farber. I don't want Dick in a facility. Try to put your anger aside. You need to think about Dick right now. Make the best decision for him.*

We had recently made a trip to the dermatologist, as Dick had developed lesions on his face, chin, and legs and the itching had become increasingly worse. There were new symptoms every day and we were both tired of going out to doctor's appointments. In the end, hospice agreed to the nurse coming on a daily basis. They said we could return all the equipment we had paid for and they would reissue a wheelchair through their own supplier who would deliver everything to our home at no cost. They would deliver a hospital bed. They also recommended a different type of walker and a gait belt so that Dick could be up as much as possible.

I ended up signing the paperwork that day, on April 15, with the assurance that they would help us through this next stage of life . . . and death.

CHAPTER 70

Adjusting to Hospice and Kerry's Girls

I had an interview the following day with Kerry from Prescribed Care, who reassured me that her staff could help us out. She said she herself might have to fill in at the beginning until she could organize a regular schedule. All her girls were trained CNAs and some of them were LPNs. Most of them had many years of experience in working with hospice patients. We discussed terms of payment and I hired her to start right away. I was so relieved that we had the help needed to keep Dick at home—where many days he was his old self, so happy to be in our new home.

Some furniture had to be moved to make way for the hospital bed. I emailed the neighborhood breakfast gang, and we had many more helpers than we needed in no time. I was glad Dick saw that if

I needed help, I just had to ask. It was an adjustment for both of us when the hospital bed arrived. Words like "egg crate" (the mattress topper), which had never been in my vocabulary before, were now a part of our lives. Although we had planned well to have our bathroom built handicapped accessible, there were still obstacles. At first, we managed using the shower seat. Then we had to have the shower door taken off to get the wheelchair in, and within another week's time, the aides determined they needed to switch to bed baths. The same was true of the bathroom. Shortly after we had the bathroom door removed for easier access, Dick was no longer able to control his bowels and bladder.

You have to have special qualities to do the kind of work those aides did. Kerry's girls, as they called themselves, were just like Juliana's friends—loving and caring, and they treated Dick with great respect. He, in turn, was always polite, thanking them for everything. Kerry's girls kept a daily log and the hospice nurse kept a communication notebook. The aides checked the nurse's notes at the beginning of each shift for updates. When I recently read through the aide's notes, I noticed they occasionally wrote personal comments.

Dr. Gross is a nice and kind man. It is a pleasure to work with him; Dr. Gross keeps urging me to make sure I wear gloves for my own safety. He is always concerned for others.

I chuckled as I read: *Ate a good supper. Now watching "The Good Wife" with his (good wife).*

Kerry's Girls had an excellent sense of what Dick's needs were, and I learned early on to trust their judgment and recommendations. Dick liked to dress more formally, but the girls suggested that clothing with no buttons or zippers would be more practical, and they recommended sweatpants and T-shirts for comfort. My three daughters were happy to provide a new wardrobe for their dad. They also got him a collection of wool caps, sweatshirts, and fleeces, which he liked to wear indoors. Even though it was April, he was always cold.

Transfers had become much more difficult. My back was killing me from trying to help the girls. One day there was a gap in shifts, and I had to call two male neighbors to help get Dick back into bed. When Dick's legs began to fail him, Kerry's girls suggested we get a Hoyer lift, an assistive medical device with a hydraulic lift, which allows a person to be lifted and transferred in a specialized sling. When I asked hospice about the Hoyer lift the following day, they said they had just discussed that in a meeting and were going to suggest it. Within days the girls told me Dick would be more comfortable in a Broda chair during the day. That way he could recline and sleep right in the chair and would not have to make so many transfers in and out of bed. Hospice agreed and it was ordered and delivered. I was annoyed with hospice for not making more timely recommendations. Kerry's girls were always one step ahead of them in anticipating Dick's needs.

The staff and I were trained to operate the Hoyer lift, as two people were required to perform a transfer. It was hard to position the lift and get the sling harness in just the right place. One person needed to crank the handle to the right height and another to guide the sling as the Hoyer lift was pushed away from the bed. Dick was then lowered down and positioned in the wheelchair. It took a lot of strength to push the lift. I was grateful that most of the aides were experienced with it, and over time, I got to be a pro.

Although we had an excellent round-the-clock crew overall, there were still challenges. There were last-minute staffing changes, a smoker who reeked of stale cigarettes, an aide who couldn't complete the shift because she threw her back out and they couldn't find a last-minute replacement. There were things that drove me crazy—when I couldn't find where an aide put something, like the TV remote or Dick's bathrobe, or when they forgot to raise the wheelchair to a full upright position before giving Dick food or drink. Although they had a communication book, things still got overlooked or forgotten. I tried not to get aggravated over the little stuff, but I felt like I always had to stay on top of everything.

The hospice aide came from 8 to 9 a.m., and when it got to be too difficult for one aide to do morning care alone, I extended the shift for Kerry's girls so there was an overlap at that hour. Dick and the aides were always chattering and laughing in the morning. It was his best time of day.

The aide noted in the log one day, *Gave sponge bath, shaved and trimmed nails—Dr. Gross tolerated it well and was making jokes the whole time.*

We had our first meeting with the hospice chaplain, Rosemary MacKay, whom we liked instantly. She had a strong, reassuring, spiritual presence. Her signature was always wearing purple. Dick enjoyed visits with our rabbi and the cantor, but Rosemary was different. She had a special way of interacting with Dick, which allowed him to open up about his feelings.

I remember hearing her ask Dick, "How is all of this for you?" gesturing her hands wide for emphasis. Her open-ended question made it easier for him to talk about dying. I always treasured those moments, which were rare, because his loving spirit was an inspiration for me.

Dick paused and said, "I know I'm dying. I am ready. I couldn't be in better hands with my wife, my family, friends, and Kerry's girls. Dr. Bharani and Dr. Friedman are always checking in on me."

He talked about how much love he felt for me and his family and all the blessings he had in his life. He was so pleased that he had lived to see our children reaching their independence. He felt rewarded that his life's work had been appreciated by his patients and their families. He was grateful for all the friends, patients, and acquaintances who had reached out to him when he was sick. He told Rosemary that I had orchestrated much of this.

We both felt fortunate to have found each other at a young age and to have had such an extraordinary relationship. Dick saw life as a way people could give of themselves to one another, and he felt he had given and received in abundance. His philosophy of life and his faith in me were reassuring and gave me confidence that I could go on by myself and continue to enjoy life's blessings.

We had been assigned a different hospice social worker than the one who did the intake, and I had a much better rapport with her. She offered us some services provided by hospice volunteers. We both took advantage of Reiki sessions. It was interesting to me that Dick wanted to try the Reiki treatment, as he had never been one to believe in something that wasn't clinical. More frequently, I didn't know what to expect of him. I think it's natural that as people become closer to death, they become more spiritual in their outlook and beliefs, and this was true of Dick. The Reiki seemed to calm him and put him to sleep.

My reactions to the Reiki treatments varied by the day. During my first experience, I felt completely energized and ready to tackle the day. The second time, I cried from the moment I hit the pillow, through the entire session. The third time, I fell into a deep sleep.

When it was time for Dick's medications that day, the aide decided not to wake me out of a sound slumber, so she gave Dick his medications herself. Although I know she meant well, I was furious that she hadn't woken me because she didn't know about some recent med changes and had given him the wrong pills. I always gave Dick his meals and his medications myself. I was upset that I had allowed myself to relax so deeply and fall asleep, although, looking back, I'm sure I needed it.

We also enjoyed performances from the volunteer hospice choir. On their first visit, they sang a few songs as we sat in the living room together. I was concerned that Dick was sleeping in his rocking chair through the mesmerizing performance and said I thought I should wake him.

The choir director responded, "Dick can hear everything even though his eyes are closed."

I wasn't so sure. I called his name so he wouldn't miss the music.

Dick surprised me when he opened his eyes and said calmly, "It's beautiful. Don't worry, Robin, I can hear everything."

The choir had asked what kind of music we enjoyed, and we were very appreciative when they added a Hebrew song, "Bashana Haba'ah," to their usual repertoire. It is a beautiful melody, and I joined them in singing the familiar refrain.

The song translates:
You will yet see, you will yet see,
how good it will be next year.
Next year we will spread out our hands
towards the radiant light.
A white heron like a light, will spread her wings
and within them the sun will rise.

Additional verses offered hope for the next year. My emotions were close to the surface and the healing power of the music made me cry, which it still does to this day.

We had a family party for Sandra's twenty-ninth birthday on April 20. Sandra was so excited that she would be graduating from nursing school in six weeks. This semester she had requested an internship at a hospital near Plymouth so she could visit home often. She loved talking to her dad about the different experiences she had at her hospital internships. We were all sitting at the dining room table after cake and ice cream when Sandra asked, "Do you think you'll be able to come to my graduation, Dad?"

I watched Dick's face closely, wondering how he would respond to Sandra's question. I didn't think he would be alive by then, and if he was, I feared he would be too weak to attend. Although Sandra was coping well with her studies and her clinical internship at the hospital, I worried that losing her dad would rock her stability. I prayed that she completed her program. I knew Dick worried about her too. Sandra had been through some rough times and was just now reaching a period in her life where she was feeling competent and self-assured.

"If it's at all possible to get there, I wouldn't miss it, but I don't know if I will be able to make it," Dick replied. "I am so proud of you, honey. I know you will make an excellent nurse. You have a caring way of interacting with people, and that is so important."

"A lot of things you taught me have been very helpful in my training, Dad. Thank you for always explaining things to me. I learned a lot from you while working in your office. Thank you for giving me your stethoscope and your black bag. That meant a lot to me. I'm so proud of what a good doctor you were. I saw how much your patients loved you."

"I'm glad I was able to teach you a few things and I hope you will always remember those lessons," Dick said.

"I will, Dad."

"Come here, let me give you a big hug," Dick said.

Dick was most alert and clearheaded in the mornings. In the late afternoons, he often became fearful, agitated, or delirious. We had more disturbing incidents with Dick's delusions; he became convinced that the FBI was after him, or that the KGB was listening, and we weren't safe. When he became agitated, he would pull off his Depends or try to take down the bed railings. It was challenging for me and for the staff.

We tried the drug Ativan to calm him down. The aides finally convinced me to use the Haldol, from the hospice emergency kit. I had been very reluctant to use any of the narcotic drugs because of Dick's concerns about hospice overmedicating, but as periods of distress became more intense and frequent, I gave in.

On one of those rough days, Dick was insistent that he see an independent doctor. He said his "team" was not giving him the help he needed. I could not console him or distract him. I called Dr. Friedman in a panic and he was at our door a half hour later. He saved the day with a combination of talking Dick down, medications, and never-ending patience.

One day, after watching a movie where a home had blown up in a fire, Dick had a delusion about a fire. Kerry's girls told me we shouldn't be watching any movies except the Hallmark Channel, as they could trigger delusions, making Dick paranoid and then harder to redirect. I hadn't pieced this together before, but it made sense. The hospice staff confirmed that we should stay away from television shows with action or violence. Instead, we started watching family videos, listening to music, and looking through old photo albums. Gena was always sending us little surprises in the mail and had recently sent us a CD of Steve's favorite songs from the '60s and it also became a favorite of ours.

We thoroughly enjoyed watching videos of the children's birthday parties, gymnastic and dance recitals, holidays, and day-to-day life in the Gross household. We would sit on the couch and laugh and reminisce about all the good times we had. We talked about the rough spells with the kids as well and how we helped each other get through them. We were so thankful the children all seemed to be on a good path right now. Dick had almost always shot and narrated the videos. Although I was sorry that we didn't have more video of Dick, it was priceless to hear his dry sense of humor as he narrated the action.

CHAPTER 71

Last Weeks

We enjoyed short periods of time in the courtyard whenever the weather permitted. It was tricky to guide the wheelchair down the narrow ramp and make the turn, at just the right angle, to the next ramp from the porch, but our little piece of heaven was worth it. On May 3 we spotted the first male hummingbird, with its shiny, iridescent red neck, at our hummingbird feeder, and I dragged the camera out of hibernation. Within a week, the hummingbirds became regulars. The previous summer, they were not attracted to our stark courtyard, but with the addition of the landscaping and branches for them to land on, they were fluttering about profusely. I knew the butterflies would follow. The tulips and grape hyacinths greeted us in full bloom.

On two occasions in the second week in May, I was sure I had seen a bird flying through our courtyard toward the birdhouse. I didn't have time to scout it out, but I was rewarded on May 14, when I got photos of a chickadee flying in and out of the birdhouse. We were so excited that the chickadee family had taken up residence in the birdhouse we had brought with us from Lakeville. Our high hopes that all our photographic subjects would follow us to our new courtyard were becoming a reality.

We continued to have human visitors, as well, on a regular basis, including cousins from New York, Atlanta, Maryland, and Boston. Our cantor, Nathaniel Schudrich, came to visit, and Dick and I enjoyed the familiar Hebrew prayers he sang with us. I continued to speak to my therapist every week by phone. Not only did she help me through this difficult stage, but she asked if she could come to see me at my home. I was so appreciative of her personal visit. Her hug never felt so good. One of Dick's previous employees, Beth, came to visit. Dick was so proud of her, as she had just become a nurse practitioner. Beth was Dick's first visitor when he was initially hospitalized at the Brigham, and it seemed appropriate that she was one of the last.

My younger sister Priscilla took some time off from work and came to stay with us for five days. It felt like such a blessing to have her there to confide in and support me. I also loved that she spent a lot of quality time with Dick. She often lay down on our bed, next to him, and they talked.

I was in the next room, filling the weekly med boxes, when I overheard Priscilla telling Dick, "You've been like a dad to me. You were already in my life when my father died, and you became my substitute dad. I am going to miss you so much."

Dick told Priscilla how much he loved our entire family.

Priscilla was twelve when I met Dick and fourteen when we got married. She was only eighteen when our dad passed away. I knew she had been very emotional lately, and I worried I was putting too much strain on her when I confided in her. But that day, I realized it was much more than that. She was reliving my father's death. The loss of Dick would be another hard blow to her. I was glad we had this time together.

The hospice choir came for a second visit while Priscilla was visiting, and this time we both cried through their performance. Another evening, I was in the bedroom when Priscilla was reassuring Dick that I would have lots of help when he was gone. "Robin has the kids to help her, she has us, she has her old friends, her new friends in the neighborhood, her Shalom Pinehills group; she has her photography friends, her synagogue friends, her childhood friends . . . , and . . . ," Dick interrupted, "She has herself."

That is when I knew that it was okay for Dick to die. He knew I could take care of myself. I did have a lot of support, but Dick had seen, through the past two years, that I could be independent. He also knew that if I did need help, I was not afraid to ask for it. *I* also made the realization that day that *I* would be okay. Dick was right—I had myself. His confidence in me helped me to recognize that, and I shared my insight with him.

CHAPTER 72

In the End,
It's All About Love

In many ways, the end of life mirrors the beginning of life—we need to be cared for with love and affection, and it's all about hydration and elimination. With the hospice nurse's advice, the aides were charting bowel movements, and giving Dick Senna and MiraLAX, but there were still periods of constipation. After one such bout, the laxatives finally worked, and Dick had a huge bowel movement. One of the newer aides didn't know that you shouldn't flush large, hard fecal matter down the toilet. The toilet got clogged and the whole house smelled foul.

Our friends Bob and Barbara called that afternoon to say they'd like to visit and asked if there was anything we needed. I told them Dick was sleeping but asked if they could pick up a bottle of Drano, as the toilet was clogged. When Bob arrived, he advised us that

Drano was not the appropriate solution. Unfortunately, the shape of our plunger was not the right type for the elongated opening at the base of the toilet bowl. Bob was smart and creative and tackled the problem just like Dick would have. He went down to the basement to see what he could use to unclog the toilet. He marched up and down the stairs gathering supplies—a hose, a knife, some wire, gloves, a bucket.

My sister Priscilla and I got a case of the giggles. Each time Bob walked by with another implement, we started laughing again until we had tears streaming down our faces. By the time the aide walked past us to deliver the goods to the garbage can in the garage, we were out of control with laughter. The aides told me later that they saw a "new me" while Priscilla was there. They were so glad to see me smiling, laughing, and acting silly.

One of my favorite springtime activities was nursery hopping. I was itching to get out to pick up some hanging planters for the side porch in the courtyard and some annual larval plants for the butterflies to lay eggs on. Another goal I had was to stop by our old house and pick up some frog's eggs for our new pond. I had gotten the new resident's permission to come by. I rarely left the house anymore, but I decided to go to my favorite nursery, which was a thirty-minute drive away. That morning there was an aide that had only come twice before. It was a beautiful day and I couldn't wait to scour the nursery for the most lush, beautiful planters I could find. It felt so good to get outside. I was able to relax and enjoy my independent outing. I even stopped to get the frog's eggs and checked out a second nursery on my way back.

I knew something was wrong the minute I walked through the door. Dick was sitting in a corner of the room and he wore a fearful, angry expression. The aide said he had become paranoid and wouldn't let her help him. Apparently, he didn't recognize her and was scared because he didn't know what she was doing there. All the joy over my purchases quickly fell by the wayside as I tried to reassure Dick that everything was all right; I was home now, and I wouldn't leave him.

I spent more time on the Women Warriors site. It made me feel better to complain to my cohorts about not being able to leave the house, to hear stories of their husbands' paranoia and delusions, and to know I was not alone.

After Priscilla left, Dick's sister, Cindy, came for several days to spend time with her brother, which again allowed me some freedom to work out in the courtyard and have some time for myself. Three of my closest friends from Lakeville called to say they would like to take me out one afternoon when I had family coverage. When they asked what I would like to do, I knew exactly where I wanted to go.

"Peaceful Meadows," I said without hesitation.

It was our favorite homemade ice cream spot. Dick had asked for Peaceful Meadows' coconut chocolate almond ice cream recently, but it was too hard to get out anymore. It was a nice reprieve to enjoy some time out of the house, conversation that was not focused on caregivers, schedules, and Depends, and best of all, to bring back a sundae for Dick with his favorite ice cream.

On Mother's Day, Sandra came to stay with her dad so that I could go to visit my mom. I was thrilled that my mom was doing well, but I missed not seeing her more often.

At the beginning of May, our nurse practitioner, Jenn, emailed to check how we were doing with the transition to hospice. She had successfully run the Boston Marathon.

She wrote, "Tell Dick mile 26 was a terrific one. He pushed me along to the finish line."

Dick smiled broadly when I gave him Jenn's message.

When Dick could no longer go out for breakfast, his friends from Lakeville came to see him at our house. When it became too confusing for him to have a group of visitors, they came two at a time. It broke my heart when Dick would wake up and say, "I want to take you out to dinner tonight," or "Let's go to the pond and take photos today." The furthest we got was the courtyard, so I was glad we had created such a peaceful oasis.

Dr. Friedman called every morning to check on Dick's status, and most mornings he drove the thirty-five minutes to our home to see him. The hospice nurses became reliant on Dr. Friedman, who became an unofficial part of the team. I was so grateful for that morning phone call. In addition to asking about Dick's symptoms, Bob always asked how I was doing. I felt like I could ask him anything and tell him my worst fears.

Just like with Bharani, we were blessed to have our own personal physician. Bob was called back to work at a new job shortly after Dick passed away. I felt like it was divine intervention that he was off for those exact five weeks when we needed him.

When I previously brought up the idea of having some kind of memorial in Dick's memory, Dick had never been receptive. I discussed it with the chaplain, Rosemary, and she helped me to broach the subject with Dick again. I told Dick it was important for me to do something in his memory as my family had done in memory of my father. He understood, as he had attended the annual breakfast in memory of my father for thirty-five years, where we presented a scholarship to a Fall River, MA, B.M.C. Durfee High School senior.

I gave Dick some suggestions I had been considering, including giving a scholarship to a student from Middleboro High School who was going into the field of health care.

"The recipients might be inspired to come back to practice in town someday. Also, the scholarship might benefit many of your patients' children or grandchildren," I told Dick.

That was the clincher. When Dick realized it would be a legacy that might continue to benefit his patients, he agreed to the scholarship idea for a Middleboro High senior. Dick was not the type who liked a big fuss made over him, but I knew that we would have an annual affair where we would remember and celebrate Dick and the values he stood for, as we presented the scholarship in his name, just as we had done for my dad. My four children never knew my father, but they learned about him as we gathered every year for the Sam Kaplan Memorial Breakfast and shared stories about him. I knew then that our grandchildren would also remember and learn who their zayde was as they heard friends, family, patients, and colleagues talk about him and what he represented.

CHAPTER 73

Crisis

Our hospice nurse told me that Dr. Browning was coming to the house to see Dick the following day, on May 12, after office hours and would like to speak to me. I felt anxious when Dr. Browning asked if we could go out on the back porch to talk privately. *Was this it? Was he going to tell me this was the end?* I wasn't prepared for the conversation that followed.

"How are you managing?" Dr. Browning asked. "Are you getting enough sleep? I'm worried about you."

"It's hard, but I am doing okay," I told him.

"Have you considered a hospice home?" Dr. Browning asked. "There is an excellent private nursing home in Plymouth called Newfield House."

My immediate response was that I wanted to keep Dick at home. Dr. Browning was concerned how we could keep going as Dick's needs became greater. I wondered about that myself some days. I looked down at my nails, which were red and raw, bitten down to the quick. I'm sure Dr. Browning could see the bags under my eyes from lack of sleep. My weight was so out of control that I had stopped getting on the scale.

"Well, I can't go on like this forever," I admitted. "Can you give me some idea? Do you think we are talking about months? Weeks?"

"Probably weeks, maybe less."

"Then I can do it."

"Please promise me you will at least go have a look at Newfield House. I can arrange it for you."

I agreed to go see it because Dr. Browning felt so strongly, and I respected his opinion.

That afternoon, I took Dick for a walk in his wheelchair down the street in the neighborhood. It was hard to maneuver the heavy wheelchair down the ramps and out on the road, but his reaction was well worth it. He loved seeing the trees in bloom, the neighbor's decorative pots with colorful flowers, and smelling the freshly cut grass. He loved greeting the first spring in our new neighborhood. I had put annuals, herbs, and some potted plants in our courtyard garden over the past week, and Dick delighted in seeing my accomplishments. I knew Dr. Browning and Kerry's Girls were concerned about me, but there was really no question in my mind that we were just fine right where we were.

Much later, I realized it may have been Kerry and the girls, themselves, who felt like they couldn't keep up the difficult caregiving regimen, but they never communicated that to me. Two girls had hurt their backs in the process of moving Dick, and one was out of work because of it. It was getting harder to fill the shifts for the aides, and sometimes one of them had to do a double shift. Hospice had recently added a second hour of aide service in the later afternoons which often was a challenging time of day.

Because I thought of Kerry's girls as invincible, I hadn't been sympathetic to their position. It never occurred to me that it might be too much for me, and it certainly never occurred to me that it might be too much for them.

Although Dick wasn't always able to express pain directly, I could usually tell when he was in pain by his facial grimacing, his behavior, or his language. I worked with the staff to make decisions when Dick needed pain medication or when a call to hospice was in order. When the aide and I were in the process of transferring Dick in the Hoyer one day, he announced in an angry voice, "I'm going to have to call the police on her. I'm being assaulted." I was trying to figure out why he was angry, but I quickly realized he was in pain. I often had to use detective skills to interpret what he meant. I could see the bottom of the sling was grabbing him too tightly. We lowered and stopped the lift at my command, took off the sling, and put him back in the Broder chair.

When the hospice nurse came to assess the situation, she discovered the Hoyer straps had been placed too tightly on the groin area and Dick was red and sore. We now had to place towels between the Hoyer straps to prevent further irritation and pain. They instituted a stricter program where one person would operate the Hoyer pump and the other would lift Dick's legs up as he was being transferred in order to take the pressure off the groin area. He seemed more comfortable after these interventions.

The day after my conversation with Dr. Browning, we had a disaster. The nurse had put in a condom catheter two weeks earlier.

It was irritating to Dick and sometimes he pulled it out and it had to be replaced.

That afternoon, Dick started yelling repeatedly, "Sally circumcised me, but she forgot to call the rabbi."

Sally was one of Dick's favorite aides and he kept telling her over and over, "I forgive you for not calling the rabbi. I forgive you, Sally."

I knew instantly that Dick was in excruciating pain.

Generally, the hospice emergency system worked well, and the on-call nurse came quickly, but that particular day she was busy with another patient some distance away. It was an agonizing wait for me, and I know it was much worse for Dick. Apparently, he had tried to take off his catheter and when the balloon was misplaced, it caused a great deal of pain. I was so upset, I called hospice repeatedly to find out when they would be coming, and I lost my temper with them over the delay. The last straw for me was when the dispatcher said that they had sent over the extra aide that afternoon and she didn't have anything to do.

I yelled at her that we couldn't predict when there would be a crisis. But I needed someone *now*. He was in pain and that was all she needed to know.

A few hours seemed like an eternity. When the nurse finally arrived, resolved the problem, and Dick was safely asleep, I vented some of my anger and frustration to the online Women Warriors Facebook Support Group. They were extremely supportive, as always. The women in the group who were nurses all wrote back to me to say in a situation like that you can pop the balloon to stop the pain. Dick would have known that, of course. I wished I had known. I wished a lot of things. I wished the aide had known. I wished the hospice on-call nurse had been on time that day. I wished the glioblastoma was just a nightmare and would go away when I woke up in the morning.

The fact that there are sometimes delays meant nothing to me at the time. I was furious and felt it was inexcusable that Dick had to be in pain for so long. I was grateful that we had not been dealing with pain throughout Dick's illness. I don't know how I would have gotten through the stress of watching him in pain long term.

I couldn't even do it for three hours.

CHAPTER 74

Coma

The following day, on May 15, I went, as scheduled, to visit Newfield House. It was unusual that Dick was still sleeping when I left, but I figured he was exhausted from the trauma of the day before. Just a day earlier, he had eaten an unusual amount for breakfast: four waffles, yogurt, bananas, strawberries, and hot chocolate; then, later that morning, a chocolate glazed donut that one of the staff brought him. I wonder if he knew it would be one of his last meals.

I felt like I gave Newfield House a fair shot, but I knew in my heart that Dick wanted to die at home. When I returned from the visitation around 10:30 a.m., I was surprised to see that Dick was still sleeping. I had missed the hospice nurse's visit that morning, but the caregivers told me the nurse had said it was okay for Dick to be sleeping so late.

Our friend Malkah was stopping by later that afternoon, so I thought Dick would be wide awake to enjoy her visit after such a good sleep. Close to noon, I went in to remind Dick that Malkah was coming by, but he didn't respond. I sat by Dick, talked to him, and held his hand. I told him I went to Newfield House to look around because Dr. Browning asked me to visit, but that I would not consider sending him there. We were going to stay together in the beautiful house we built. I told him about the new buds bursting open in the garden and that I thought the chickadee had babies. I told him about Sarah's call that morning.

I was scared. I called hospice a few times in desperation. I thought Dick hadn't woken up because of the trauma or drugs from the day before, but they thought that Dick had just slipped into a coma, unrelated to the events of the previous day. I didn't feel ready to accept that. I wanted somebody to *do* something. Hours passed. I lay down on the bed and periodically drifted into a fitful sleep.

I kept talking to Dick because I didn't know what else to do. I thought maybe I could reach him. I told him how grateful I was for the remarkable life we had together, what a great team we were. I believe I thought my love for him could will him back. Tears streamed down my cheeks and I realized that Dick couldn't even wake up to tell me not to cry.

After a while, I started pleading with him, "Please wake up. I'm not ready yet. I know we can't be together forever, but I just want a little more time. I want you to see Sandra graduate from nursing school. I want you to see Samantha's new house. It's supposed to be a "smart house." You would really get a kick out of that. I want to have one last summer together, just one summer.

"I'm going to be okay. You know I will. You taught me well. You set me up with everything I need. I love you so much." I kissed him on the cheek. "Please wake up."

Hospice didn't consider Dick's not waking up an emergency, but I did. They said they would send someone over later that evening. I searched for the business card that my neighbor Annie, a retired physician's assistant, had given me at the pool that summer. She had looked at me, so knowingly, with her clear, blue eyes, telling me to call anytime. And so, I did.

By the time my friend Malkah arrived around 4 p.m., I was frantic. I had a ferocious headache and my stomach was uneasy. When I heard her car pull up, I raced outside. As Malkah exited her car, I grabbed hold of her, hugged her tightly, and burst into tears.

"Dick didn't wake up today. He hasn't eaten or drunk anything all day."

Malkah had been widowed at a young age and she understood the emotional ups and downs.

"It's okay to cry, just let it out. Tell me what's going on."

It felt so good to have a shoulder to cry on. My feelings were still raw, and I needed to vent.

My neighbor Annie arrived shortly after Malkah and I told them what had transpired the day before. They allowed me to rant and rave and cry tears of anger, fear, and despair. I felt like I couldn't stop. It all came tumbling out, the frustration . . . the panic. They encouraged me to call the kids. Annie examined Dick and helped me to understand and accept that the current situation was not related to the events of the day before. It felt a lot easier hearing it from her than from hospice. Annie and Malkah stayed well into the night to help me cope with the reality that Dick was in a coma and it might be permanent.

I was worried Dick might have a seizure, since he wasn't able to take his medications orally, but Annie was able to give him his evening meds with a syringe. She talked to the hospice nurse about ordering Dick's seizure medication and Tylenol as a suppository. Annie was so knowledgeable and compassionate, I felt like I'd known her forever.

Dick didn't look like himself and when he opened his eyes, he made no eye contact. I missed his beautiful smile and soulful eyes. *Could this really be the end?* We'd prepared, we'd lived, we'd laughed and loved, but I was still not ready. I would never really be ready.

That night I cried harsh tears of reality, recognizing that the love of my life was drifting away from me.

Seth was granted emergency leave and flew home. The girls all came in. My two sisters flew in from California. We always had at least one family member staying in the bedroom with Dick, usually several. Two days later, Dick opened his eyes and seemed to make eye contact with the family and attempted to communicate. When I gave him a kiss, he puckered up to kiss me.

We sang songs to Dick, from "The Hills are Alive" from *The Sound of Music*, to the Yiddish lullaby, "Shlof Mayn Kind," that my mom had sung to us, and that I had sung to all of our children. We talked to Dick and each other, sharing stories and memories, and we all snuggled up on the bed next to him. Rabbi Kanter came and led us in the recitation of the Hebrew prayer, "shema." The shema is a central prayer in Judaism, a statement of faith, and is the last thing a Jew is supposed to say before death. We formed a circle around Dick and held hands as we recited the prayer. I felt like Dick was sharing that holy moment and God's spirit was with us. Tears flowed freely.

Sandra said she had something important to tell her Dad. I stayed nearby. Sandra held her dad's hand in hers. "Dad, my graduation is the first week in June. They just told us we could have our favorite faculty member, family, or friend, who is a doctor or nurse, pin us at our graduation ceremony. I want you to do it." Her voice faltered but she continued, "But I know you won't be able to. I asked Dr. Bharani to pin me to represent you. I thought you would like that."

"I love you, Dad," she said, as she leaned over and hugged him.

We all knew that having Bharani stand in for Dick would be exactly what Dick would have wanted. I was pleased that Sandra gave him that honor, as he was like a brother to Dick during his illness.

I asked the hospice nurse how long someone could live without eating and drinking and she responded, "a week." The hospice staff suggested that sometimes people wouldn't let go if one of the family members has unfinished business or hasn't given the patient permission to leave this earth. We all felt that was not the case. We had all told Dick that week that it was okay to let go. We reassured him we were going to be fine. I think he just held on as long as he could because he was still sharing his love.

There were a few occasions during the week where Dick became alert and spoke a few words. I lived for those moments. Once he said he was in pain but did not want more morphine. He wanted us to rub his temples. His familiar refrain was "I love you," and when he couldn't verbalize it, he would mouth the words. He would pucker up to kiss me when he heard my voice. He gave us a beautiful smile just a few days before he left. Samantha, Sarah, Sandra, and Seth each had special time with their dad. Jacob and Aerin ran in and out of the room, although it was hard for them to see their zayde nonresponsive, as he had always been so animated with them.

When my cousin Sasha's weekly phone call came in, I carried the phone into our bedroom, told Dick that Sasha wanted to speak to him, and held the phone up to his ear. We were all astounded when Dick spoke clear as could be and said, "Hi Sasha." I burst into tears; I was so happy to hear the sound of his voice. I had been confident that Dick was aware of our presence and conversations and this confirmed it for me.

Samantha approached me a few days after Dick went into the coma and asked me if her dad had arranged to give his brain to research.

"No, he didn't."

"It was important to him to contribute to glioblastoma research. I'm sure he would have wanted to donate his brain," Samantha said.

"I think you're right, but we didn't talk about that. I'm not sure how to go about arranging it but I could call and ask Dr. Reardon."

Adam offered to make the inquiries. He found out from the Brigham that in order to donate Dick's brain, Dick would have to die in the hospital. We discussed this new information but decided we wanted Dick to die at home. I thought about another possibility. We had a friend, Dr. David Housman, who did research on glioblastoma and worked with groups who carried out brain donations for neurodegenerative diseases around the world and at Massachusetts General Hospital (MGH).

I asked Adam to call Dr. Housman to see if he could help. Dr. Housman said he would try to figure this out through his contacts at MGH. Although MGH and the Brigham were both under the Partners medical system, he was concerned that MGH may not be able to assist since Dick had not been a patient of theirs.

Instead, Dr. Housman contacted Dr. Melanie Feeney, one of the pathologists at the Brigham and she graciously agreed to coordinate the donation. The end was getting close and we were anxious that we might not be able to make arrangements in time. Dr. Feeney prioritized a meeting with the Brigham and was successful in coming to an agreement with them that Dick would immediately be transported to the Brigham when he died.

Because Dick was treated there from the beginning and they had all his records, they told Adam it would be very helpful to their research to have his brain. Adam made arrangements with a local funeral company, which would transport Dick's body to the Brigham. Adam would stay with him at all times and then the funeral company would wait and transport his body to the Shalom Memorial Chapel in Cranston, Rhode Island. Dick and I had decided together that he would be buried in the Hebrew Cemetery in Fall River, where my father, grandparents, and extended family were buried.

We all felt good about donating Dick's brain, as we knew how strongly he felt about contributing to research, especially since there was the possibility of a genetic predisposition to glioblastoma.

We made it through the two-year anniversary on May 20, the day that forever changed our lives.

On May 21, Dick's breathing became more rapid and he was flushed. He developed a temperature and a weak cough. The caregivers told us it would be soon. They had worked with dying patients so long that they knew when the time was near.

On May 22, the hospice choir came again. They sang a few songs, including "Bashana Haba'ah" again, and they sang an additional Hebrew song, "Eli, Eli."

It translates:

Oh Lord, my God,
I pray that these things never end,
The sand and the sea,
the rush of water,
the crash of the heavens,
the prayer of the heart.

The angelic music was very emotional for me. I didn't even try to muffle my cries, as I thought again, *Dick isn't able to tell me not to cry anymore.*

In the middle of the night of May 23, the caregivers woke us and said Dick wouldn't make it until the next day. We were all there surrounding him with love, holding his hands, as he slipped from us that night.

Monet's Garden Reunion

I n the months that followed, I missed Dick more than I thought possible. I was still struggling to get through each day. I joined the gym at Mirbeau, with its beautiful Monet's Garden theme and cried my way through savasana in every yoga class. My compassionate instructor, Grace, had a strong spiritual aura and created a safe space to grieve. The Mirbeau's healing environment became a second home for me.

Mid-winter, I received a phone call from Charles Needle, the photographer who led our Monet's Garden/Keukenhof trip. It was so good to hear his enthusiastic voice.

"I've been talking to Gena," he said. "We thought it would be fun to have a Monet's Garden photography reunion in the spring in memory of Dick. We're considering Callaway Gardens in Georgia, where they have a spectacular butterfly conservatory. It would be a special way to remember Dick and a time for you to spread your wings."

I had gone outside to take the call as I was at a noisy restaurant. My hand on the phone was frozen, but despite the bitter cold outside, I felt warm inside. It was one of the first times I felt any excitement trickle through since Dick had died.

I could feel myself well up and wasn't able to say anything at first. Then, in a faint voice, I managed to tell Charles how much a photography reunion would mean to me. It was a beautiful idea and would give me something to look forward to.

Charles contacted the rest of the gang and the reunion began to take shape. When he reached Martha, he found out that her husband, Bob, had died a few months earlier, at the age of eighty-four. The reunion was dedicated in Bob's memory as well.

In April 2015, I flew to Atlanta, where I met up with Gena and we drove down to Callaway together. I got very little sleep the night before I left. I was nervous about traveling by myself, but I was even more anxious about photographing and managing all the equipment on my own. *Dick wouldn't be there to help me. How would I manage without my other half? Could I do it all on my own?*

It was wonderful to see everybody again as we gathered in the hotel lobby. As I hugged and greeted old friends, I shed tears through my smiles, thinking how much Dick would have loved being there beside me. Rene and John H. brought their spouses, who had not been with us on the original trip, and they quickly became part of the gang. We all shared our condolences with Martha on the loss of her husband. We donned the baseball caps Charles had made for us, imprinted in script with *Monet's Garden Reunion 2015,* embroidered with a butterfly and accessorized with a camera pin.

Gena had asked me to room with her and I was so relieved not to be by myself. She helped me with some of the technical aspects of the photography, such as downloading my photos onto an external hard drive, one of the many tasks Dick had always done for me.

We spent five glorious days photographing the Callaway Gardens, which were alive with luscious shades of pink and purple rhododendrons and azaleas. We had an opportunity to try out some of the techniques Charles taught us in Europe. He received special permission for our group to go into the butterfly conservatory before it opened to the public. It was one of the first times I used the new tripod Dick had bought for me.

Although I was becoming a more independent photographer, it sure felt good knowing I had a cavalry of people around me the whole week who could answer questions and help me with any challenges. When we weren't in the field shooting, we shared photos and laughter, enjoyed southern cuisine, caught up on each other's lives, and talked about the latest photo gadgets and technology.

We had a slide show of our best photos of the France and Holland trip. Tears sprang to my eyes as I saw images of Dick and me, so joyful in the gardens. The photo Charles had taken of us walking in the rain with the Monet's Garden umbrella overhead popped on the screen and I saw it differently now. I felt like the rainstorm symbolized the impending doom that was to come but the umbrella represented all our Helping Hands friends and family who protected us and watched over us. I was forever thankful that we had celebrated our fortieth anniversary early.

As I spent time with each member of the gang, they shared their intimate memories of Dick.

John C. told me, "You could see how much Dick loved you by the way he looked at you. I know you have four children, but Dick still considered you his bride. I got a great shot of the two of you that last night. You had that look of a couple who was so in love. You don't often see that in couples who are married for forty years."

I spoke to Martha about everything she had gone through with her husband's decline. We talked about how photography was a blessing to both of us in our grief, as it kept us focused on the moment and helped bring us back to life. When I was focusing through the lens on a forest of azalea bushes in various shades of purple, I was fully present to the beauty of nature and could think of nothing else.

Charles knew how important that last photo excursion we ever took together had become for us. "I think there was a higher power at work orchestrating that trip! It gives me a warm heart to know I helped facilitate that special time for you."

Gena and I have a special bond—we call ourselves "soul sisters." I told her how much her support had meant to both of us: her letter, which had become our guide through Dick's illness, and her emails, calls, notes, and gifts.

"Dick really admired you and how you went on with your life after Steve died. Thank you for being such a good friend and role model."

Gena said, "I remember you telling me once you had never lived alone and you didn't know if you could make it. I am so proud of you, Robin. Dick would be proud of you. He believed in you. He knew you could do it."

We all started talking about when and where we would have our next reunion. I thought about Dick's only directive to me, "I want you to go on a photo trip and smile like Gena." I felt sure Dick knew that this would be the first of many adventures that Gena and I would enjoy together.

I remembered the first time we gathered in a circle to introduce ourselves. I had been so impressed by Gena and Rene's independence, and now I was headed down my own independent path. I was eager to pursue my goals of writing a book, helping others who were grieving, traveling, and advancing my photography. I finally felt ready to spread my wings.

As we headed out of the gardens on that last day, a profusion of butterflies fluttered alongside, leading us down the path. Rene said, "Dick is with us," and I knew she was right.

Acknowledgments

In gratitude to all of our Lotsa Helping Hands friends and family. In addition to all the physical help you provided, your constant, loving, support is what made Dick feel like it was the best two years of his life. We couldn't have done it without you.

Thank you to the dedicated members of the Plymouth Creative Writing Meetup Group, who listened and critiqued every two weeks over three years, as I read chapter by chapter. Your feedback helped me to become a much better writer and I am grateful for your support in sharing my emotional journey.

Thank you to my friend Marcia Landa whose superb editing skills helped me to trim my manuscript even further when I thought I was done.

Thank you to Gena Reebs for both technical and emotional support, and becoming my trusted travel buddy.

Thank you to my editor, Sara Stratton, whose direction, patience, and assistance were invaluable.

Made in the USA
Columbia, SC
14 May 2020